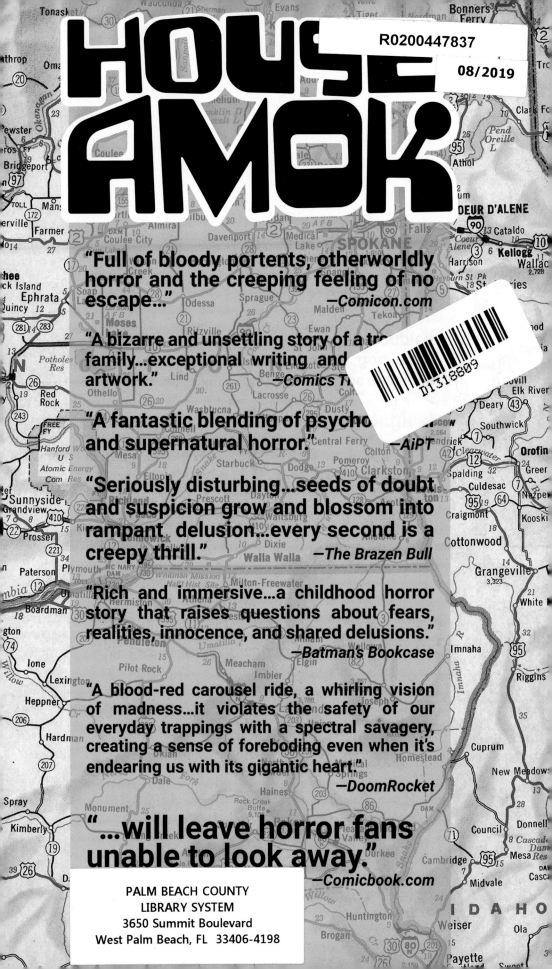

HOUSE AMOK

"Full of bloody portents, otherworldly horror and the creeping feeling of no escape..." —Comicon.com

"A bizarre and unsettling story of a troubled family...exceptional writing and artwork." —Comics T...

"A fantastic blending of psycho... and supernatural horror." —AiPT

"Seriously disturbing...seeds of doubt and suspicion grow and blossom into rampant delusion...every second is a creepy thrill." —The Brazen Bull

"Rich and immersive...a childhood horror story that raises questions about fears, realities, innocence, and shared delusions." —Batman's Bookcase

"A blood-red carousel ride, a whirling vision of madness...it violates the safety of our everyday trappings with a spectral savagery, creating a sense of foreboding even when it's endearing us with its gigantic heart." —DoomRocket

"...will leave horror fans unable to look away." —Comicbook.com

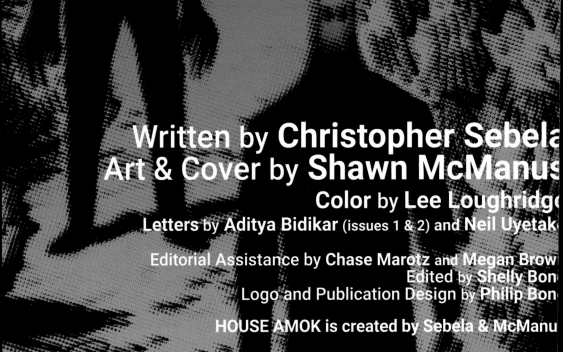

Written by **Christopher Sebela**
Art & Cover by **Shawn McManus**
Color by **Lee Loughridge**
Letters by **Aditya Bidikar** (issues 1 & 2) and **Neil Uyetak**

Editorial Assistance by **Chase Marotz** and **Megan Brown**
Edited by **Shelly Bond**
Logo and Publication Design by **Philip Bond**

HOUSE AMOK is created by Sebela & McManus

BLACK CROWN HQ
Shelly Bond, Editor • **Chase Marotz** and **Megan Brown,** Editorial Assistants • **Arlene Lo,** Proofreader
Philip Bond, logo, publication design and general dogsbody • **Chris Ryall, President**/Publisher & Chief Creative Officer

BLACK CROWN is a fully functioning curation operation based in Los Angeles by way of IDW Publishing.
Accept No Substitutes!

For international rights, contact licensing@idwpublishi

IDW
www.IDWPUBLISHING.com

Chris Ryall, President/Publisher & Chief Creative Officer • **Robbie Robbins,** EVP/Sr. Graphic Artist • **John Barber,** Editor-in-Chief • **David Hedge**
Associate Publisher • **Anita Frazier,** Senior Vice President of Sales & Marketing • **Lorelei Bunjes,** VP of Digital Services • **Eric Moss,** Senior Dir
Licensing & Business Development
Ted Adams, Founder & CEO of IDW Media Holdings

Facebook: **facebook.com/idwpublishing** • Twitter: **@idwpublishing** • YouTube: **youtube.com/idwpublishing**
Tumblr: **tumblr.idwpublishing.com** • Instagram: **instagram.com/idwpublishing**

HOUSE AMOK

blackcrown.pub

INTRODUCTION
by CHRISTOPHER SEBELA

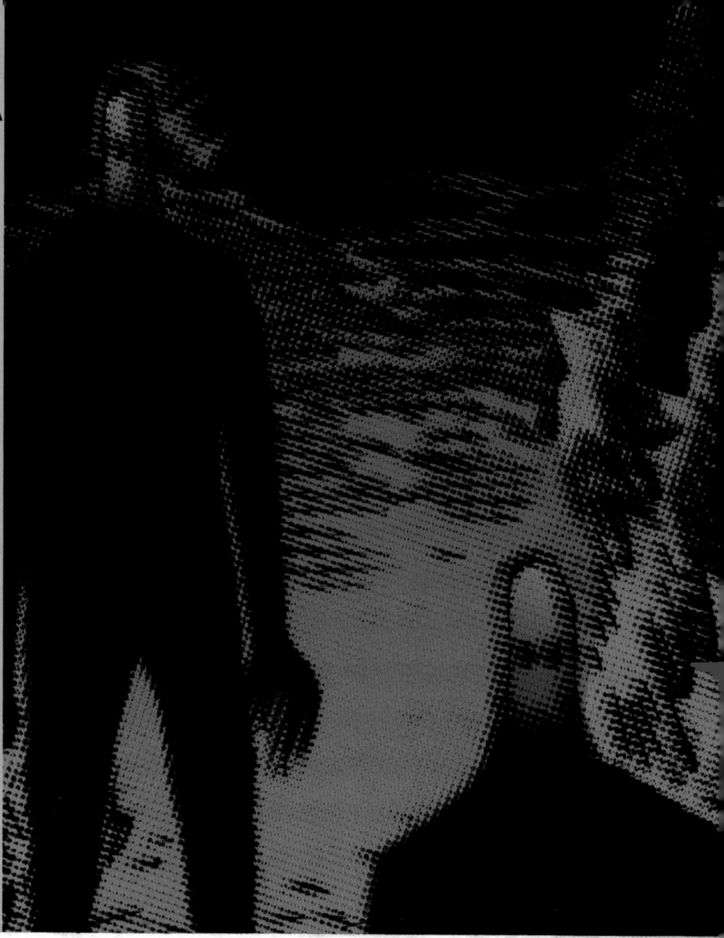

Conspiracies used to be fun; a party game with no pieces required, played worldwide, trying to chisel a divot of doubt into some of the biggest world events ever. I grew up in an age where the JFK assassination became a choose-your-own adventure of cabals, secret gunmen and shadowy puppet masters. Enough time had passed where it felt like a distant thing, actual history in actual textbooks, and going over it with a fine-tooth (if often wildly deranged) comb wasn't like trampling all over his grave.

Conspiracies used to be rare. Before I left Chicago and headed west, I got caught up in a conspiracy theory of my own. Weekly single-page digests explaining how an ancient order would use laser rays and mendelevium and the passages of George Orwell's 1984 to control school shooters, start World War One and down JFK Jr.'s plane. I collected over 70 of them within a two-and-a-half-year span, trying to parse out the whole timeline and ethos of this stranger's conspiracy worldview. It felt magical and singular. I never discovered who the person making them was, or even laid eyes on him, but I felt like we shared a secret.

Conspiracies used to be the province of world history. One of the first websites I ever bookmarked on the Internet was a forum for people who claimed to be the victims of mind control and gang stalking. Each one had their own page where they'd dump tens of thousands of words to lament the microphones in their walls which had recently been repainted by strangers. Pointing out the cameras in the streetlights to every family member and friend who was secretly reporting on their behavior. None of it linked to anything bigger than themselves, just a victim of one at the mercy of the world's bad intentions.

Conspiracies stopped being fun. They stopped being rare and started becoming personal. Somewhere along the line, tin foil hats were traded in for red baseball caps and the birth cycle of a conspiracy, which used to take years to gestate, moved into light speed, where an entire alternate explanation of events could be manufactured before the bodies got cold. They've become a panacea for a world that doesn't make sense to lots of people, that is too violent and unfair and awful to chalk up to "this is just how things are" and a balm for people whose lives haven't quite turned out the way they pictured. It's not their fault; it's a game of chess and it's rigged against them.

Just driving the Sandifer family insane felt too easy, too simple. In a world where conspiracy is part of the 24-hour news cycle and has wormed its way into messages from heads of state, this family drowning in bad luck and bad

choices would look outside themselves to find out where the rot is coming from. And the world offers an endless menu of cabals and secret agendas for people to choose from. This diagramming of the past to root out the weak spots used to feel like a thought experiment you'd play to pass the time; now it's become a philosophy, a belief system, a sickness that's spreading wider and wider, taking over the whole country. Taking over one family feels like a pretty small feat for this invisible monster that's been stalking every page of this book and the last twenty years of our lives. Shawn McManus seemed like the unlikeliest of co-conspirators on this endeavor, but he had all kinds of monsters lurking in his head and all I had to do was point him towards a door and let him decide what was behind it. And the trick with Shawn is, he can make those doors look so good that you have no choice but to open them, but so scary that you have to think twice. For every suit full of fists and pool of blood on the pavement, Shawn can make the quietest glance radiate menace or love or some mixture of the two.

With Lee Loughridge's colors making everything sedate until it all explodes in a cloud of bugs, we built a perfect conspiracy of our own in comics; an artform that combines intent and symbology, where they can flow in tandem or against each other and create something new, where all the signs and portents are hidden on the edges in symbols and movements.

Because, despite it all, conspiracies are still compelling. Even here, in the middle of this Illuminati-esque vortex we call our daily lives, there's still something about a wall covered in notes and string and pushpins and Scotch tape, about the idea that we're not to blame for what happens to us that's irresistible and swells the self-esteem. Success is ours and ours alone. Failure is the property of backstabbers and shadowy colluders. It's an insanity we can switch on and off, a comfort in the same way that sleeping with a gun under your pillow is. You might feel as safe as you've ever been, but the chances of blowing your head off rise dramatically. But maybe that's a bad metaphor. Maybe it only makes sense if you've looked through the Sandifers' eyes or fallen. But it feels a perfect family crest, hanging over the burning door of HOUSE AMOK. Come on in and keep an eye on your things while you're here; they might be different when you come out.

Christopher Sebela
January 15, 2019
Portland, Oregon

“We were born to be partners in crime
One person accidentally split into two.

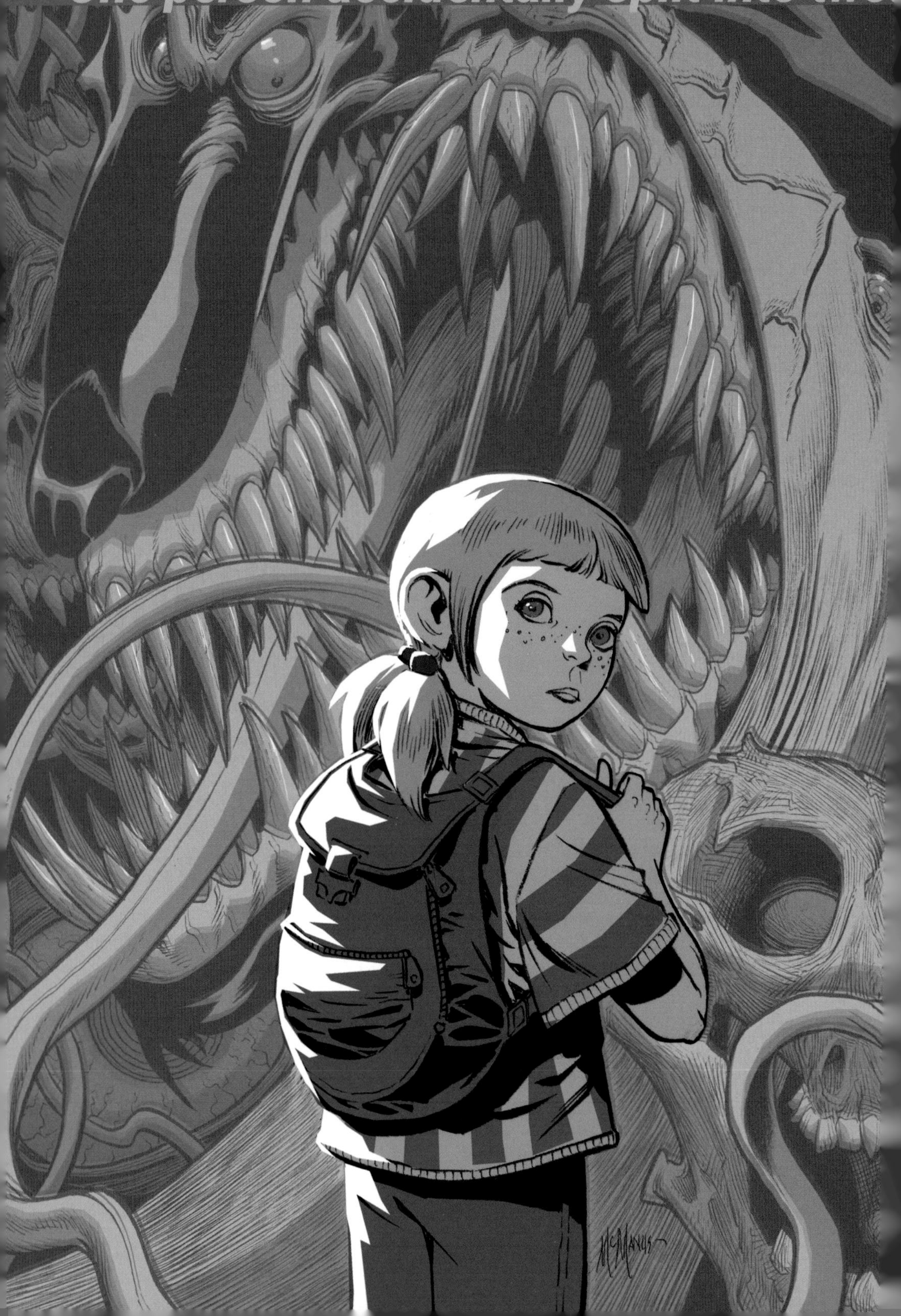
McManus

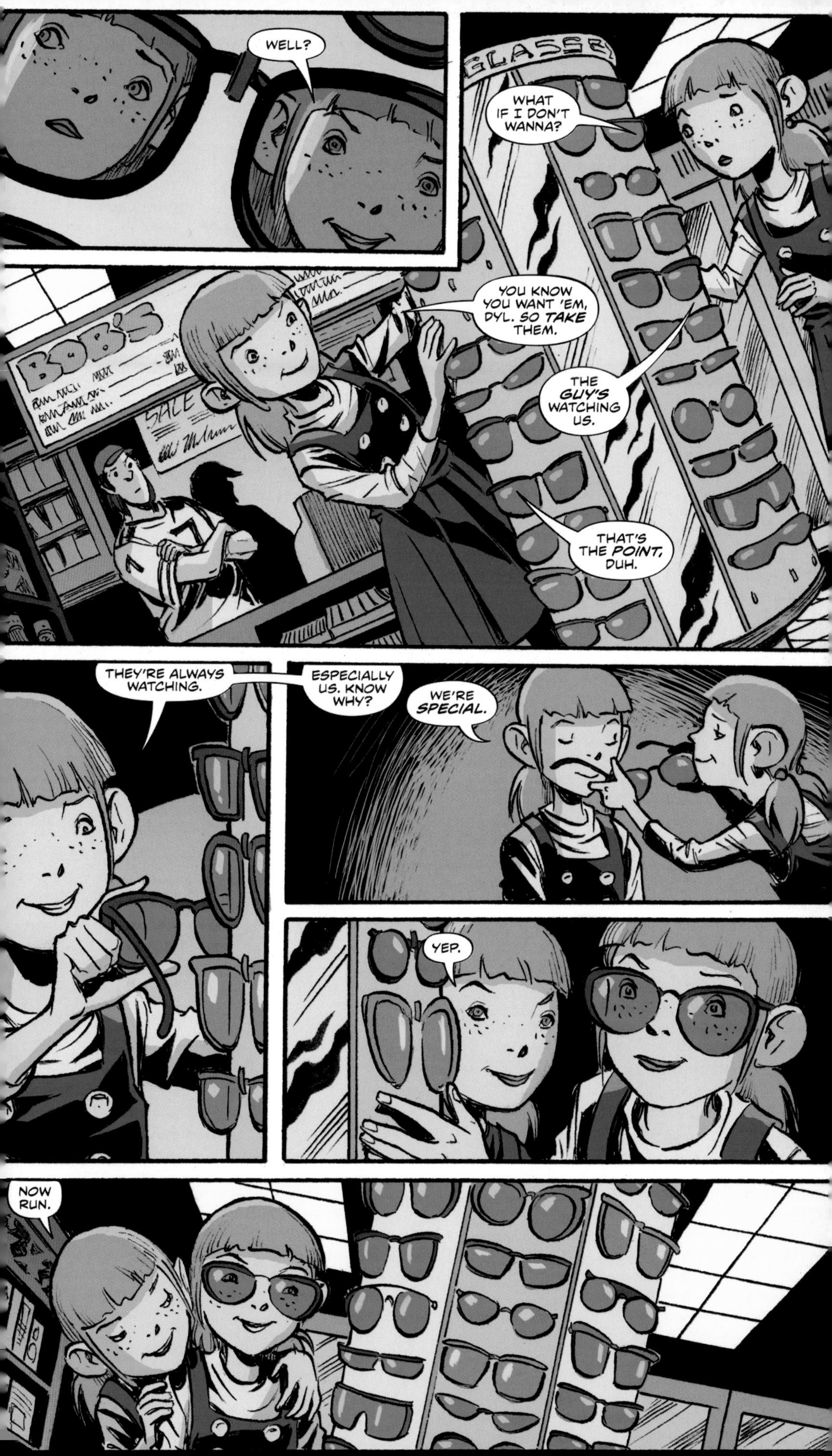
WELL?
WHAT IF I DON'T WANNA?
YOU KNOW YOU WANT 'EM, DYL. SO TAKE THEM.
THE GUY'S WATCHING US.
THAT'S THE POINT, DUH.
BOB'S
SALE
GLASSES
THEY'RE ALWAYS WATCHING.
ESPECIALLY US. KNOW WHY?
WE'RE SPECIAL.
YEP.
NOW RUN.

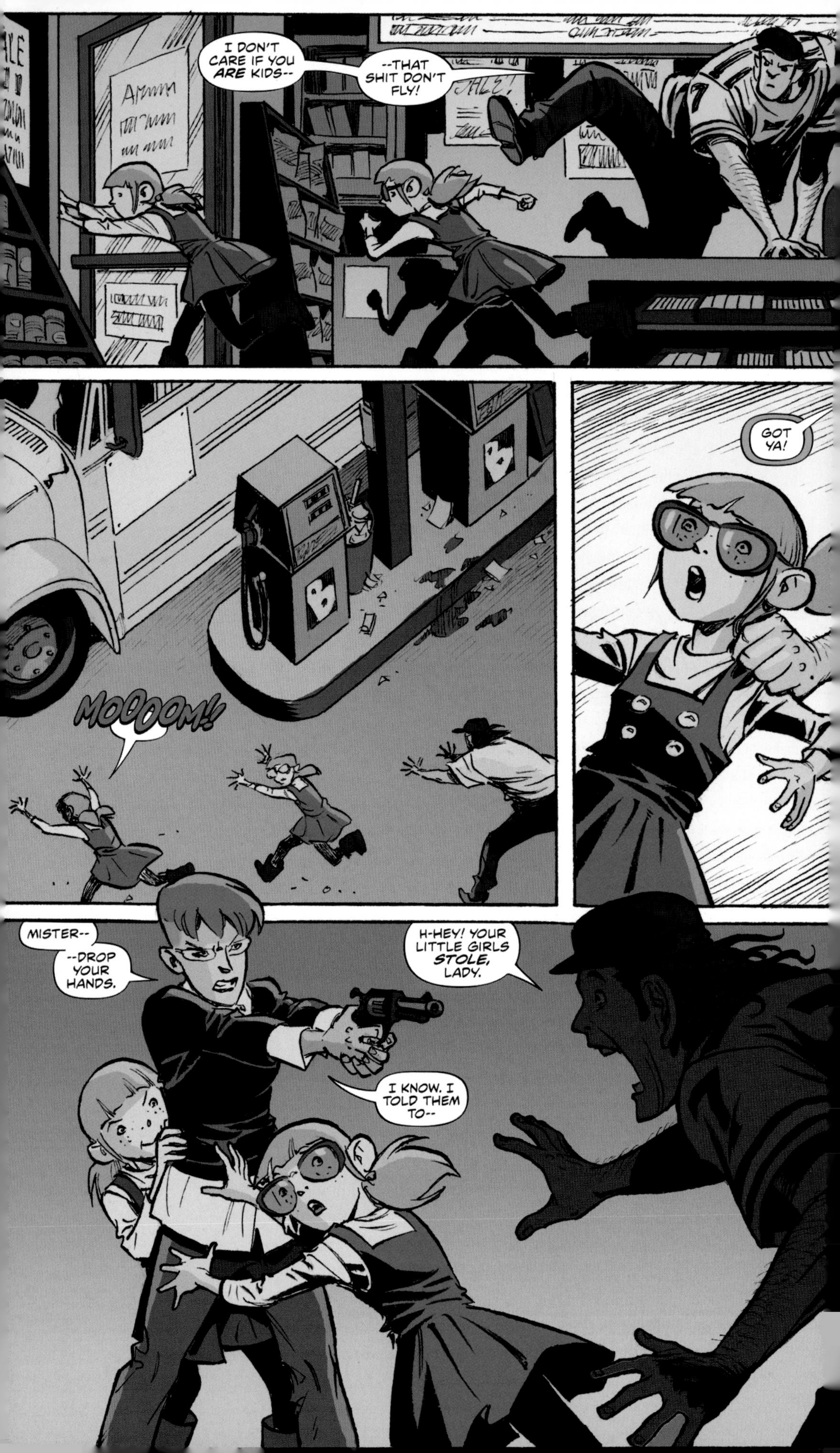
I DON'T CARE IF YOU ARE KIDS--
--THAT SHIT DON'T FLY!
MOOOOM!!
GOT YA!
MISTER--
--DROP YOUR HANDS.
H-HEY! YOUR LITTLE GIRLS STOLE, LADY.
I KNOW. I TOLD THEM TO--

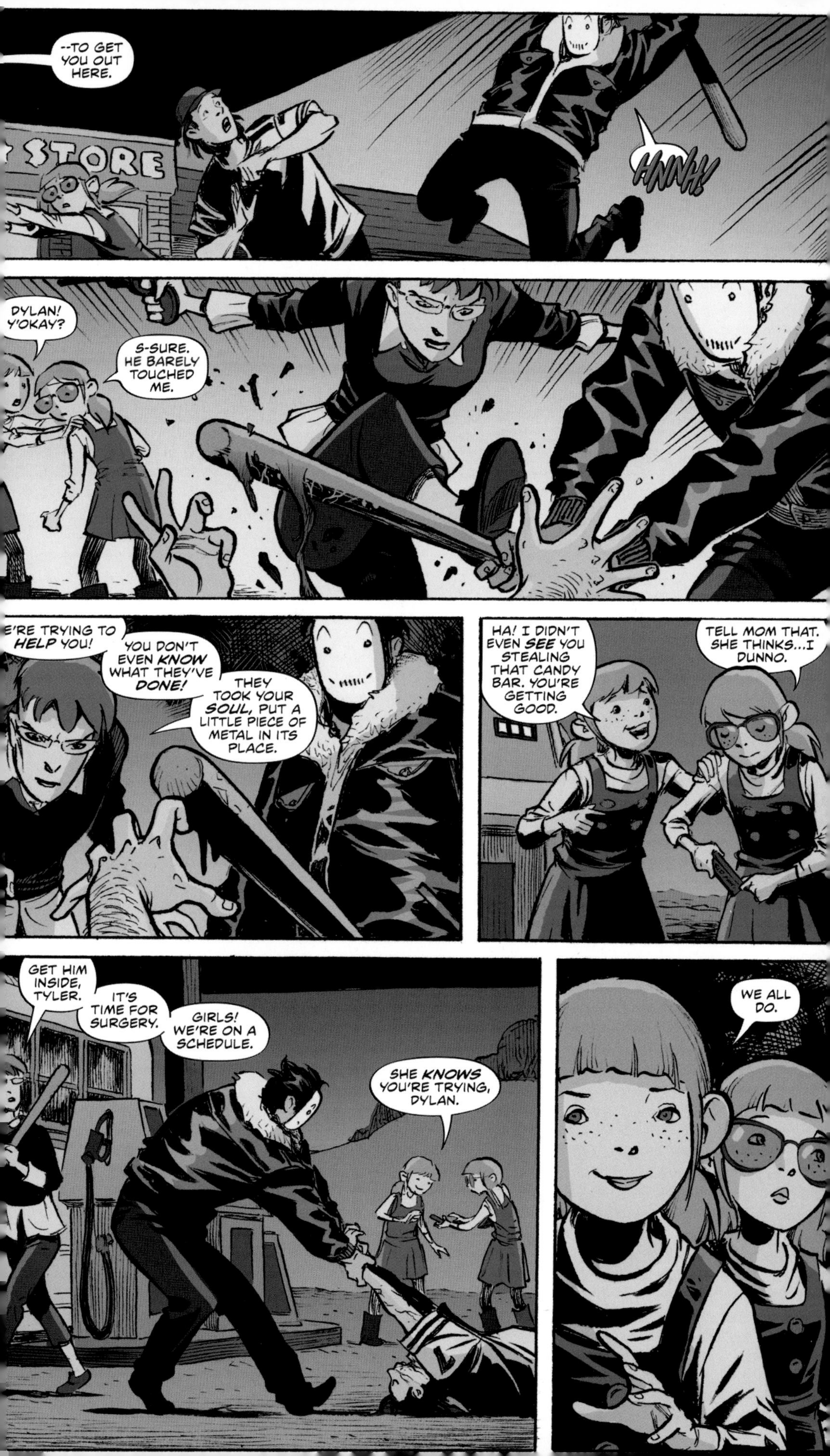

--TO GET YOU OUT HERE.
STORE
HNNH!
DYLAN! Y'OKAY?
S-SURE. HE BARELY TOUCHED ME.
'RE TRYING TO HELP YOU!
YOU DON'T EVEN KNOW WHAT THEY'VE DONE!
THEY TOOK YOUR SOUL, PUT A LITTLE PIECE OF METAL IN ITS PLACE.
HA! I DIDN'T EVEN SEE YOU STEALING THAT CANDY BAR. YOU'RE GETTING GOOD.
TELL MOM THAT. SHE THINKS...I DUNNO.
GET HIM INSIDE, TYLER.
IT'S TIME FOR SURGERY.
GIRLS! WE'RE ON A SCHEDULE.
SHE KNOWS YOU'RE TRYING, DYLAN.
WE ALL DO.

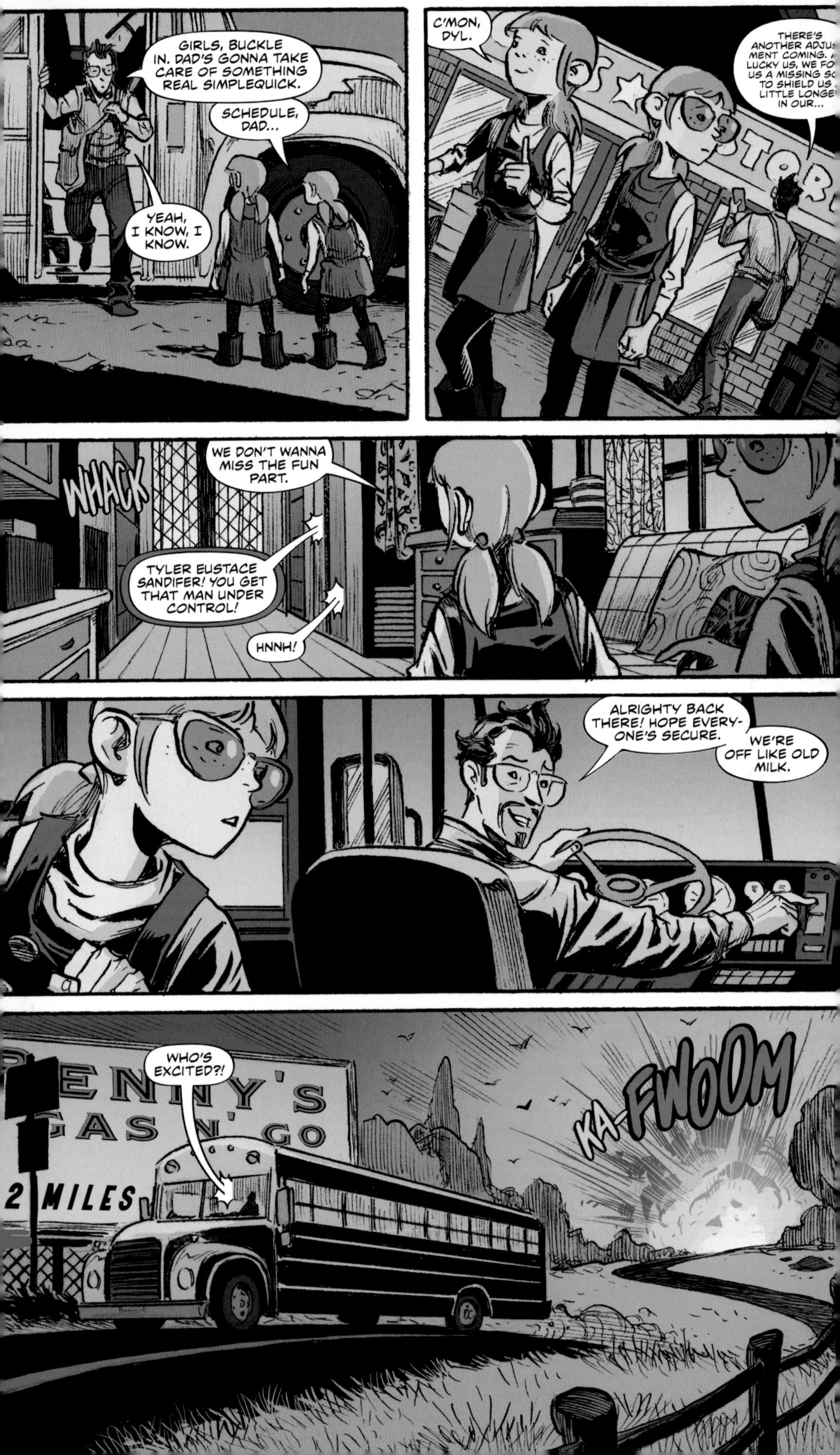
GIRLS, BUCKLE IN. DAD'S GONNA TAKE CARE OF SOMETHING REAL SIMPLEQUICK.
SCHEDULE, DAD...
YEAH, I KNOW, I KNOW.
C'MON, DYL.
THERE'S ANOTHER ADJUS MENT COMING. LUCKY US, WE FO US A MISSING SC TO SHIELD US LITTLE LONGE IN OUR...
STOR
WHACK
WE DON'T WANNA MISS THE FUN PART.
TYLER EUSTACE SANDIFER! YOU GET THAT MAN UNDER CONTROL!
HNNH!
ALRIGHTY BACK THERE! HOPE EVERY-ONE'S SECURE.
WE'RE OFF LIKE OLD MILK.
ENNY'S GAS 'N' GO
2 MILES
WHO'S EXCITED?!
KA-FWOOM

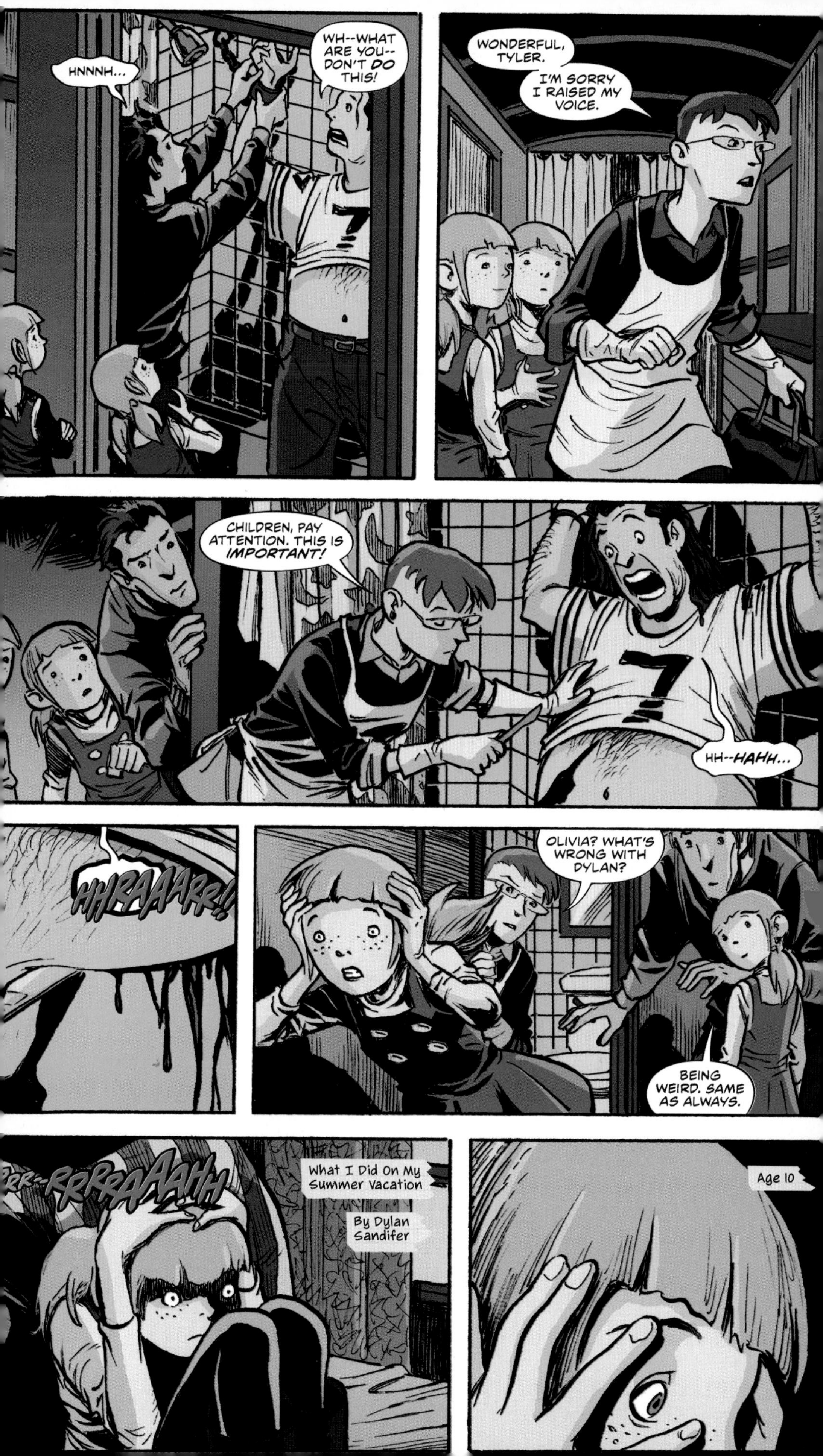
HNNNH...
WH--WHAT ARE YOU-- DON'T DO THIS!
WONDERFUL, TYLER.
I'M SORRY I RAISED MY VOICE.
CHILDREN, PAY ATTENTION. THIS IS IMPORTANT!
HH--HAHH...
HHRAAAARR!!
OLIVIA? WHAT'S WRONG WITH DYLAN?
BEING WEIRD. SAME AS ALWAYS.
RR--RRRRAAAHH
What I Did On My Summer Vacation
By Dylan Sandifer
Age 10

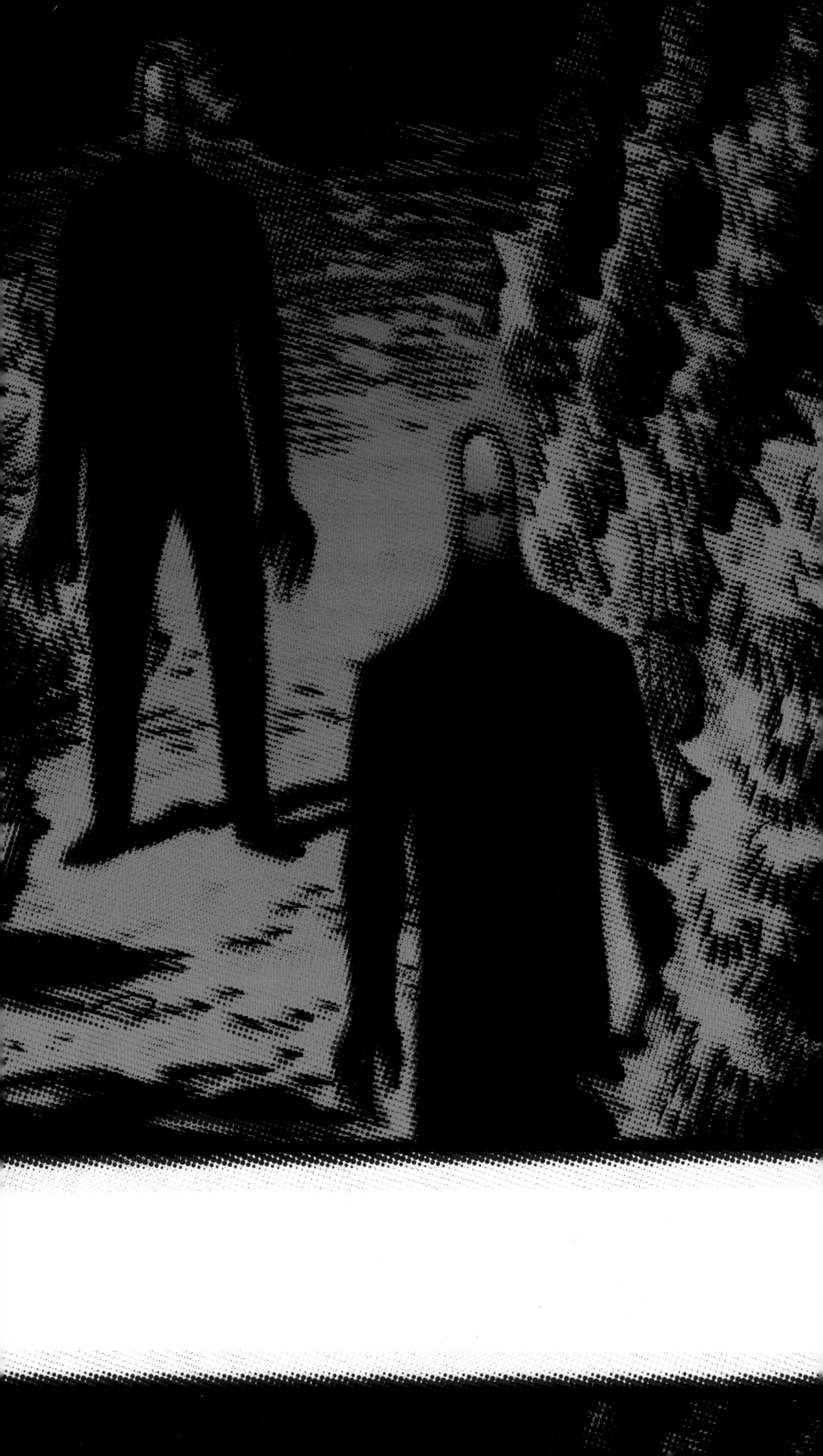

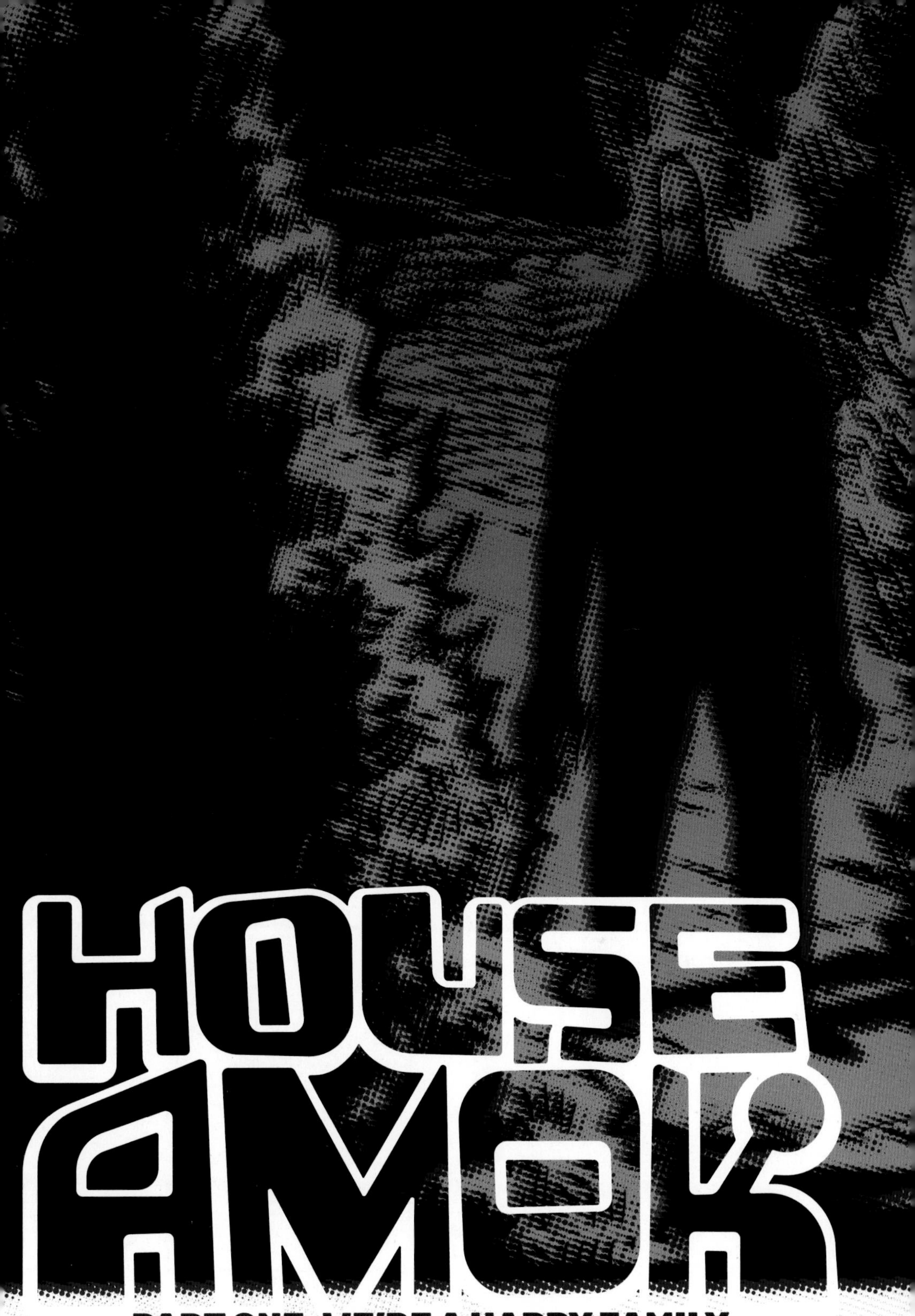

HOUSE AMOK

PART ONE: WE'RE A HAPPY FAMILY

CHRISTOPHER SEBELA
writer

SHAWN McMANUS
artist , cover A & retailer incentive

Tony Sandoval	Aditya Bidikar	Lee Loughridge	Chase Marotz	Shelly Bond
cover B	*letterer*	*colorist*	*assoc.editor*	*editor*

HOUSE AMOK is created by Sebela & McManus

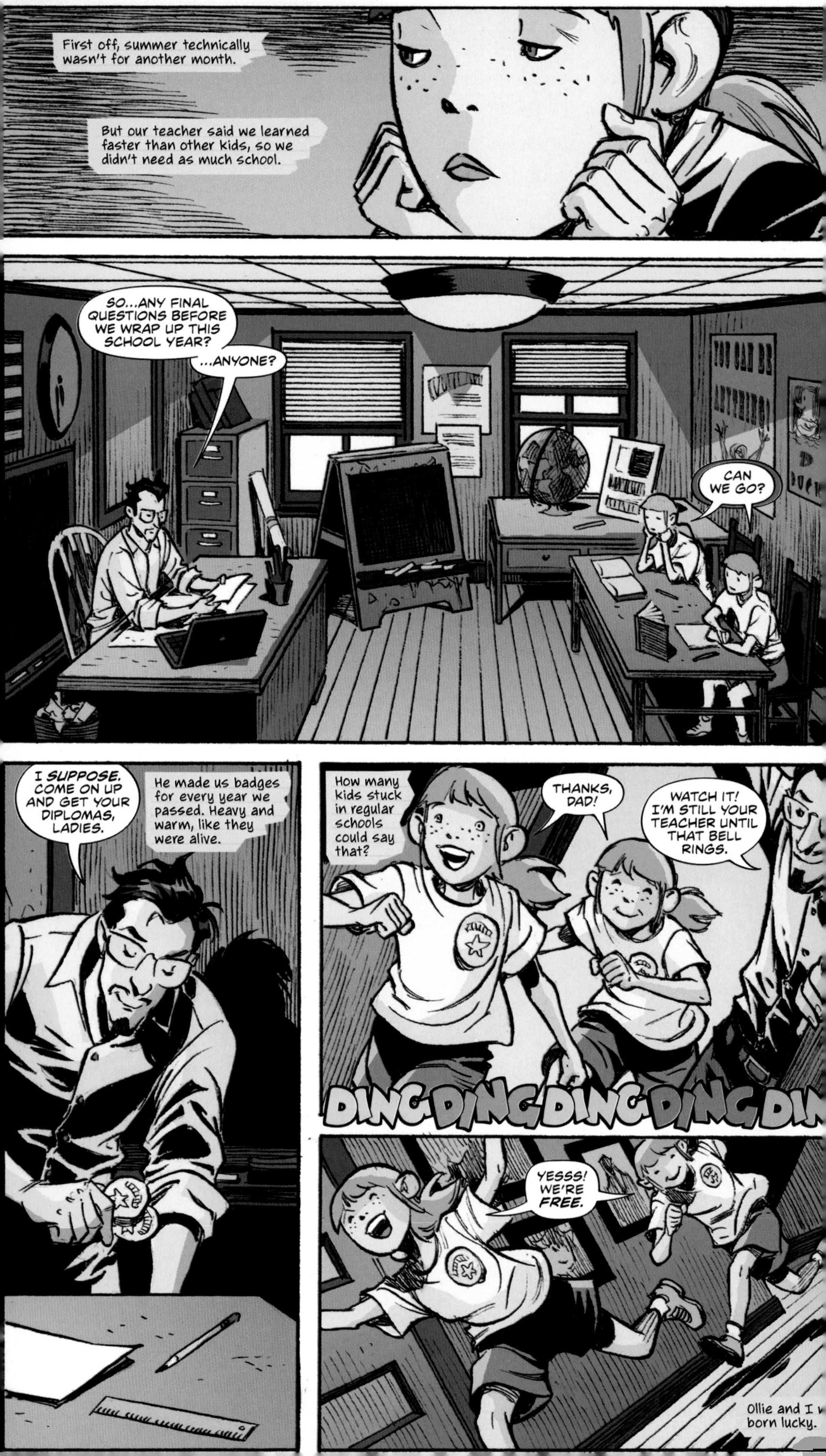
First off, summer technically wasn't for another month.
But our teacher said we learned faster than other kids, so we didn't need as much school.
SO...ANY FINAL QUESTIONS BEFORE WE WRAP UP THIS SCHOOL YEAR?
...ANYONE?
YOU CAN BE ANYTHING!
CAN WE GO?
I SUPPOSE. COME ON UP AND GET YOUR DIPLOMAS, LADIES.
He made us badges for every year we passed. Heavy and warm, like they were alive.
How many kids stuck in regular schools could say that?
THANKS, DAD!
WATCH IT! I'M STILL YOUR TEACHER UNTIL THAT BELL RINGS.
DING DING DING DING DIN
YESSS! WE'RE FREE.
Ollie and I w
born lucky.

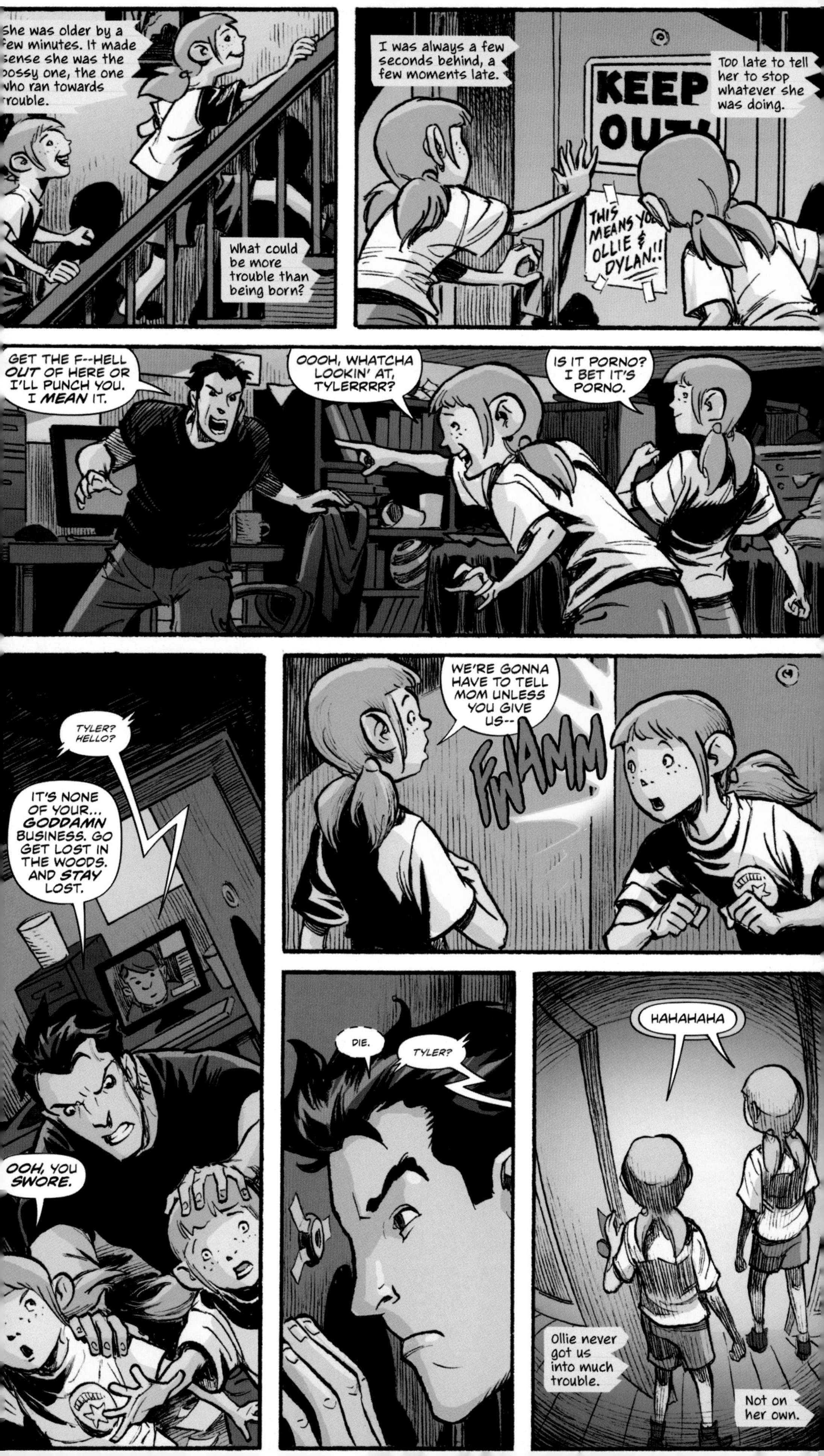

She was older by a few minutes. It made sense she was the bossy one, the one who ran towards trouble.
What could be more trouble than being born?
I was always a few seconds behind, a few moments late.
Too late to tell her to stop whatever she was doing.
KEEP OUT!
THIS MEANS YOU OLLIE & DYLAN!!
GET THE F--HELL OUT OF HERE OR I'LL PUNCH YOU. I MEAN IT.
OOOH, WHATCHA LOOKIN' AT, TYLERRRR?
IS IT PORNO? I BET IT'S PORNO.
TYLER? HELLO?
IT'S NONE OF YOUR... GODDAMN BUSINESS. GO GET LOST IN THE WOODS. AND STAY LOST.
OOH, YOU SWORE.
WE'RE GONNA HAVE TO TELL MOM UNLESS YOU GIVE US--
FWAMM
DIE.
TYLER?
HAHAHAHA
Ollie never got us into much trouble.
Not on her own.

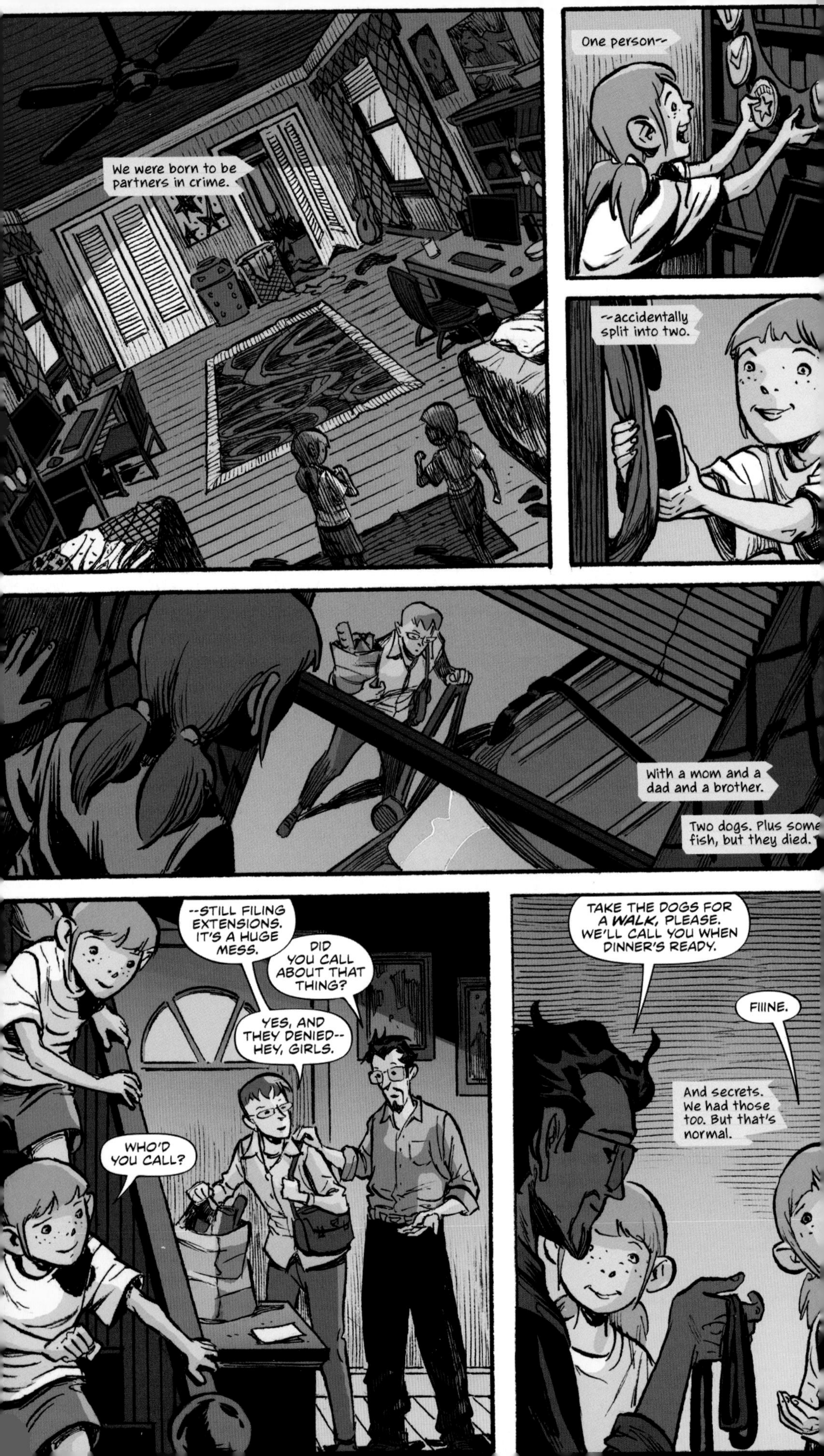
We were born to be partners in crime.
One person--
--accidentally split into two.
With a mom and a dad and a brother.
Two dogs. Plus some fish, but they died.
--STILL FILING EXTENSIONS. IT'S A HUGE MESS.
DID YOU CALL ABOUT THAT THING?
YES, AND THEY DENIED-- HEY, GIRLS.
WHO'D YOU CALL?
TAKE THE DOGS FOR A WALK, PLEASE. WE'LL CALL YOU WHEN DINNER'S READY.
FIIINE.
And secrets. We had those too. But that's normal.

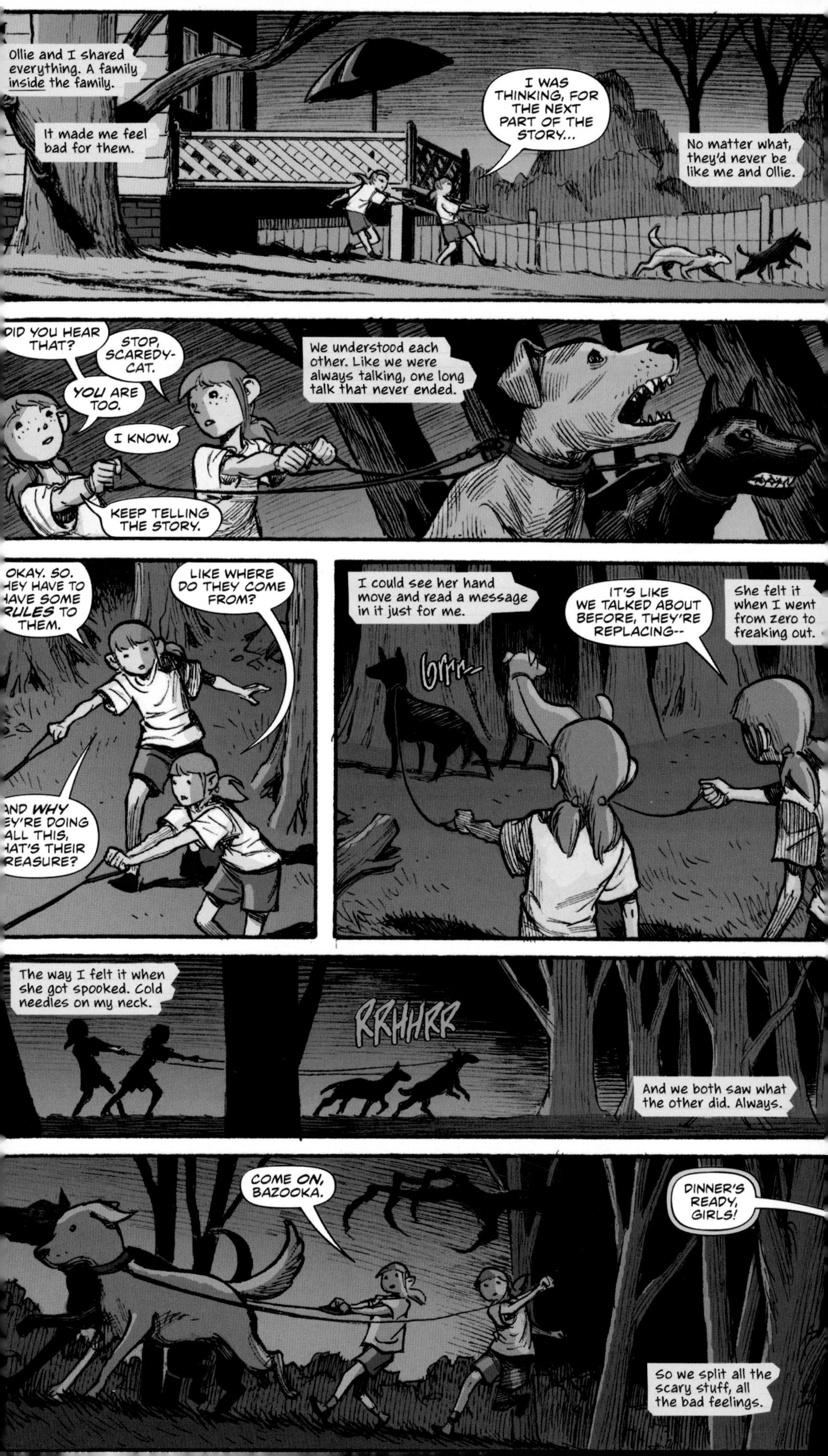

Ollie and I shared everything. A family inside the family.
It made me feel bad for them.
I WAS THINKING, FOR THE NEXT PART OF THE STORY...
No matter what, they'd never be like me and Ollie.
DID YOU HEAR THAT?
STOP, SCAREDY-CAT.
YOU ARE TOO.
I KNOW.
KEEP TELLING THE STORY.
We understood each other. Like we were always talking, one long talk that never ended.
OKAY. SO. HEY HAVE TO HAVE SOME RULES TO THEM.
LIKE WHERE DO THEY COME FROM?
AND WHY EY'RE DOING ALL THIS, HAT'S THEIR REASURE?
I could see her hand move and read a message in it just for me.
IT'S LIKE WE TALKED ABOUT BEFORE, THEY'RE REPLACING--
She felt it when I went from zero to freaking out.
GRRR
The way I felt it when she got spooked. Cold needles on my neck.
RRHHRR
And we both saw what the other did. Always.
COME ON, BAZOOKA.
DINNER'S READY, GIRLS!
So we split all the scary stuff, all the bad feelings.

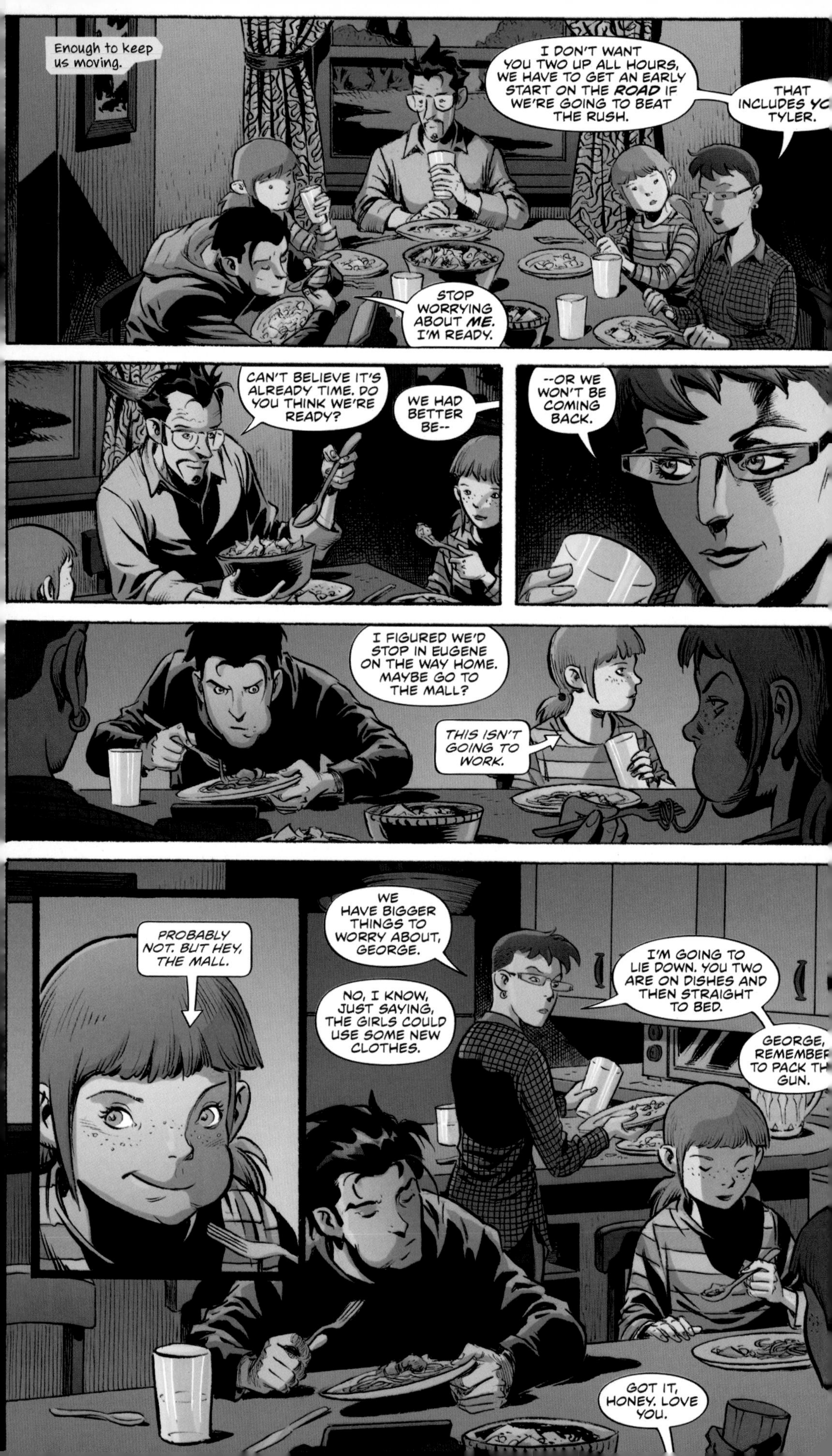

Enough to keep us moving.
I DON'T WANT YOU TWO UP ALL HOURS, WE HAVE TO GET AN EARLY START ON THE ROAD IF WE'RE GOING TO BEAT THE RUSH.
THAT INCLUDES YO TYLER.
STOP WORRYING ABOUT ME. I'M READY.
CAN'T BELIEVE IT'S ALREADY TIME. DO YOU THINK WE'RE READY?
WE HAD BETTER BE--
--OR WE WON'T BE COMING BACK.
I FIGURED WE'D STOP IN EUGENE ON THE WAY HOME. MAYBE GO TO THE MALL?
THIS ISN'T GOING TO WORK.
PROBABLY NOT. BUT HEY, THE MALL.
WE HAVE BIGGER THINGS TO WORRY ABOUT, GEORGE.
NO, I KNOW, JUST SAYING, THE GIRLS COULD USE SOME NEW CLOTHES.
I'M GOING TO LIE DOWN. YOU TWO ARE ON DISHES AND THEN STRAIGHT TO BED.
GEORGE, REMEMBER TO PACK TH GUN.
GOT IT, HONEY. LOVE YOU.

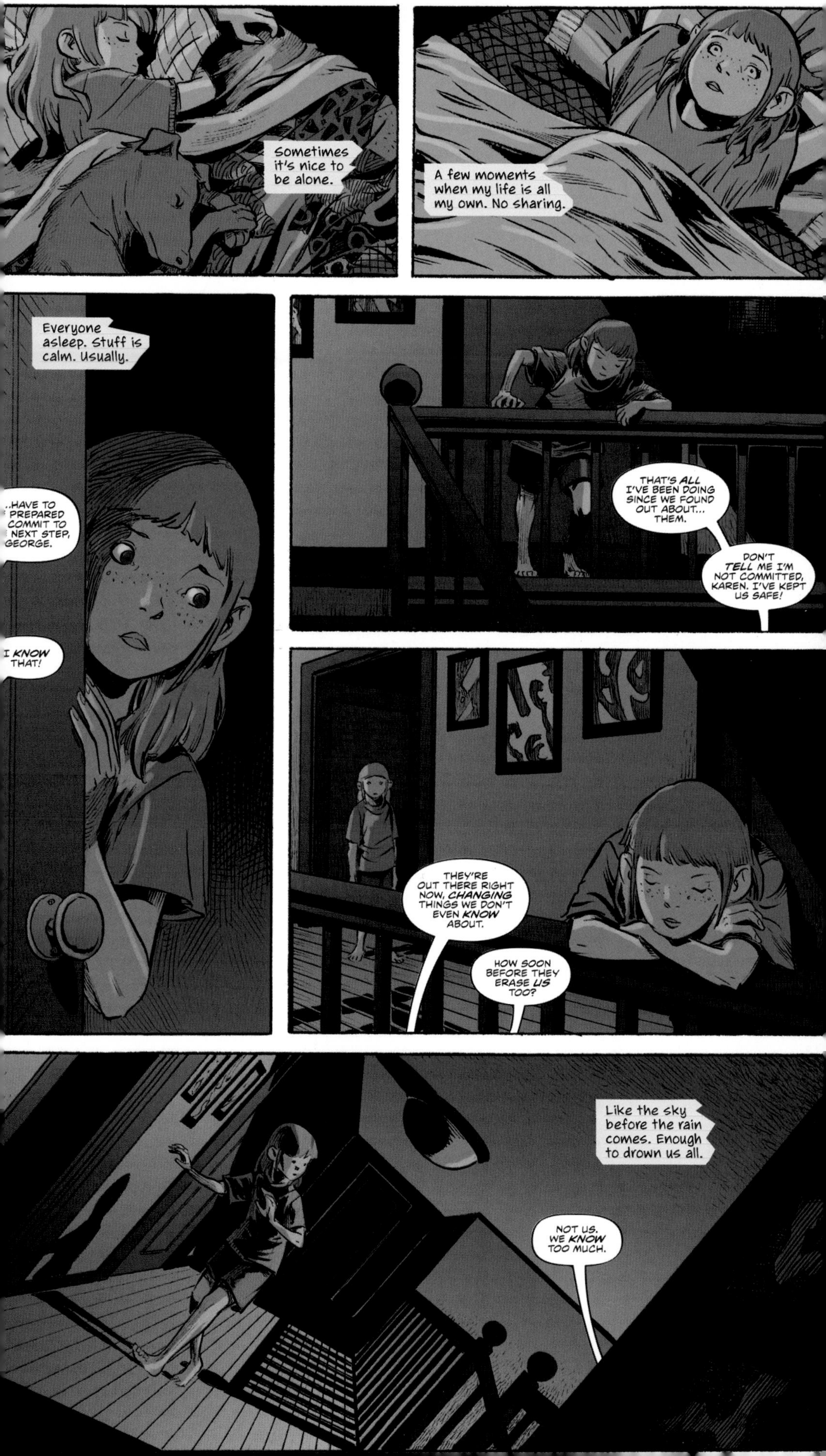

Sometimes it's nice to be alone.
A few moments when my life is all my own. No sharing.
Everyone asleep. Stuff is calm. Usually.
..HAVE TO PREPARED COMMIT TO NEXT STEP, GEORGE.
I KNOW THAT!
THAT'S ALL I'VE BEEN DOING SINCE WE FOUND OUT ABOUT... THEM.
DON'T TELL ME I'M NOT COMMITTED, KAREN. I'VE KEPT US SAFE!
THEY'RE OUT THERE RIGHT NOW, CHANGING THINGS WE DON'T EVEN KNOW ABOUT.
HOW SOON BEFORE THEY ERASE US TOO?
Like the sky before the rain comes. Enough to drown us all.
NOT US. WE KNOW TOO MUCH.

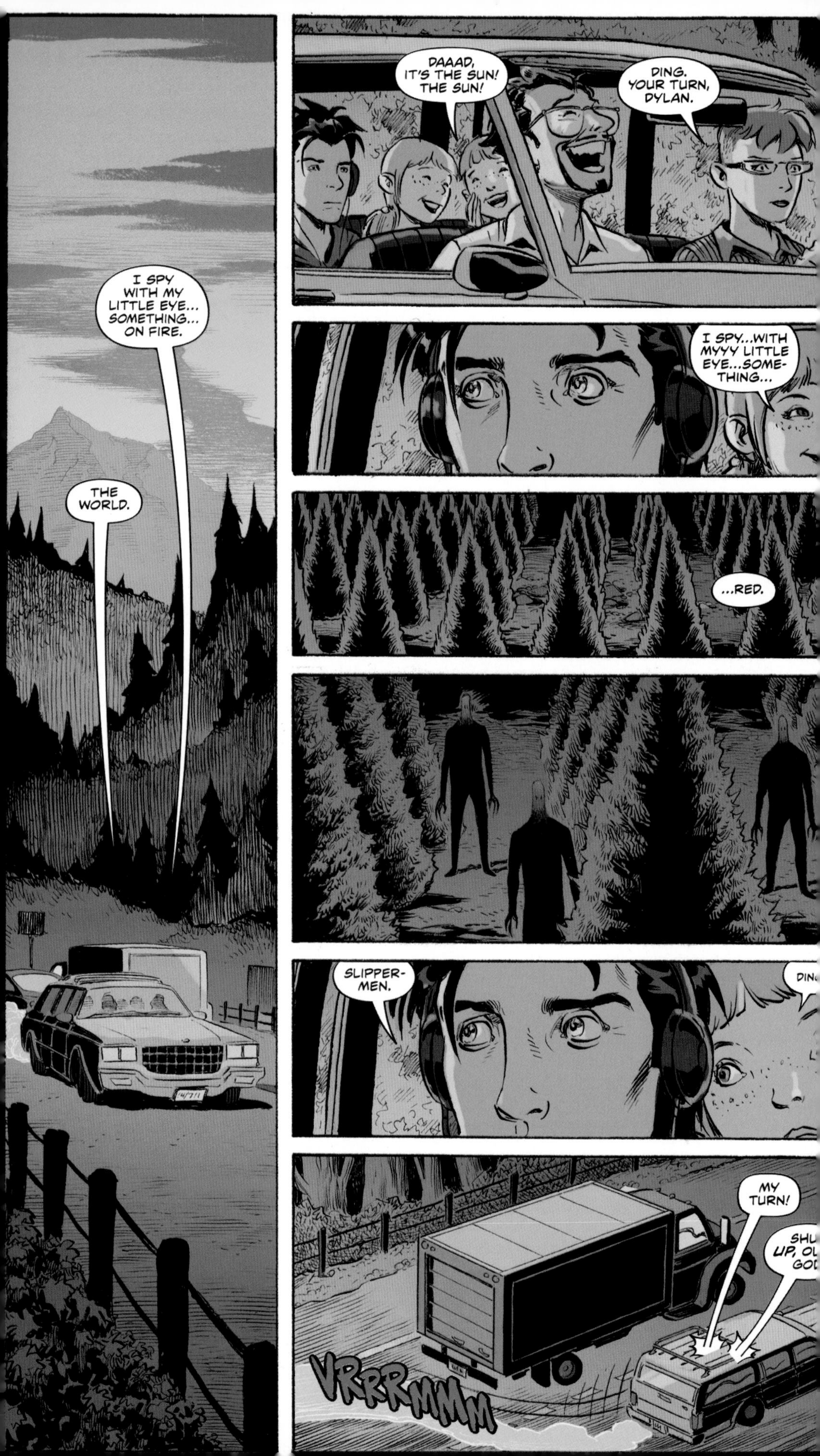
I SPY WITH MY LITTLE EYE... SOMETHING... ON FIRE.
THE WORLD.
DAAAD, IT'S THE SUN! THE SUN!
DING. YOUR TURN, DYLAN.
I SPY...WITH MYYY LITTLE EYE...SOME-THING...
...RED.
SLIPPER-MEN.
MY TURN!
VRRRMMMM

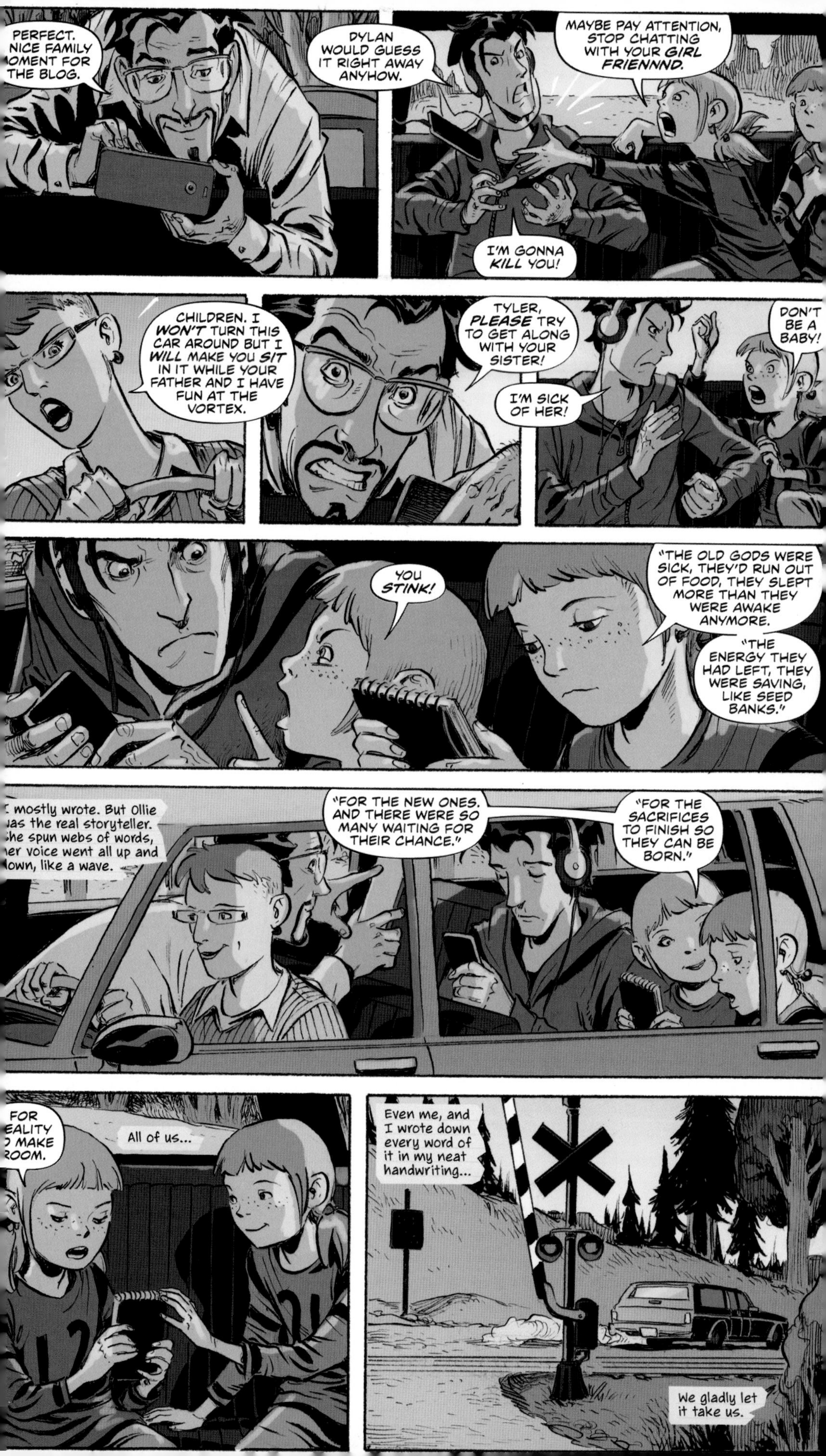
PERFECT. NICE FAMILY MOMENT FOR THE BLOG.
DYLAN WOULD GUESS IT RIGHT AWAY ANYHOW.
MAYBE PAY ATTENTION, STOP CHATTING WITH YOUR GIRL FRIENNND.
I'M GONNA KILL YOU!
CHILDREN. I WON'T TURN THIS CAR AROUND BUT I WILL MAKE YOU SIT IN IT WHILE YOUR FATHER AND I HAVE FUN AT THE VORTEX.
TYLER, PLEASE TRY TO GET ALONG WITH YOUR SISTER!
I'M SICK OF HER!
DON'T BE A BABY!
YOU STINK!
"THE OLD GODS WERE SICK, THEY'D RUN OUT OF FOOD, THEY SLEPT MORE THAN THEY WERE AWAKE ANYMORE.
"THE ENERGY THEY HAD LEFT, THEY WERE SAVING, LIKE SEED BANKS."
I mostly wrote. But Ollie was the real storyteller. She spun webs of words, her voice went all up and down, like a wave.
"FOR THE NEW ONES. AND THERE WERE SO MANY WAITING FOR THEIR CHANCE."
"FOR THE SACRIFICES TO FINISH SO THEY CAN BE BORN."
FOR REALITY TO MAKE ROOM.
All of us...
Even me, and I wrote down every word of it in my neat handwriting...
We gladly let it take us.

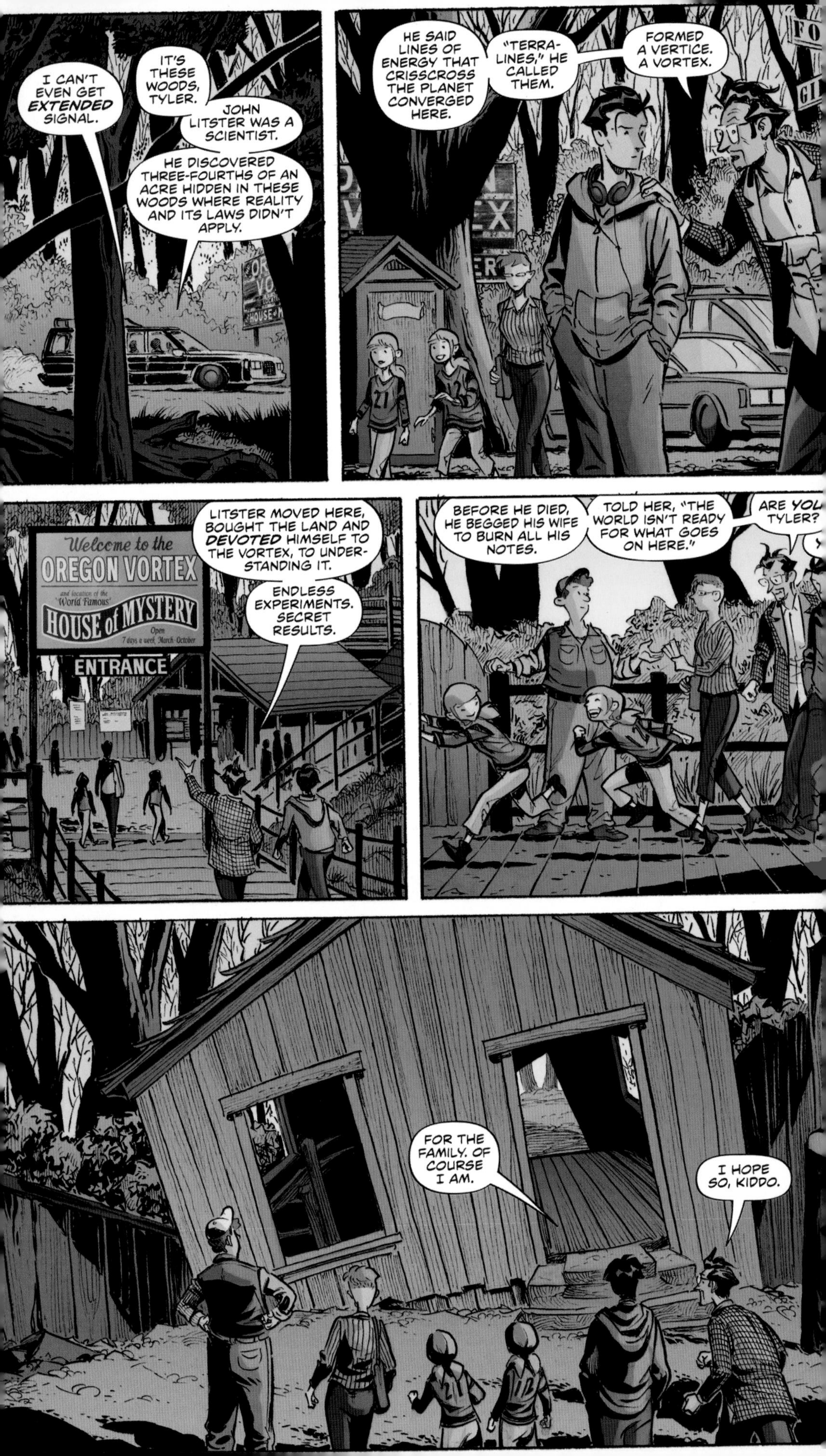

I CAN'T EVEN GET ***EXTENDED*** SIGNAL.
IT'S THESE WOODS, TYLER.
JOHN LITSTER WAS A SCIENTIST.
HE DISCOVERED THREE-FOURTHS OF AN ACRE HIDDEN IN THESE WOODS WHERE REALITY AND ITS LAWS DIDN'T APPLY.
HE SAID LINES OF ENERGY THAT CRISSCROSS THE PLANET CONVERGED HERE.
"TERRA-LINES," HE CALLED THEM.
FORMED A VERTICE. A VORTEX.
Welcome to the
OREGON VORTEX
and location of the "World Famous"
HOUSE of MYSTERY
Open
7 days a week, March-October
ENTRANCE
LITSTER MOVED HERE, BOUGHT THE LAND AND ***DEVOTED*** HIMSELF TO THE VORTEX, TO UNDERSTANDING IT.
ENDLESS EXPERIMENTS. SECRET RESULTS.
BEFORE HE DIED, HE BEGGED HIS WIFE TO BURN ALL HIS NOTES.
TOLD HER, "THE WORLD ISN'T READY FOR WHAT GOES ON HERE."
ARE ***YOU*** TYLER?
FOR THE FAMILY. OF COURSE I AM.
I HOPE SO, KIDDO.

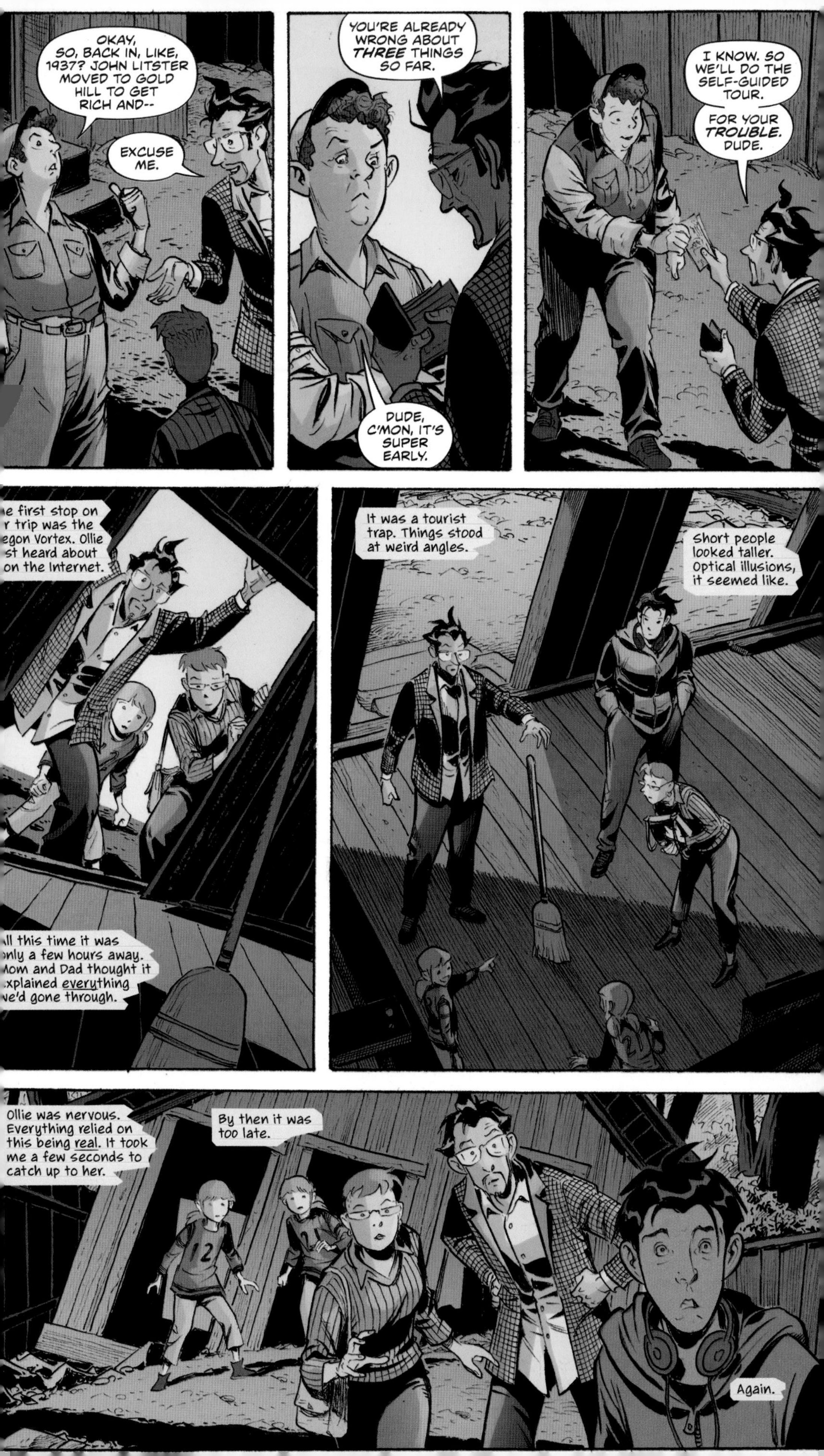
OKAY, SO, BACK IN, LIKE, 1937? JOHN LITSTER MOVED TO GOLD HILL TO GET RICH AND--
EXCUSE ME.
YOU'RE ALREADY WRONG ABOUT THREE THINGS SO FAR.
DUDE, C'MON, IT'S SUPER EARLY.
I KNOW. SO WE'LL DO THE SELF-GUIDED TOUR.
FOR YOUR TROUBLE. DUDE.
e first stop on r trip was the egon Vortex. Ollie st heard about on the Internet.
ll this time it was nly a few hours away. Mom and Dad thought it xplained everything we'd gone through.
It was a tourist trap. Things stood at weird angles.
Short people looked taller. Optical illusions, it seemed like.
Ollie was nervous. Everything relied on this being real. It took me a few seconds to catch up to her.
By then it was too late.
Again.

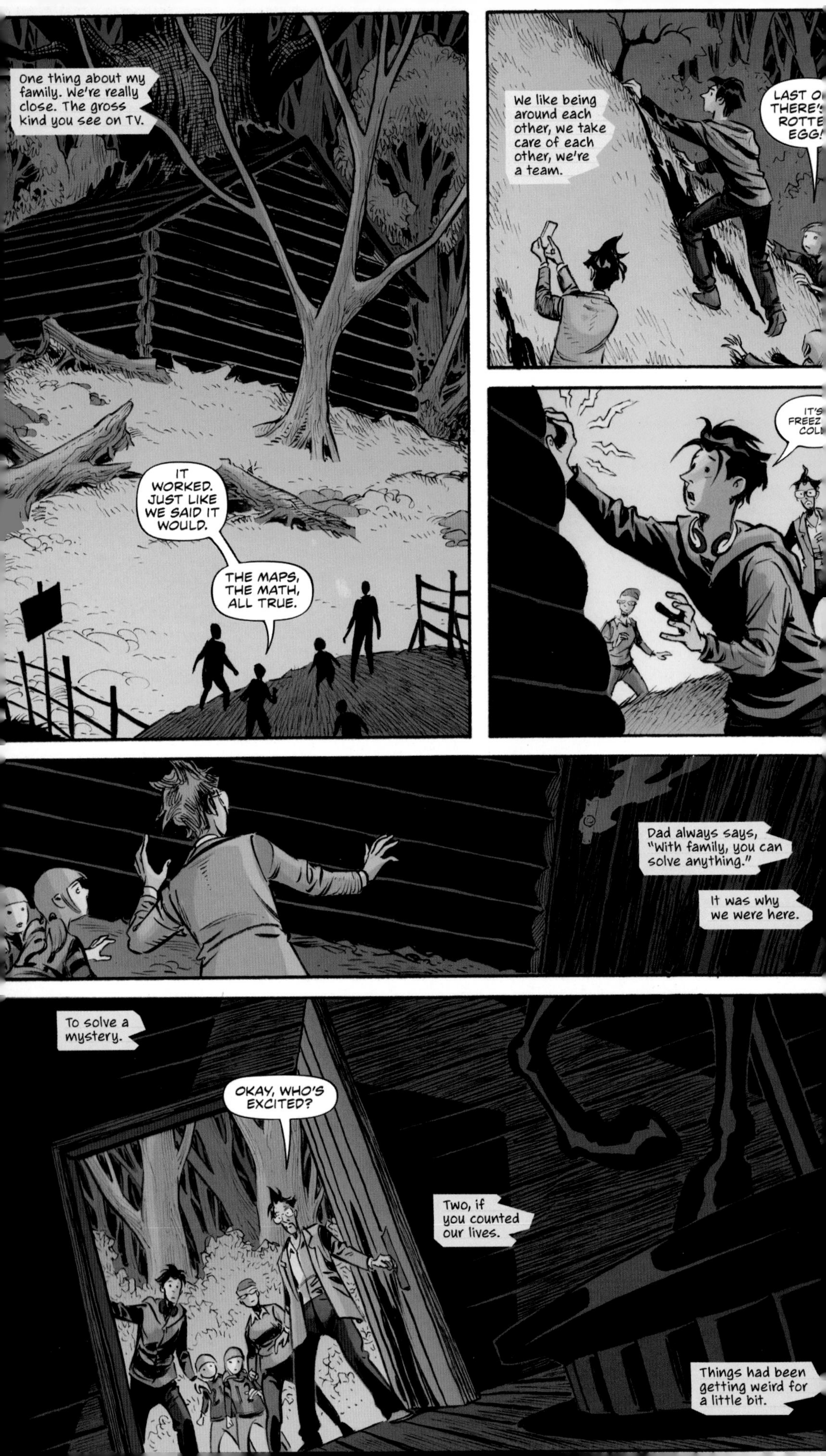
One thing about my family. We're really close. The gross kind you see on TV.
IT WORKED. JUST LIKE WE SAID IT WOULD.
THE MAPS, THE MATH, ALL TRUE.
We like being around each other, we take care of each other, we're a team.
LAST O THERE'S ROTTE EGG!
IT'S FREEZ COL
Dad always says, "With family, you can solve anything."
It was why we were here.
To solve a mystery.
OKAY, WHO'S EXCITED?
Two, if you counted our lives.
Things had been getting weird for a little bit.

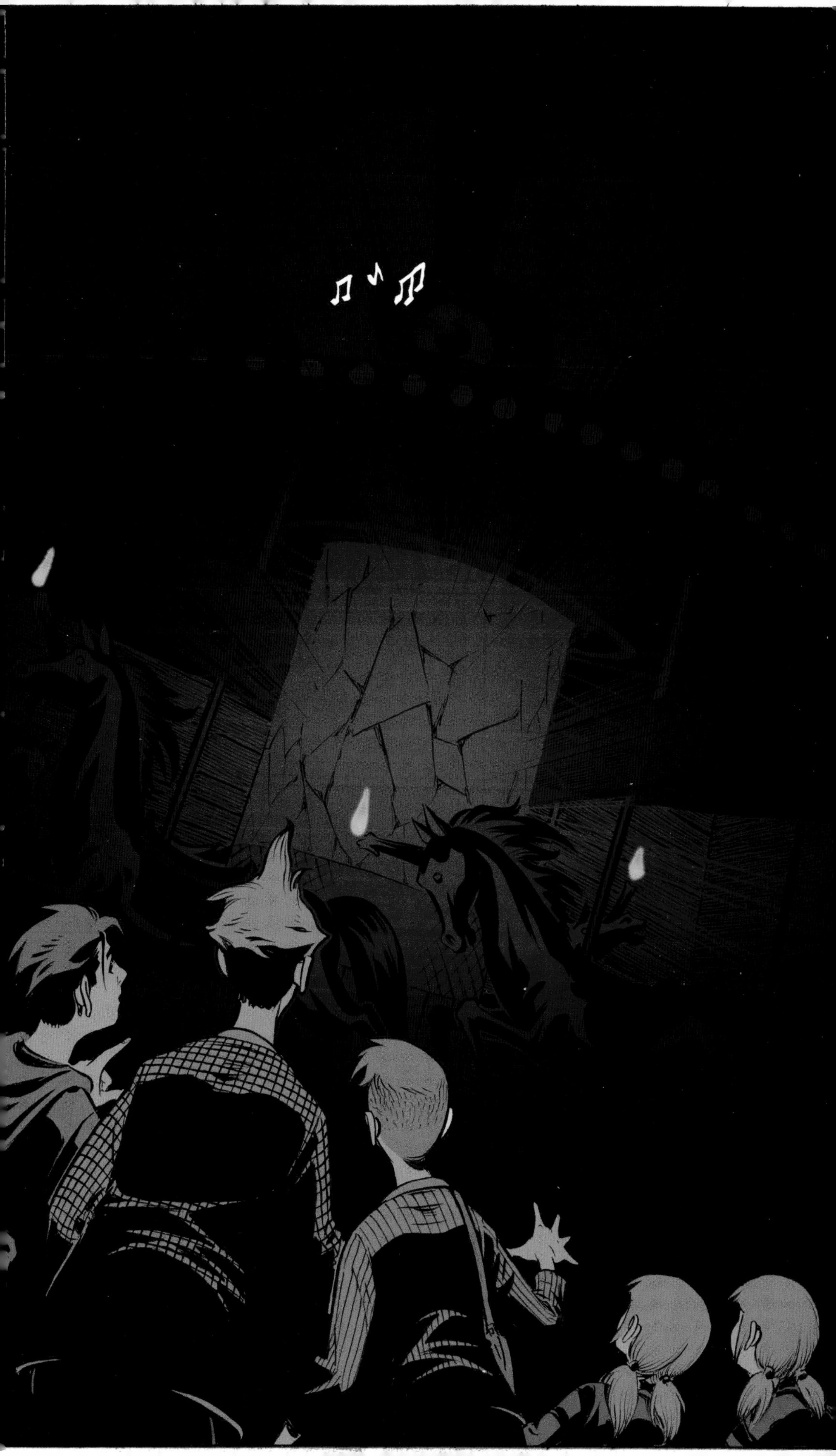

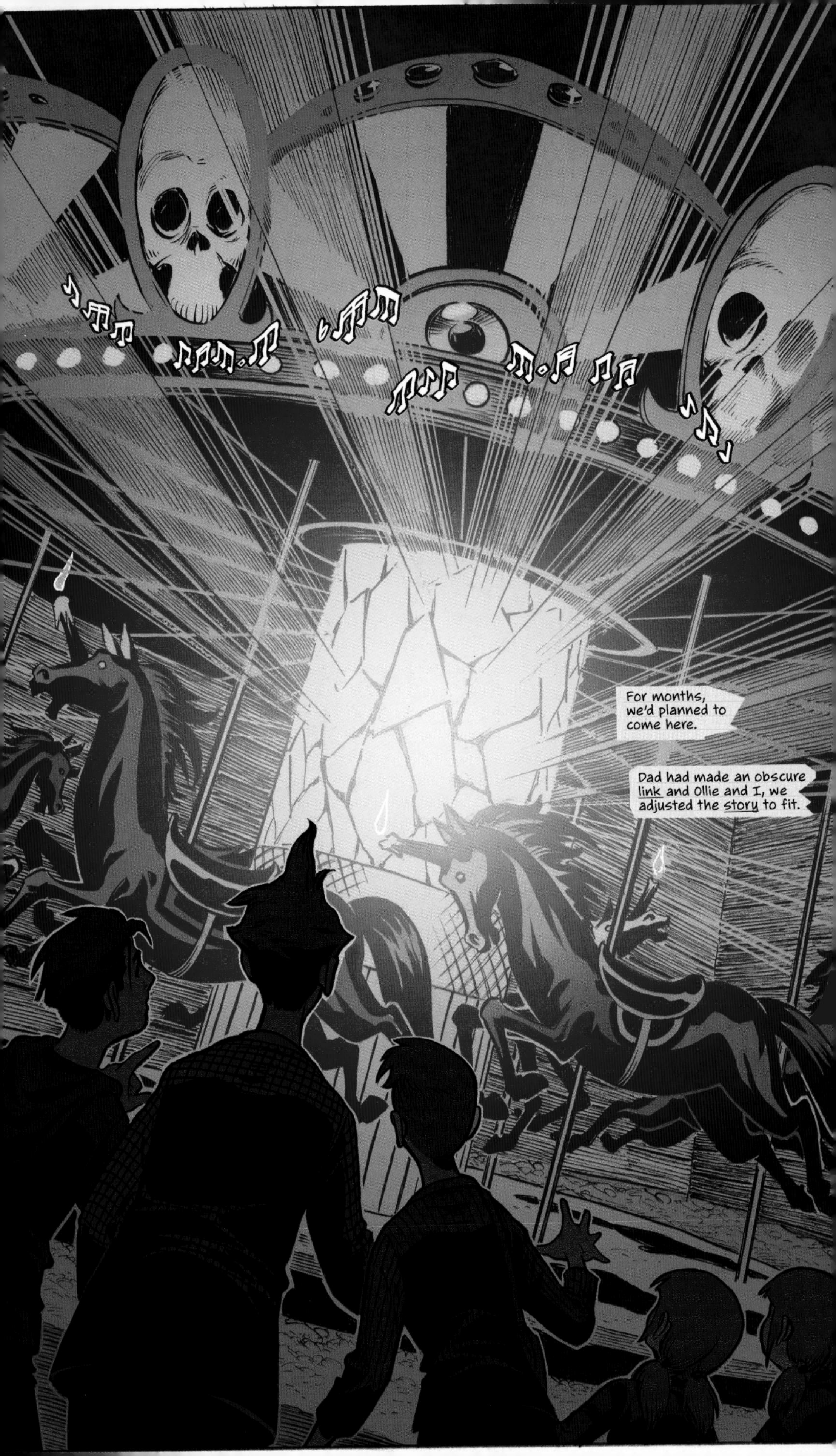

For months, we'd planned to come here.
Dad had made an obscure link and Ollie and I, we adjusted the story to fit.

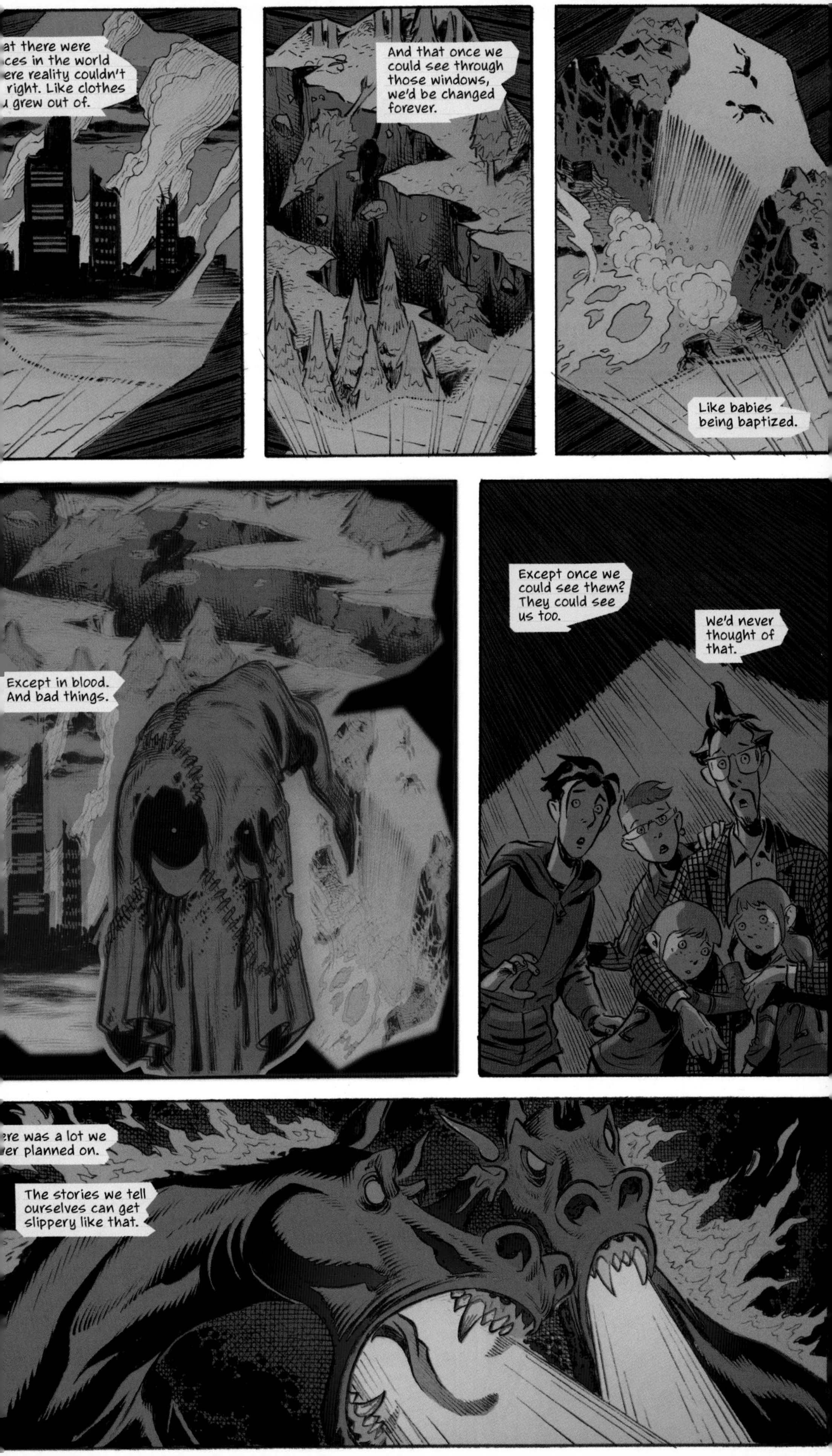
at there were ces in the world ere reality couldn't right. Like clothes u grew out of.
And that once we could see through those windows, we'd be changed forever.
Like babies being baptized.
Except in blood. And bad things.
Except once we could see them? They could see us too.
We'd never thought of that.
ere was a lot we ver planned on.
The stories we tell ourselves can get slippery like that.

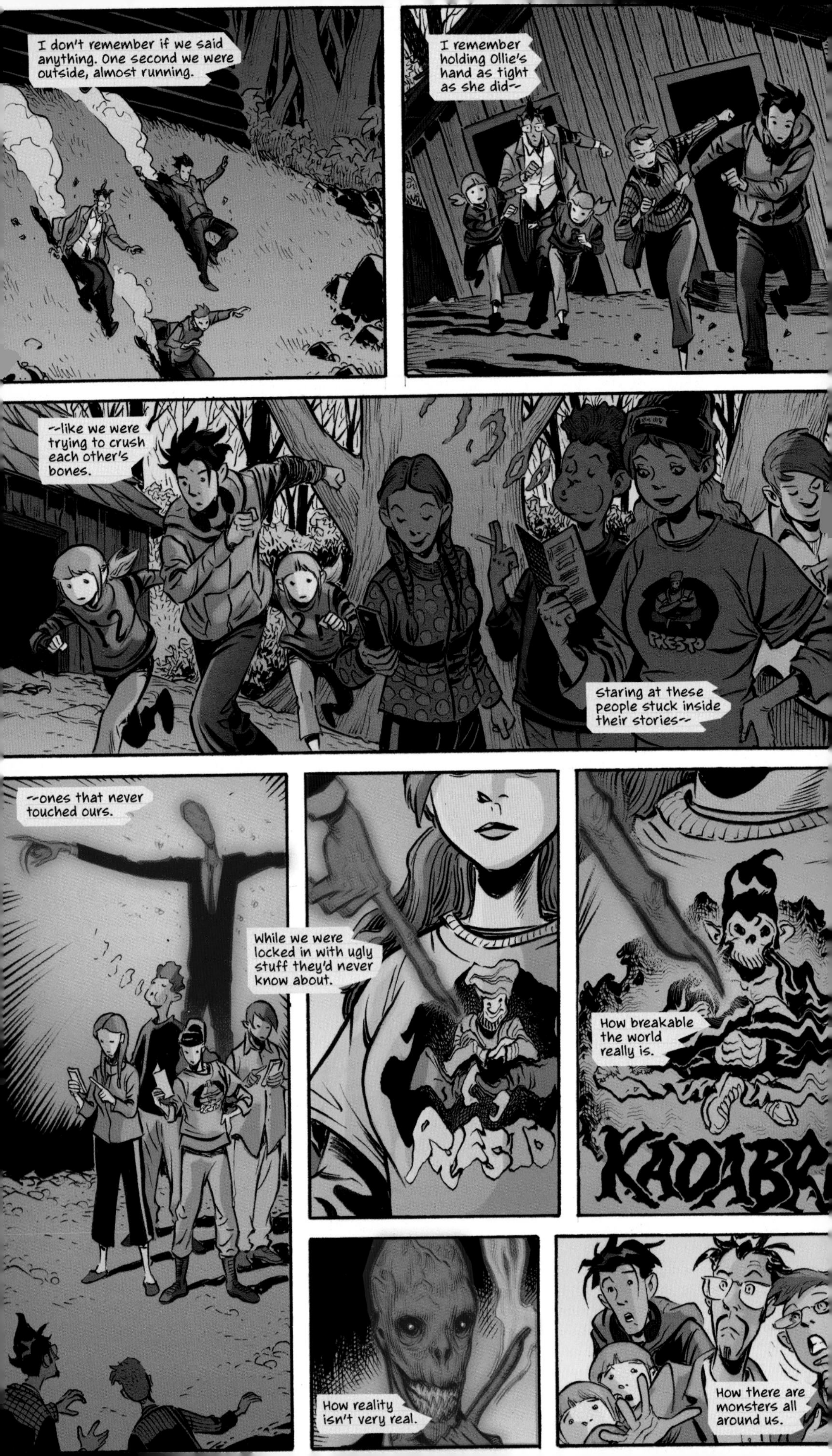
I don't remember if we said anything. One second we were outside, almost running.
I remember holding Ollie's hand as tight as she did--
--like we were trying to crush each other's bones.
PRESTO
Staring at these people stuck inside their stories--
--ones that never touched ours.
While we were locked in with ugly stuff they'd never know about.
PRESTO
How breakable the world really is.
KADABR
How reality isn't very real.
How there are monsters all around us.

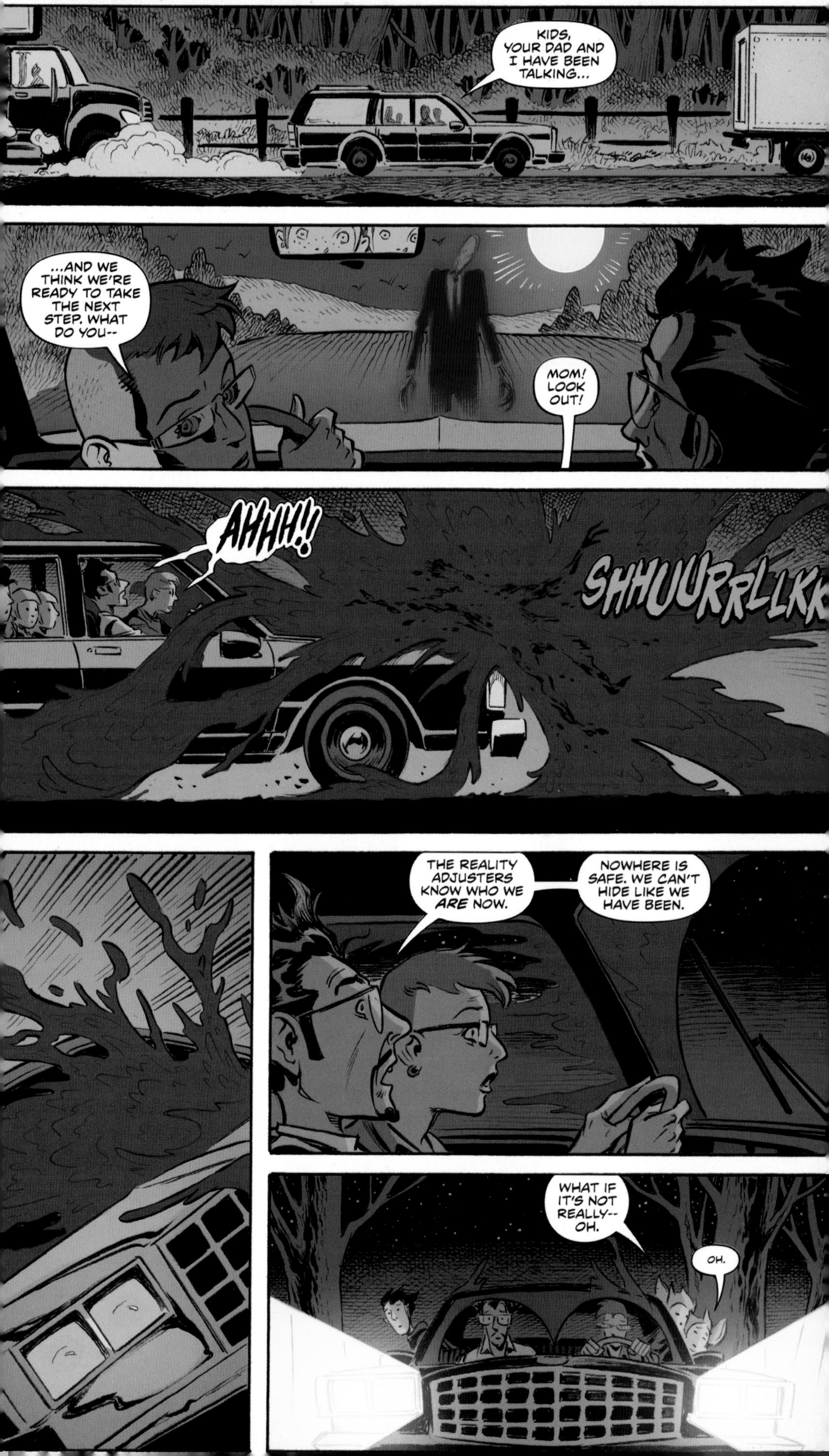

KIDS, YOUR DAD AND I HAVE BEEN TALKING...
...AND WE THINK WE'RE READY TO TAKE THE NEXT STEP. WHAT DO YOU--
MOM! LOOK OUT!
AHHH!!
SHHUURRLLKK
THE REALITY ADJUSTERS KNOW WHO WE *ARE* NOW.
NOWHERE IS SAFE. WE CAN'T HIDE LIKE WE HAVE BEEN.
WHAT IF IT'S NOT REALLY-- OH.
OH.

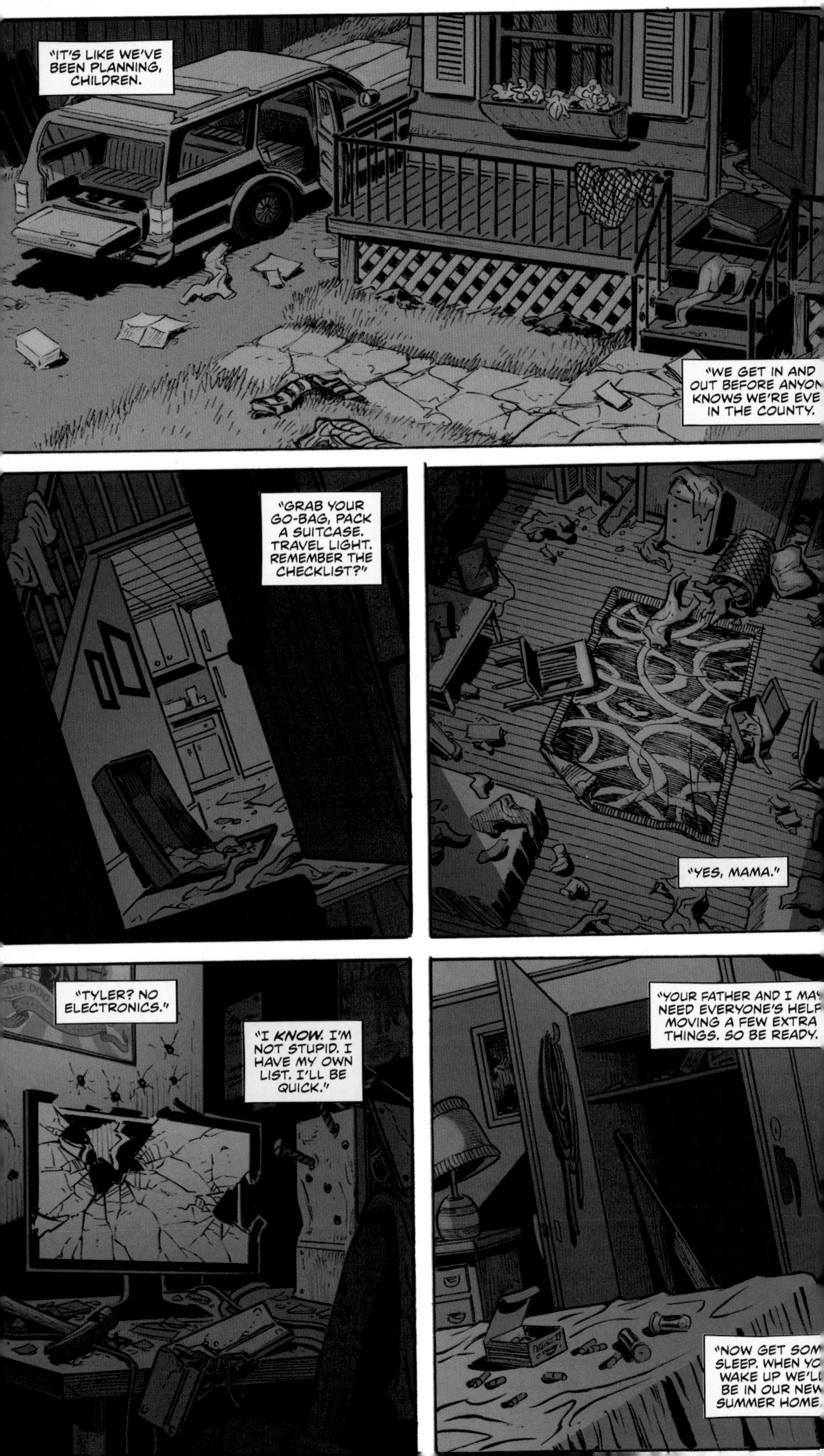
"IT'S LIKE WE'VE BEEN PLANNING, CHILDREN.
"WE GET IN AND OUT BEFORE ANYON KNOWS WE'RE EVE IN THE COUNTY.
"GRAB YOUR GO-BAG, PACK A SUITCASE. TRAVEL LIGHT. REMEMBER THE CHECKLIST?"
"YES, MAMA."
"TYLER? NO ELECTRONICS."
"I *KNOW*. I'M NOT STUPID. I HAVE MY OWN LIST. I'LL BE QUICK."
"YOUR FATHER AND I MA NEED EVERYONE'S HELP MOVING A FEW EXTRA THINGS. SO BE READY.
"NOW GET SOM SLEEP. WHEN YO WAKE UP WE'L BE IN OUR NEW SUMMER HOME.

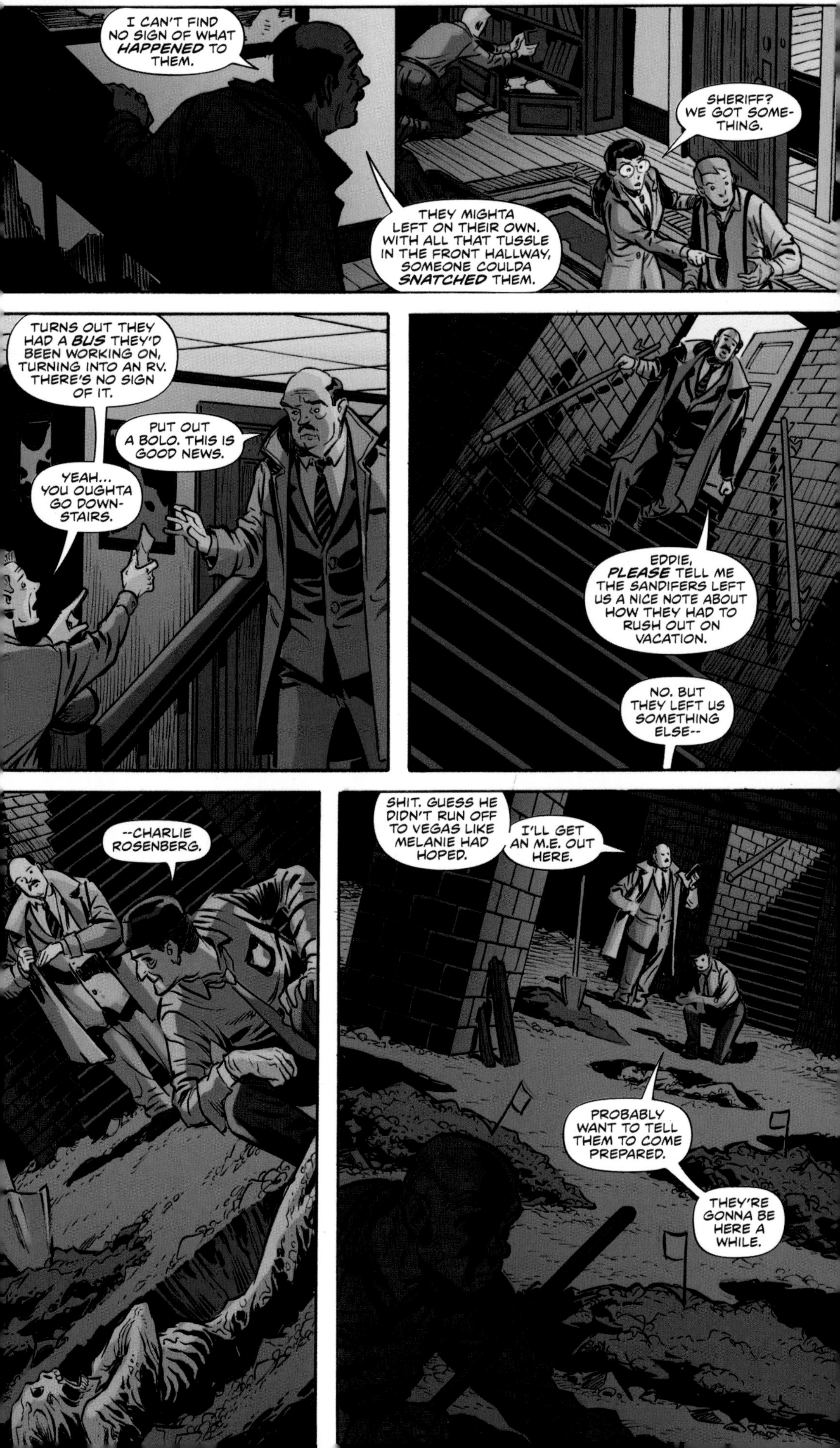
I CAN'T FIND NO SIGN OF WHAT HAPPENED TO THEM.
THEY MIGHTA LEFT ON THEIR OWN. WITH ALL THAT TUSSLE IN THE FRONT HALLWAY, SOMEONE COULDA SNATCHED THEM.
SHERIFF? WE GOT SOME-THING.
TURNS OUT THEY HAD A BUS THEY'D BEEN WORKING ON, TURNING INTO AN RV. THERE'S NO SIGN OF IT.
PUT OUT A BOLO. THIS IS GOOD NEWS.
YEAH... YOU OUGHTA GO DOWN-STAIRS.
EDDIE, PLEASE TELL ME THE SANDIFERS LEFT US A NICE NOTE ABOUT HOW THEY HAD TO RUSH OUT ON VACATION.
NO. BUT THEY LEFT US SOMETHING ELSE--
--CHARLIE ROSENBERG.
SHIT. GUESS HE DIDN'T RUN OFF TO VEGAS LIKE MELANIE HAD HOPED.
I'LL GET AN M.E. OUT HERE.
PROBABLY WANT TO TELL THEM TO COME PREPARED.
THEY'RE GONNA BE HERE A WHILE.

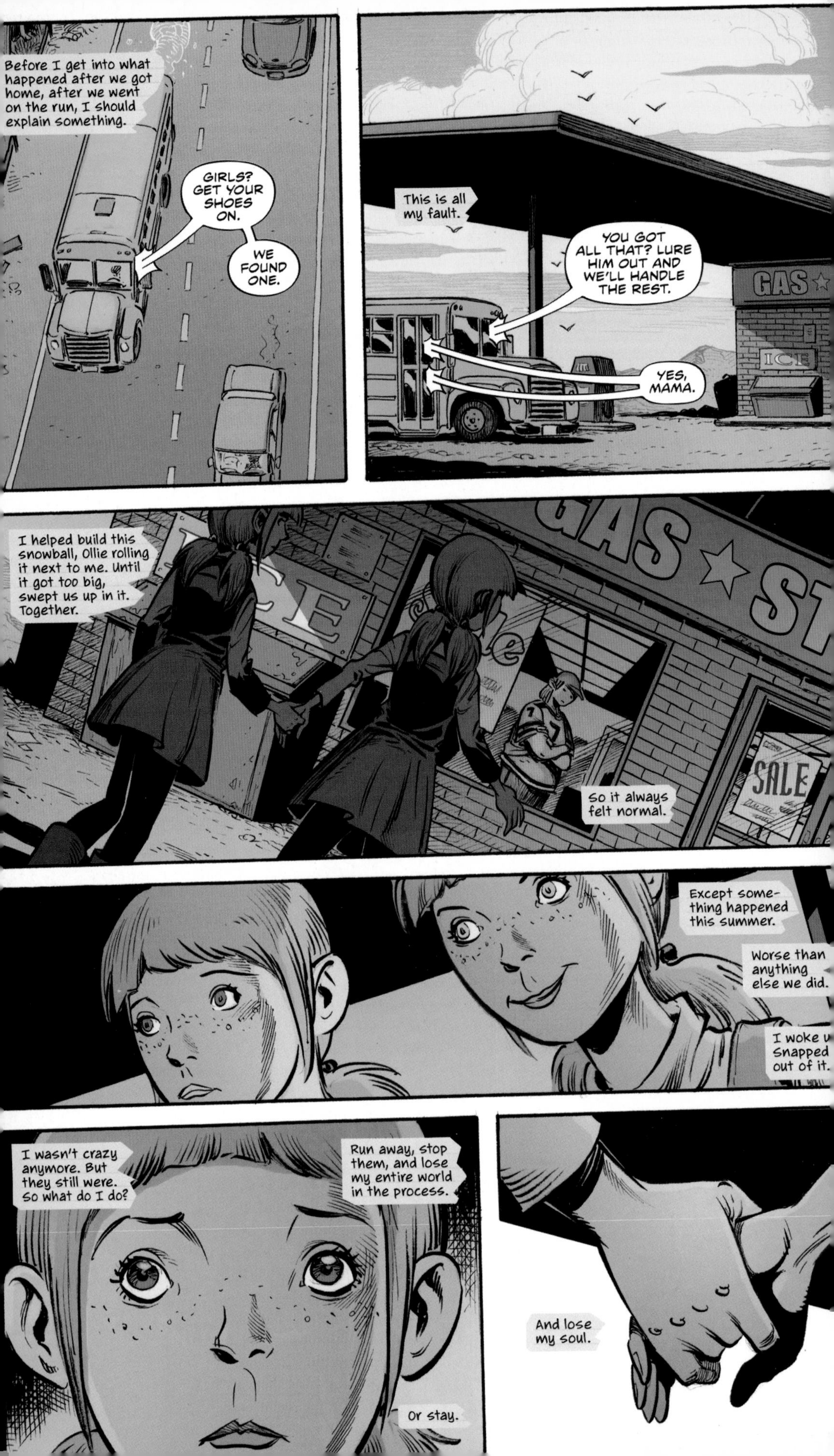
Before I get into what happened after we got home, after we went on the run, I should explain something.
GIRLS? GET YOUR SHOES ON.
WE FOUND ONE.
This is all my fault.
YOU GOT ALL THAT? LURE HIM OUT AND WE'LL HANDLE THE REST.
YES, MAMA.
GAS
ICE
I helped build this snowball, Ollie rolling it next to me. Until it got too big, swept us up in it. Together.
GAS ★ ST
SALE
So it always felt normal.
Except something happened this summer.
Worse than anything else we did.
I woke u
Snapped out of it.
I wasn't crazy anymore. But they still were. So what do I do?
Run away, stop them, and lose my entire world in the process.
Or stay.
And lose my soul.

“We wrote it down. We made it real.”

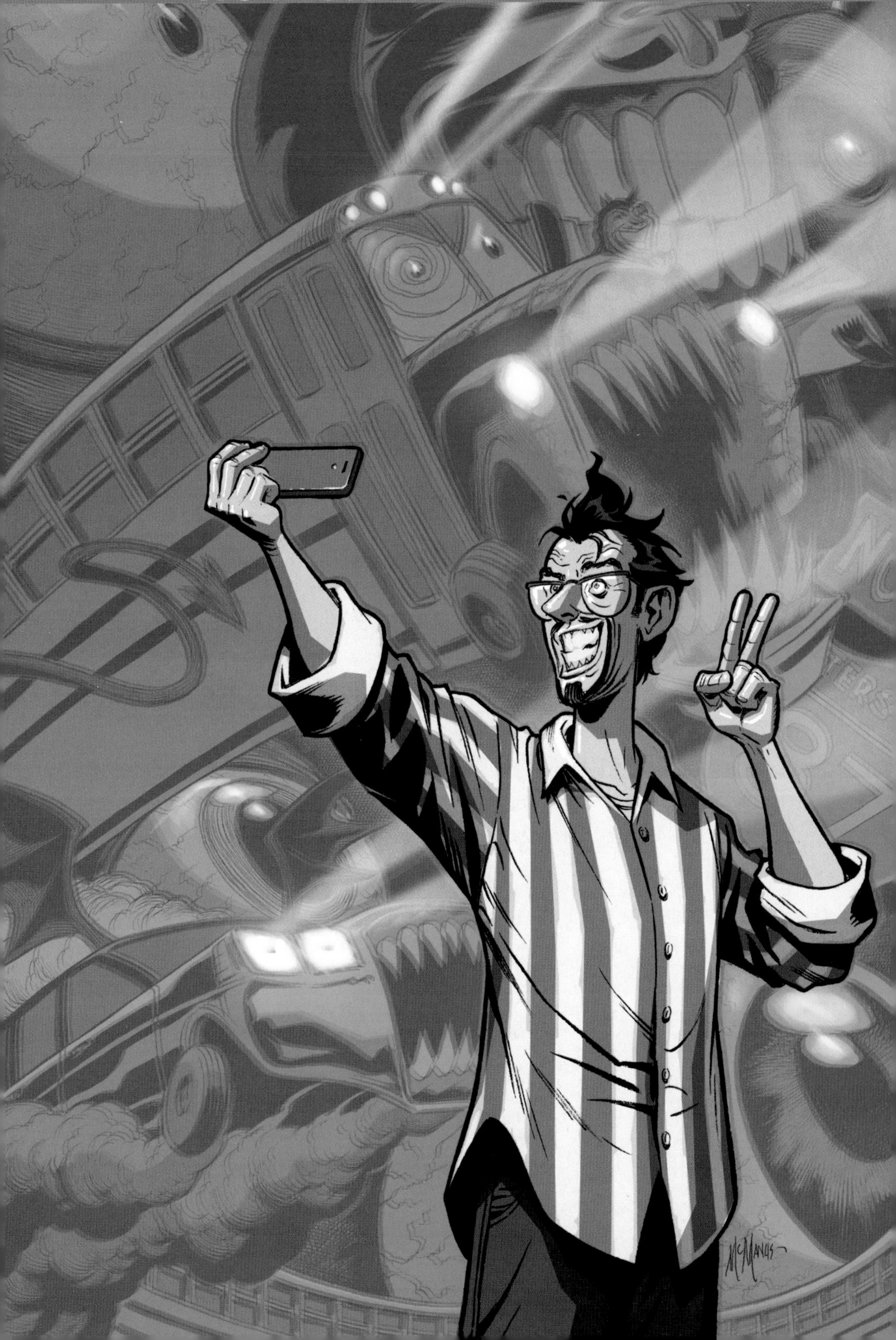

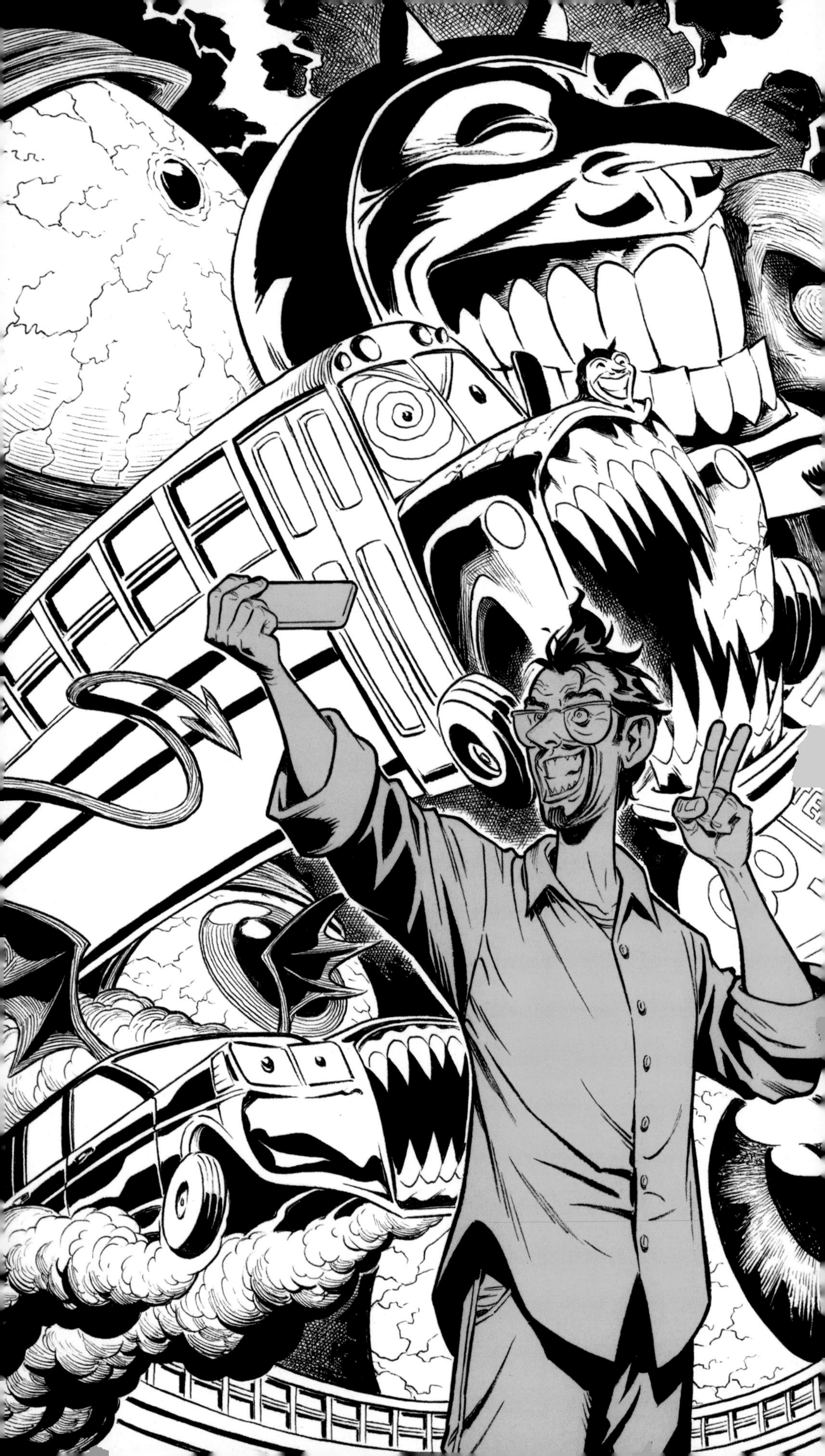

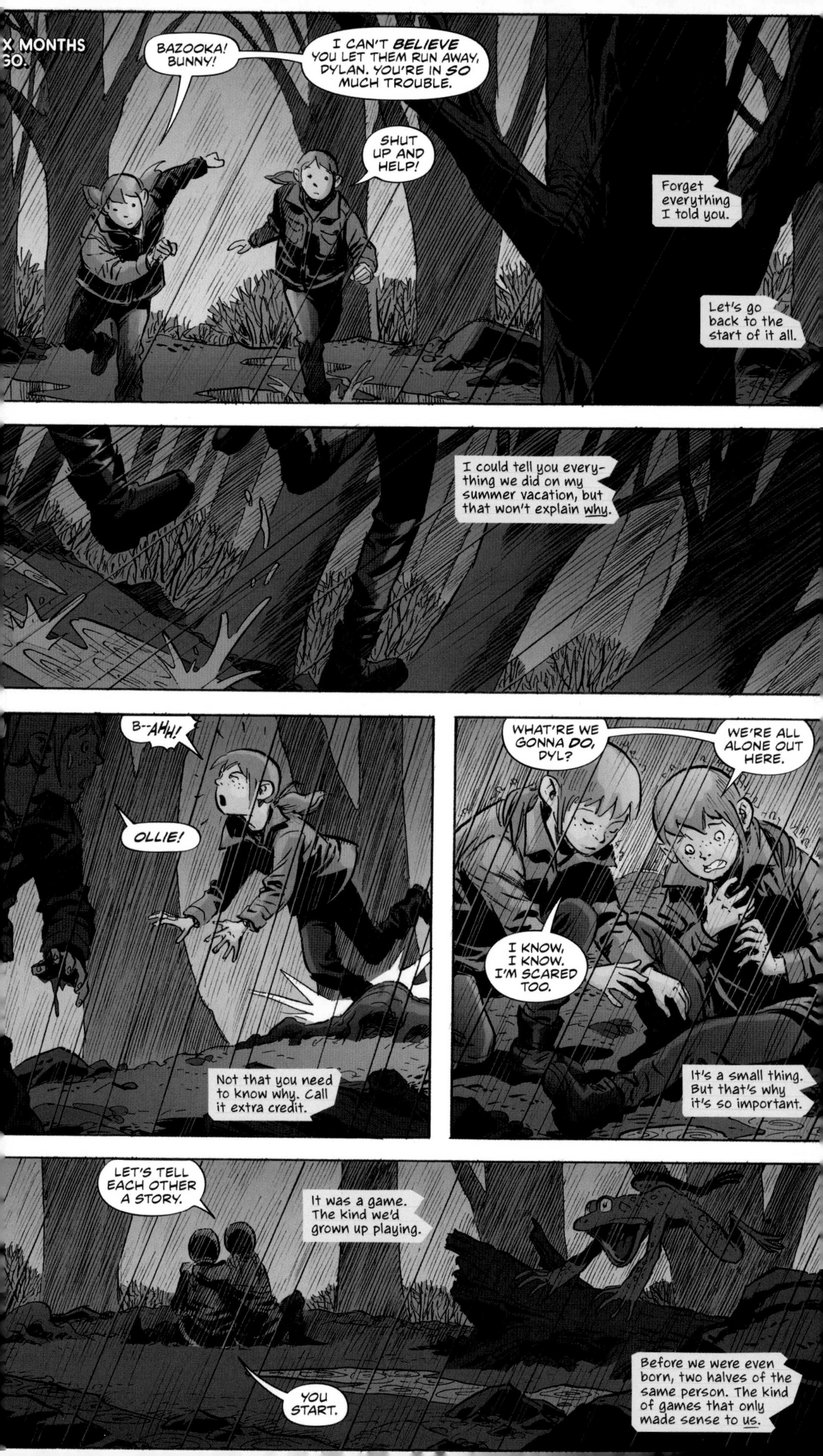
X MONTHS
GO.
BAZOOKA! BUNNY!
I CAN'T BELIEVE YOU LET THEM RUN AWAY, DYLAN. YOU'RE IN SO MUCH TROUBLE.
SHUT UP AND HELP!
Forget everything I told you.
Let's go back to the start of it all.
I could tell you everything we did on my summer vacation, but that won't explain why.
B--AHH!
OLLIE!
Not that you need to know why. Call it extra credit.
WHAT'RE WE GONNA DO, DYL?
WE'RE ALL ALONE OUT HERE.
I KNOW, I KNOW. I'M SCARED TOO.
It's a small thing. But that's why it's so important.
LET'S TELL EACH OTHER A STORY.
It was a game. The kind we'd grown up playing.
YOU START.
Before we were even born, two halves of the same person. The kind of games that only made sense to us.

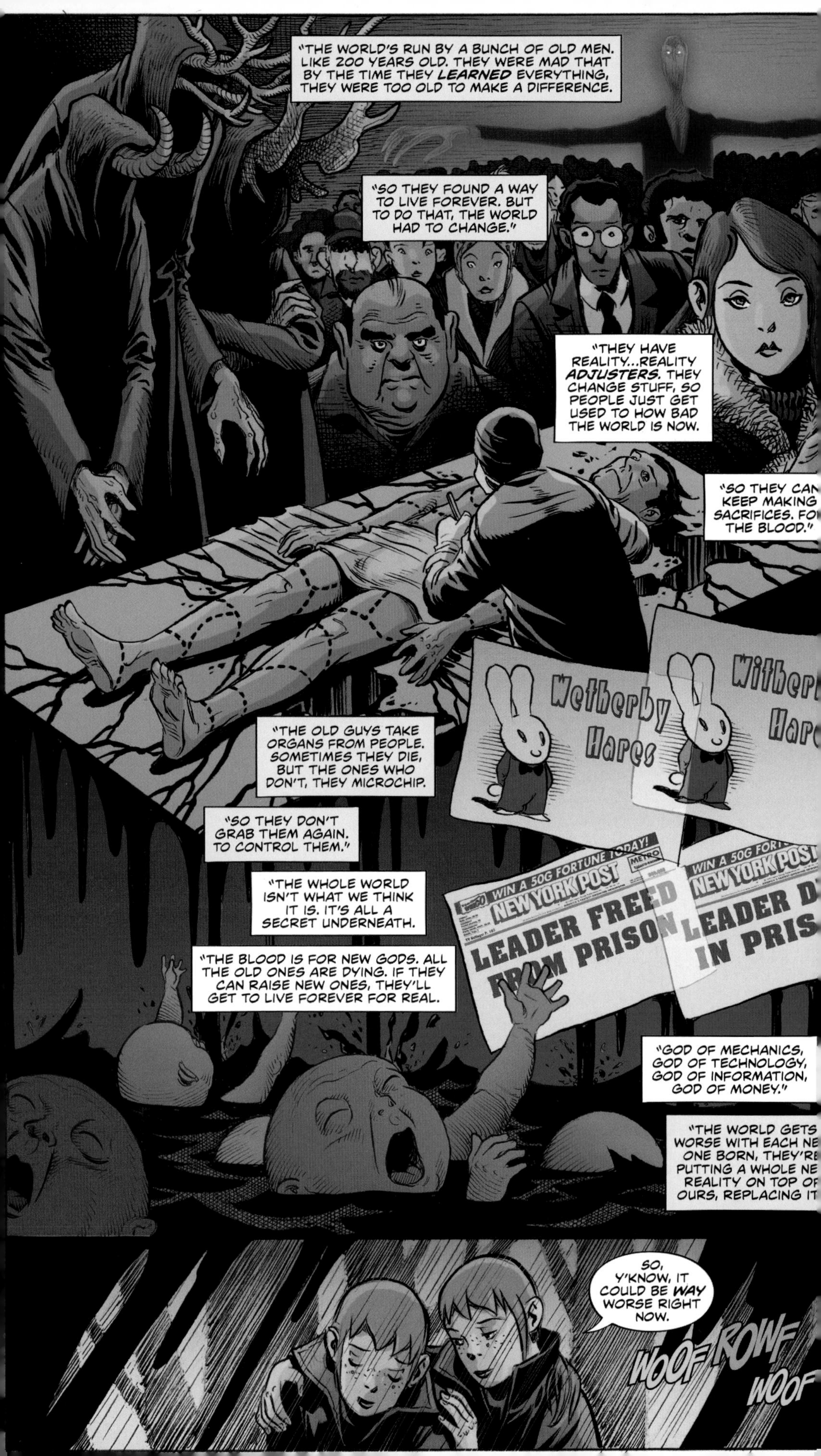
"THE WORLD'S RUN BY A BUNCH OF OLD MEN. LIKE 200 YEARS OLD. THEY WERE MAD THAT BY THE TIME THEY *LEARNED* EVERYTHING, THEY WERE TOO OLD TO MAKE A DIFFERENCE.
"SO THEY FOUND A WAY TO LIVE FOREVER. BUT TO DO THAT, THE WORLD HAD TO CHANGE."
"THEY HAVE REALITY...REALITY *ADJUSTERS.* THEY CHANGE STUFF, SO PEOPLE JUST GET USED TO HOW BAD THE WORLD IS NOW.
"SO THEY CAN KEEP MAKING SACRIFICES. FO THE BLOOD."
Wetherby Hares
"THE OLD GUYS TAKE ORGANS FROM PEOPLE. SOMETIMES THEY DIE, BUT THE ONES WHO DON'T, THEY MICROCHIP.
"SO THEY DON'T GRAB THEM AGAIN. TO CONTROL THEM."
WIN A 50G FORTUNE TODAY! NEW YORK POST LEADER FREED FROM PRISON
NEW YORK POST LEADER D IN PRIS
"THE WHOLE WORLD ISN'T WHAT WE THINK IT IS. IT'S ALL A SECRET UNDERNEATH.
"THE BLOOD IS FOR NEW GODS. ALL THE OLD ONES ARE DYING. IF THEY CAN RAISE NEW ONES, THEY'LL GET TO LIVE FOREVER FOR REAL.
"GOD OF MECHANICS, GOD OF TECHNOLOGY, GOD OF INFORMATION, GOD OF MONEY."
"THE WORLD GETS WORSE WITH EACH NE ONE BORN, THEY'RE PUTTING A WHOLE NE REALITY ON TOP OF OURS, REPLACING IT
SO, Y'KNOW, IT COULD BE *WAY* WORSE RIGHT NOW.
WOOF ROWF
WOOF

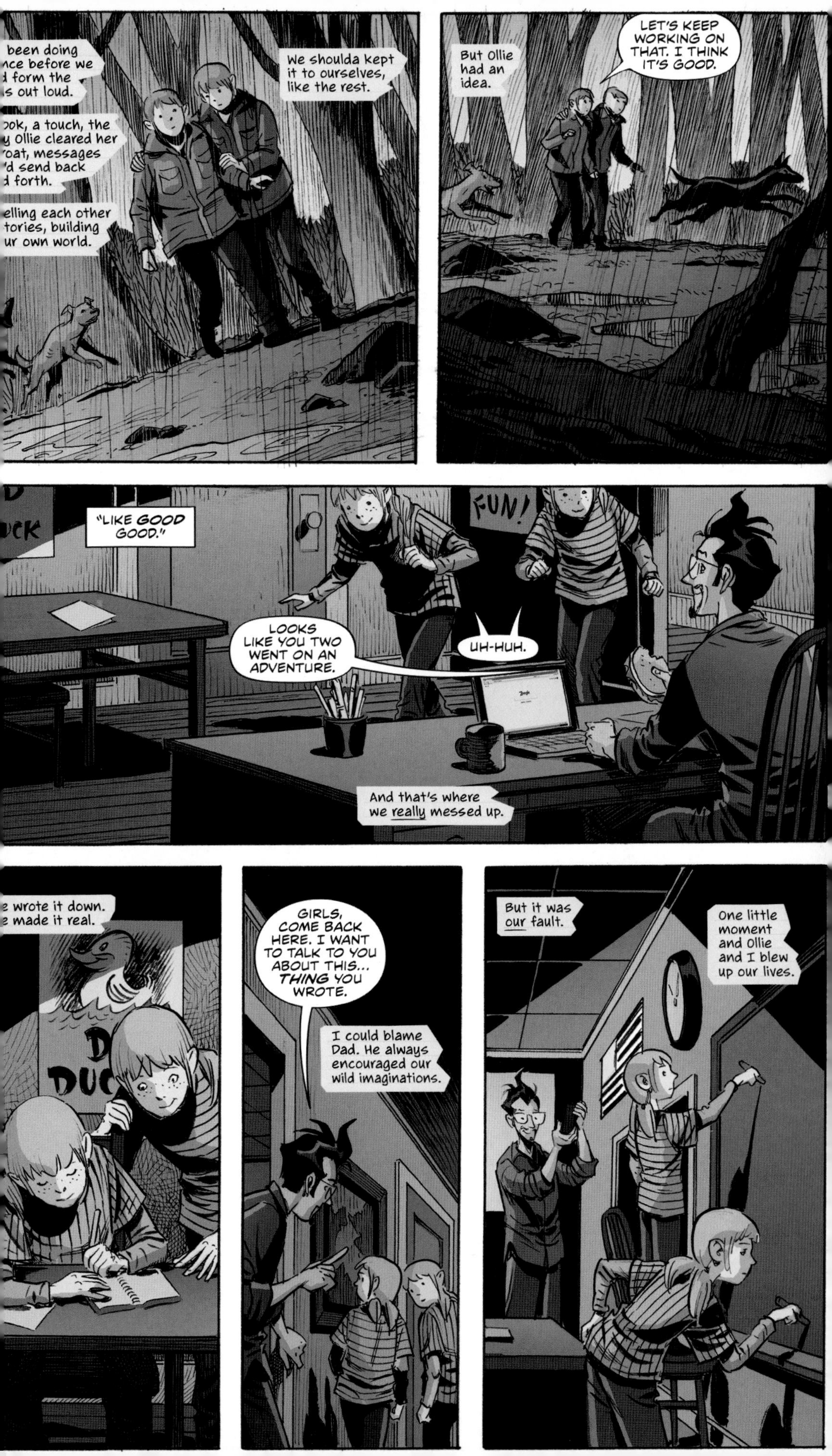

been doing
nce before we
d form the
s out loud.
ook, a touch, the
y Ollie cleared her
roat, messages
'd send back
d forth.
elling each other
tories, building
ur own world.
We shoulda kept it to ourselves, like the rest.
But Ollie had an idea.
LET'S KEEP WORKING ON THAT. I THINK IT'S GOOD.
"LIKE GOOD GOOD."
FUN!
LOOKS LIKE YOU TWO WENT ON AN ADVENTURE.
UH-HUH.
And that's where we really messed up.
e wrote it down.
e made it real.
GIRLS, COME BACK HERE. I WANT TO TALK TO YOU ABOUT THIS... THING YOU WROTE.
I could blame Dad. He always encouraged our wild imaginations.
But it was our fault.
One little moment and Ollie and I blew up our lives.

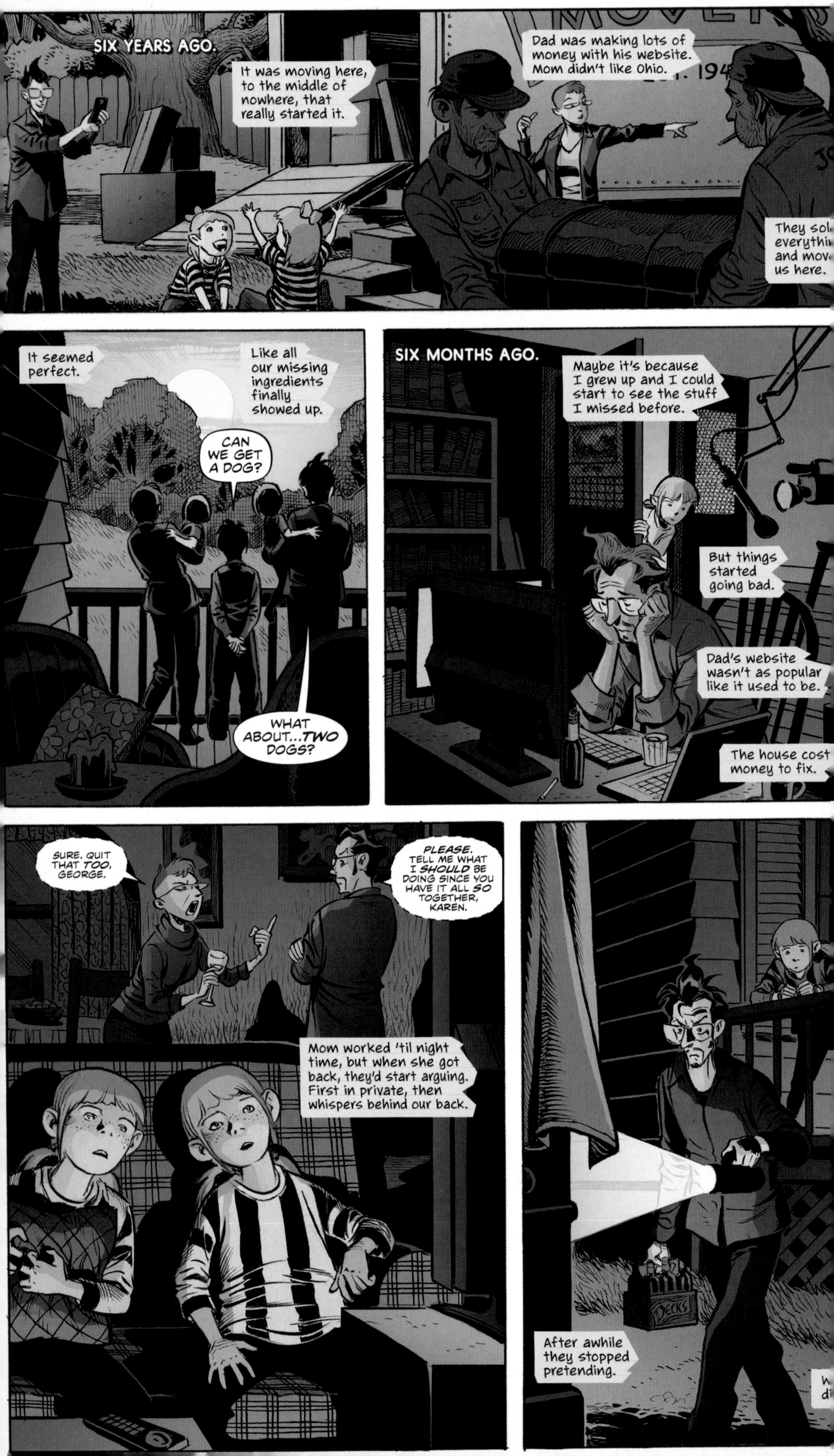

SIX YEARS AGO.
It was moving here, to the middle of nowhere, that really started it.
Dad was making lots of money with his website. Mom didn't like Ohio.
They sol
everythi
and mov
us here.
It seemed perfect.
Like all our missing ingredients finally showed up.
CAN WE GET A DOG?
WHAT ABOUT...TWO DOGS?
SIX MONTHS AGO.
Maybe it's because I grew up and I could start to see the stuff I missed before.
But things started going bad.
Dad's website wasn't as popular like it used to be.
The house cost money to fix.
SURE. QUIT THAT TOO, GEORGE.
PLEASE. TELL ME WHAT I SHOULD BE DOING SINCE YOU HAVE IT ALL SO TOGETHER, KAREN.
Mom worked 'til night time, but when she got back, they'd start arguing. First in private, then whispers behind our back.
DECKS
After awhile they stopped pretending.

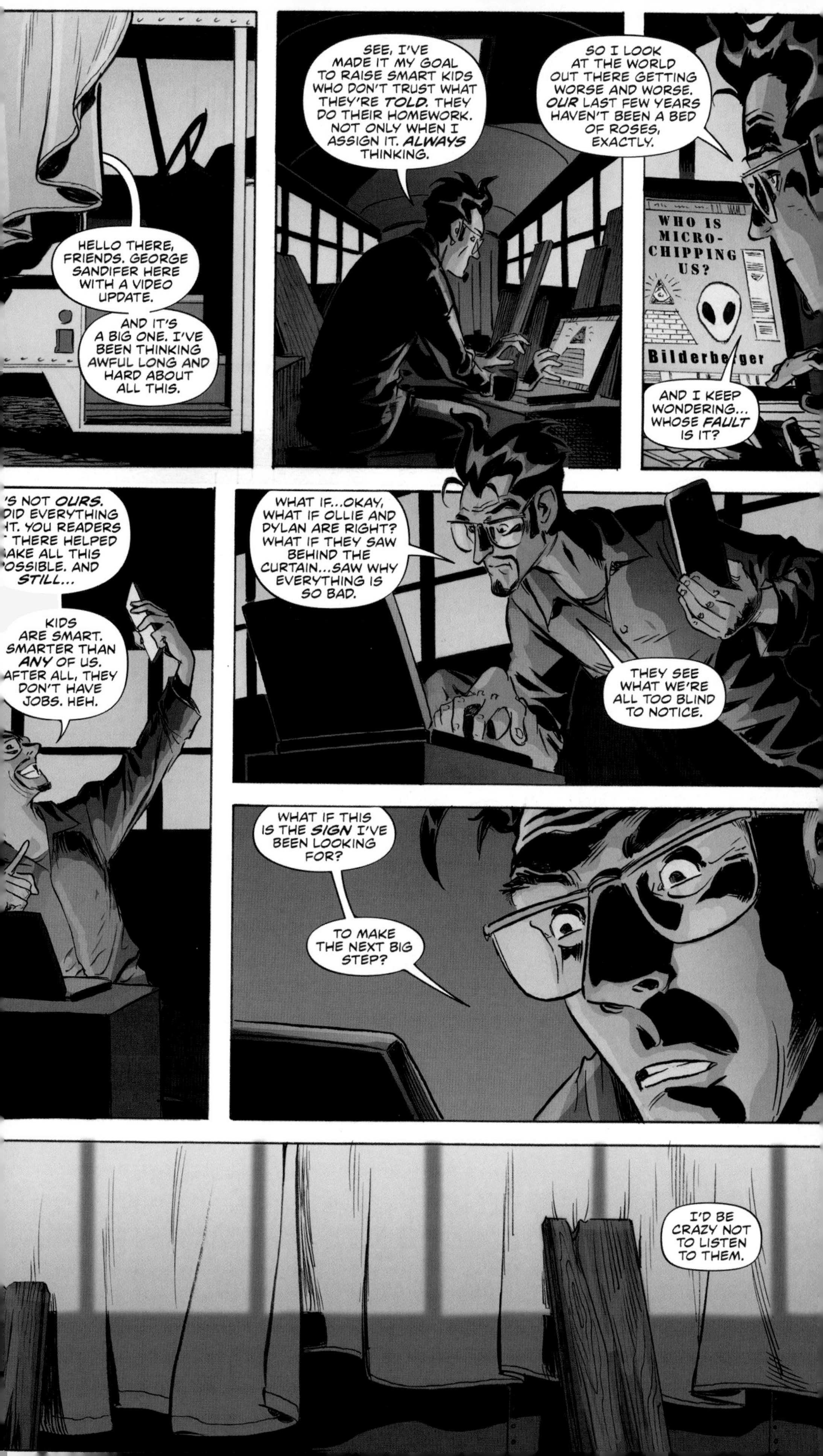
HELLO THERE, FRIENDS. GEORGE SANDIFER HERE WITH A VIDEO UPDATE.
AND IT'S A BIG ONE. I'VE BEEN THINKING AWFUL LONG AND HARD ABOUT ALL THIS.
SEE, I'VE MADE IT MY GOAL TO RAISE SMART KIDS WHO DON'T TRUST WHAT THEY'RE *TOLD*. THEY DO THEIR HOMEWORK. NOT ONLY WHEN I ASSIGN IT. *ALWAYS* THINKING.
SO I LOOK AT THE WORLD OUT THERE GETTING WORSE AND WORSE. *OUR* LAST FEW YEARS HAVEN'T BEEN A BED OF ROSES, EXACTLY.
WHO IS MICRO-CHIPPING US?
AND I KEEP WONDERING... WHOSE *FAULT* IS IT?
'S NOT *OURS*. DID EVERYTHING HT. YOU READERS T THERE HELPED AKE ALL THIS OSSIBLE. AND *STILL*...
KIDS ARE SMART. SMARTER THAN *ANY* OF US. AFTER ALL, THEY DON'T HAVE JOBS. HEH.
WHAT IF...OKAY, WHAT IF OLLIE AND DYLAN ARE RIGHT? WHAT IF THEY SAW BEHIND THE CURTAIN...SAW WHY EVERYTHING IS SO BAD.
THEY SEE WHAT WE'RE ALL TOO BLIND TO NOTICE.
WHAT IF THIS IS THE *SIGN* I'VE BEEN LOOKING FOR?
TO MAKE THE NEXT BIG STEP?
I'D BE CRAZY NOT TO LISTEN TO THEM.

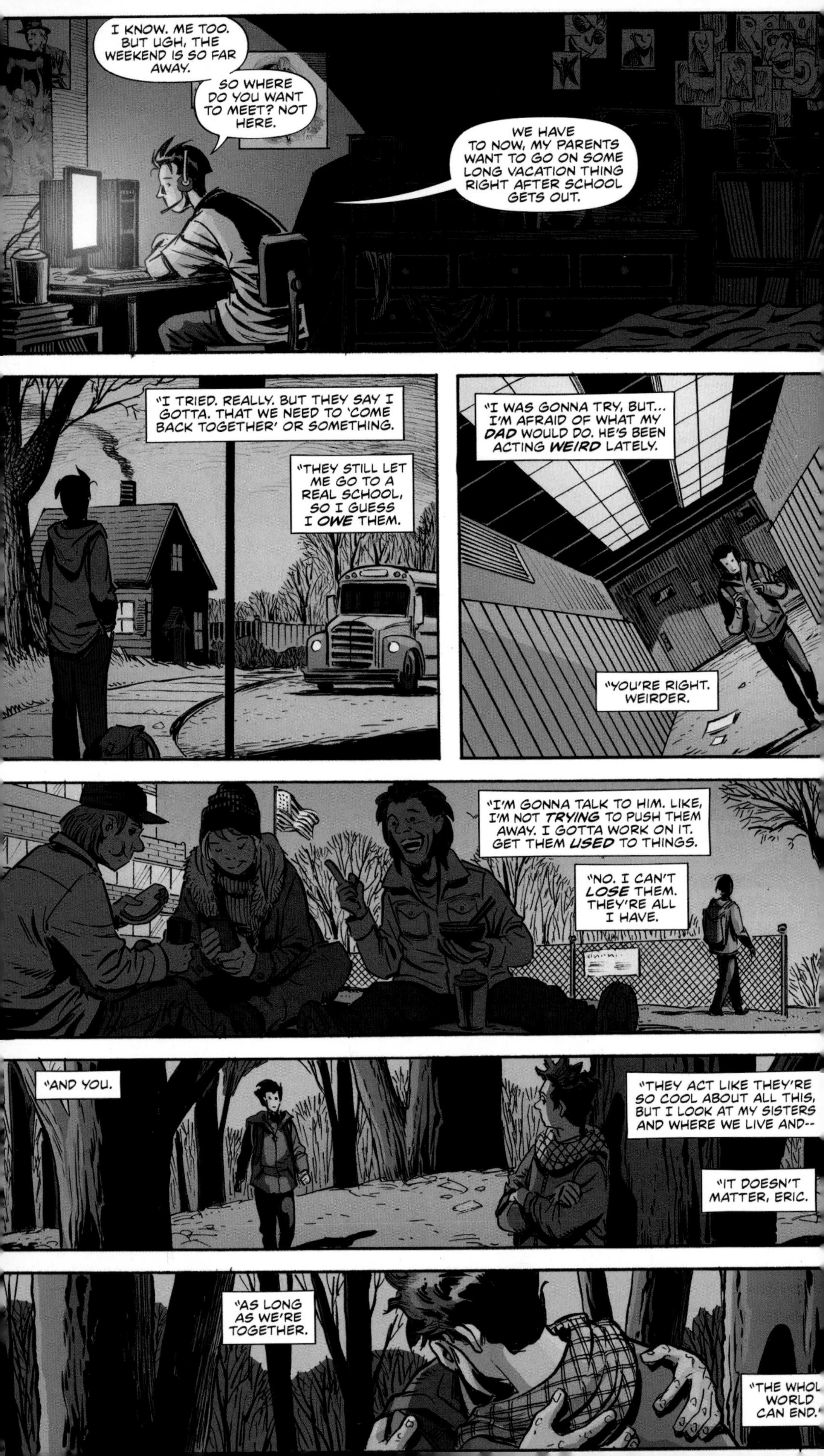

I KNOW. ME TOO. BUT UGH, THE WEEKEND IS SO FAR AWAY.
SO WHERE DO YOU WANT TO MEET? NOT HERE.
WE HAVE TO NOW, MY PARENTS WANT TO GO ON SOME LONG VACATION THING RIGHT AFTER SCHOOL GETS OUT.
"I TRIED. REALLY. BUT THEY SAY I GOTTA. THAT WE NEED TO 'COME BACK TOGETHER' OR SOMETHING.
"THEY STILL LET ME GO TO A REAL SCHOOL, SO I GUESS I OWE THEM.
"I WAS GONNA TRY, BUT... I'M AFRAID OF WHAT MY DAD WOULD DO. HE'S BEEN ACTING WEIRD LATELY.
"YOU'RE RIGHT. WEIRDER.
"I'M GONNA TALK TO HIM. LIKE, I'M NOT TRYING TO PUSH THEM AWAY. I GOTTA WORK ON IT. GET THEM USED TO THINGS.
"NO. I CAN'T LOSE THEM. THEY'RE ALL I HAVE.
"AND YOU.
"THEY ACT LIKE THEY'RE SO COOL ABOUT ALL THIS, BUT I LOOK AT MY SISTERS AND WHERE WE LIVE AND--
"IT DOESN'T MATTER, ERIC.
"AS LONG AS WE'RE TOGETHER.
"THE WHOL WORLD CAN END."

WELCOME TO YOUR FUTURE. INVEST A DOLLAR TO DIVINE THE PATH.

CHRISTOPHER
SEBELA
writer

SHAWN McMANUS
artist, cover A
retailer incentive

HOUSE AMOK

PART TWO: DREAM OF THE MACHINES

Caitlin Yarsky
cover B

Aditya Bidikar
letterer

Lee Loughridge
colorist

Chase Marotz
assoc. editor

Shelly Bond
editor

**HOUSE AMOK is created
by Sebela & McManus**

OUT THERE.

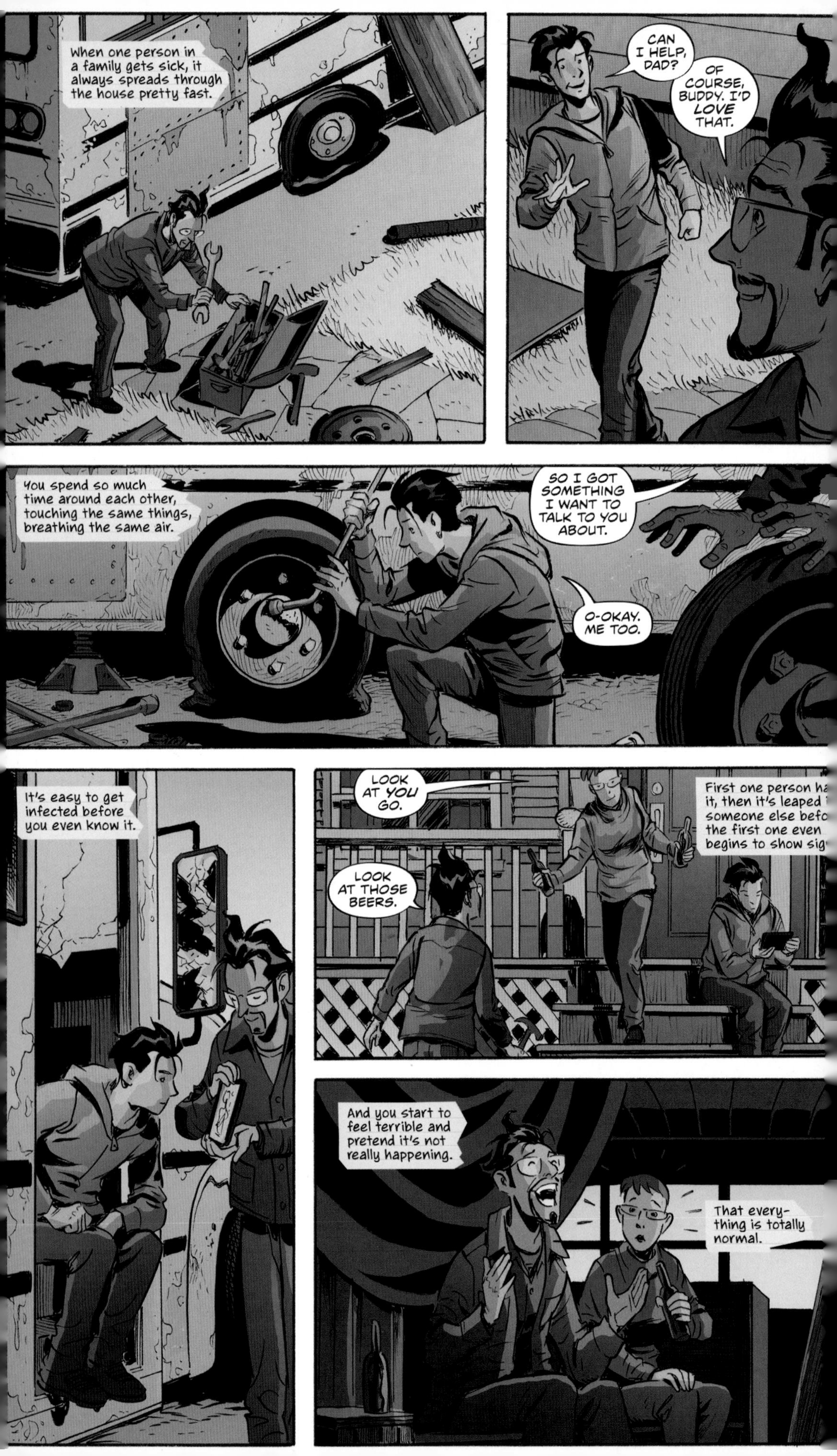
When one person in a family gets sick, it always spreads through the house pretty fast.
CAN I HELP, DAD?
OF COURSE, BUDDY. I'D LOVE THAT.
You spend so much time around each other, touching the same things, breathing the same air.
SO I GOT SOMETHING I WANT TO TALK TO YOU ABOUT.
O-OKAY. ME TOO.
It's easy to get infected before you even know it.
LOOK AT YOU GO.
LOOK AT THOSE BEERS.
First one person ha it, then it's leaped someone else befo the first one even begins to show sig
And you start to feel terrible and pretend it's not really happening.
That everything is totally normal.

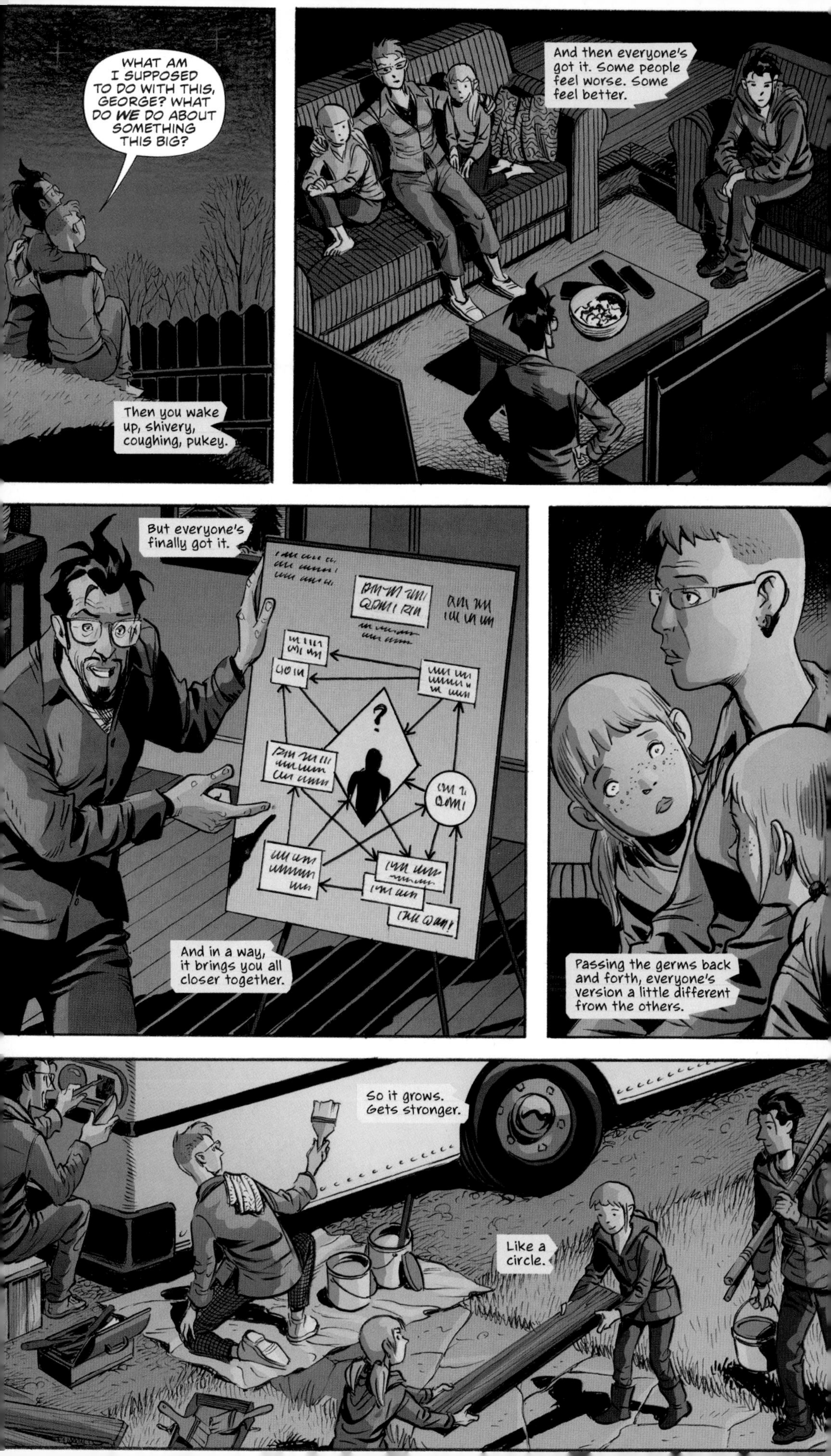

WHAT AM I SUPPOSED TO DO WITH THIS, GEORGE? WHAT DO WE DO ABOUT SOMETHING THIS BIG?
Then you wake up, shivery, coughing, pukey.
And then everyone's got it. Some people feel worse. Some feel better.
But everyone's finally got it.
And in a way, it brings you all closer together.
Passing the germs back and forth, everyone's version a little different from the others.
So it grows. Gets stronger.
Like a circle.

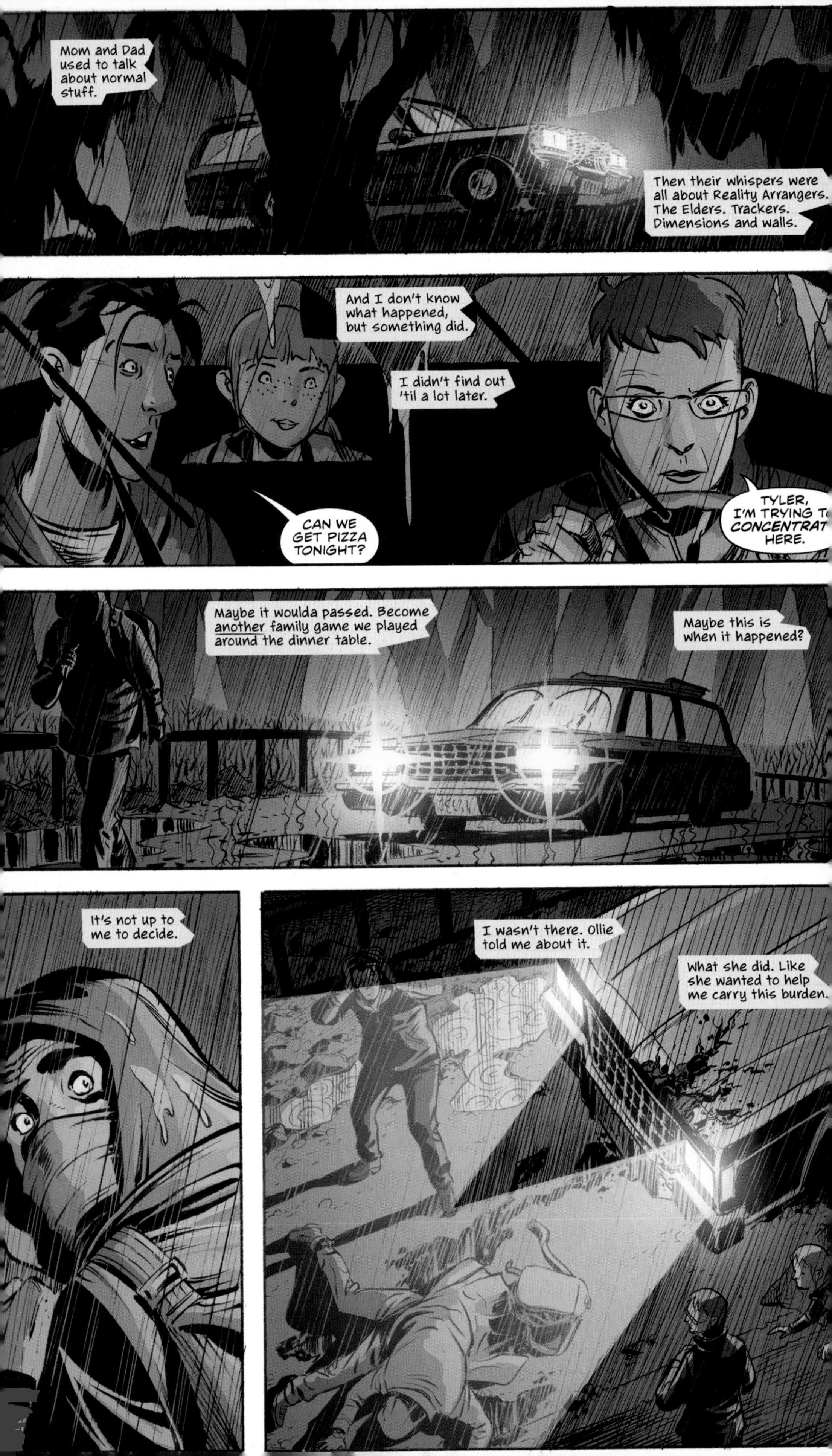

Mom and Dad used to talk about normal stuff.
Then their whispers were all about Reality Arrangers. The Elders. Trackers. Dimensions and walls.
And I don't know what happened, but something did.
I didn't find out 'til a lot later.
CAN WE GET PIZZA TONIGHT?
TYLER, I'M TRYING TO CONCENTRATE HERE.
Maybe it woulda passed. Become another family game we played around the dinner table.
Maybe this is when it happened?
It's not up to me to decide.
I wasn't there. Ollie told me about it.
What she did. Like she wanted to help me carry this burden.

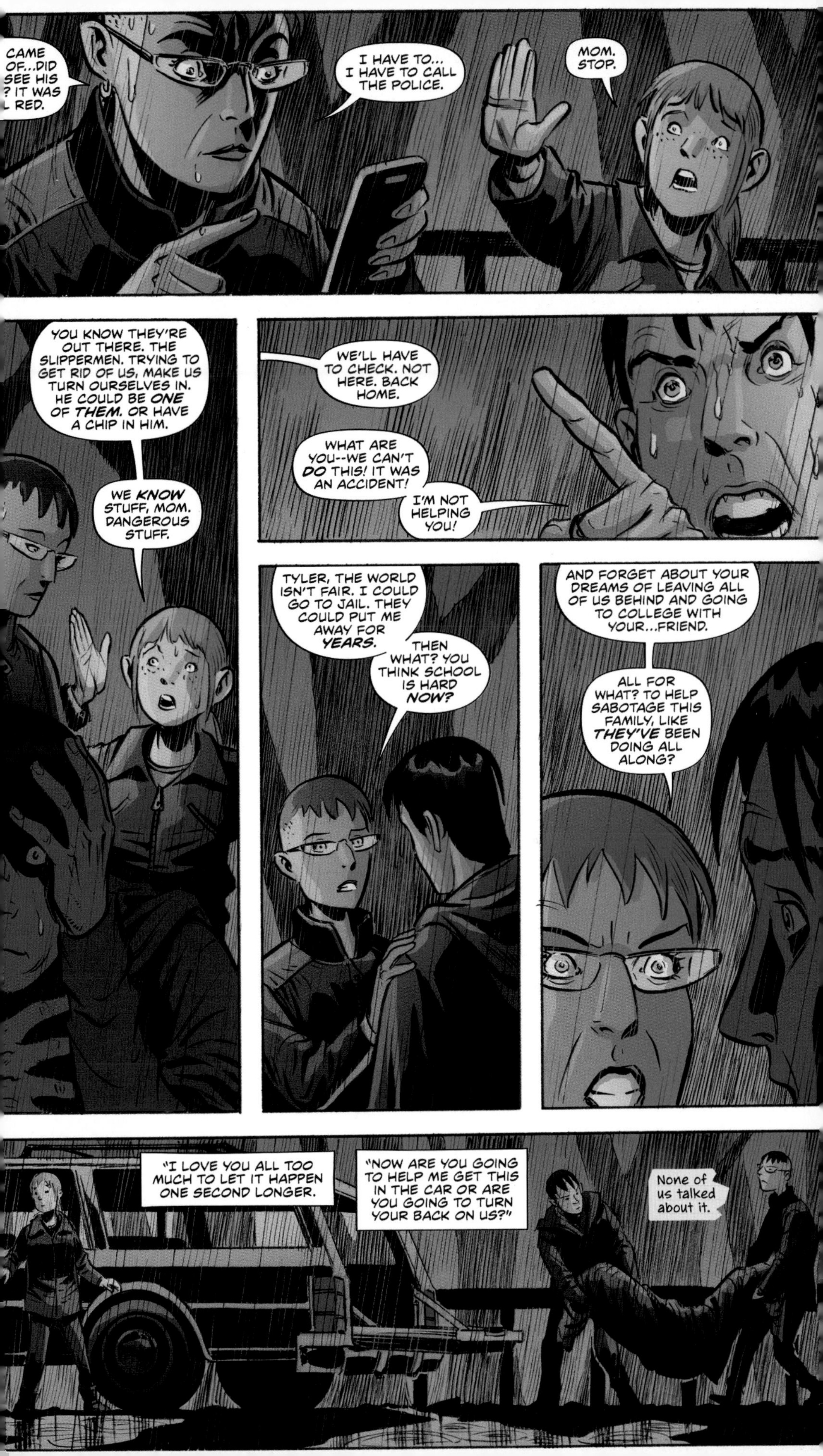
CAME
OF...DID
SEE HIS
? IT WAS
L RED.
I HAVE TO... I HAVE TO CALL THE POLICE.
MOM. STOP.
YOU KNOW THEY'RE OUT THERE. THE SLIPPERMEN. TRYING TO GET RID OF US, MAKE US TURN OURSELVES IN. HE COULD BE ONE OF THEM. OR HAVE A CHIP IN HIM.
WE KNOW STUFF, MOM. DANGEROUS STUFF.
WE'LL HAVE TO CHECK. NOT HERE. BACK HOME.
WHAT ARE YOU--WE CAN'T DO THIS! IT WAS AN ACCIDENT!
I'M NOT HELPING YOU!
TYLER, THE WORLD ISN'T FAIR. I COULD GO TO JAIL. THEY COULD PUT ME AWAY FOR YEARS.
THEN WHAT? YOU THINK SCHOOL IS HARD NOW?
AND FORGET ABOUT YOUR DREAMS OF LEAVING ALL OF US BEHIND AND GOING TO COLLEGE WITH YOUR...FRIEND.
ALL FOR WHAT? TO HELP SABOTAGE THIS FAMILY, LIKE THEY'VE BEEN DOING ALL ALONG?
"I LOVE YOU ALL TOO MUCH TO LET IT HAPPEN ONE SECOND LONGER.
"NOW ARE YOU GOING TO HELP ME GET THIS IN THE CAR OR ARE YOU GOING TO TURN YOUR BACK ON US?"
None of us talked about it.

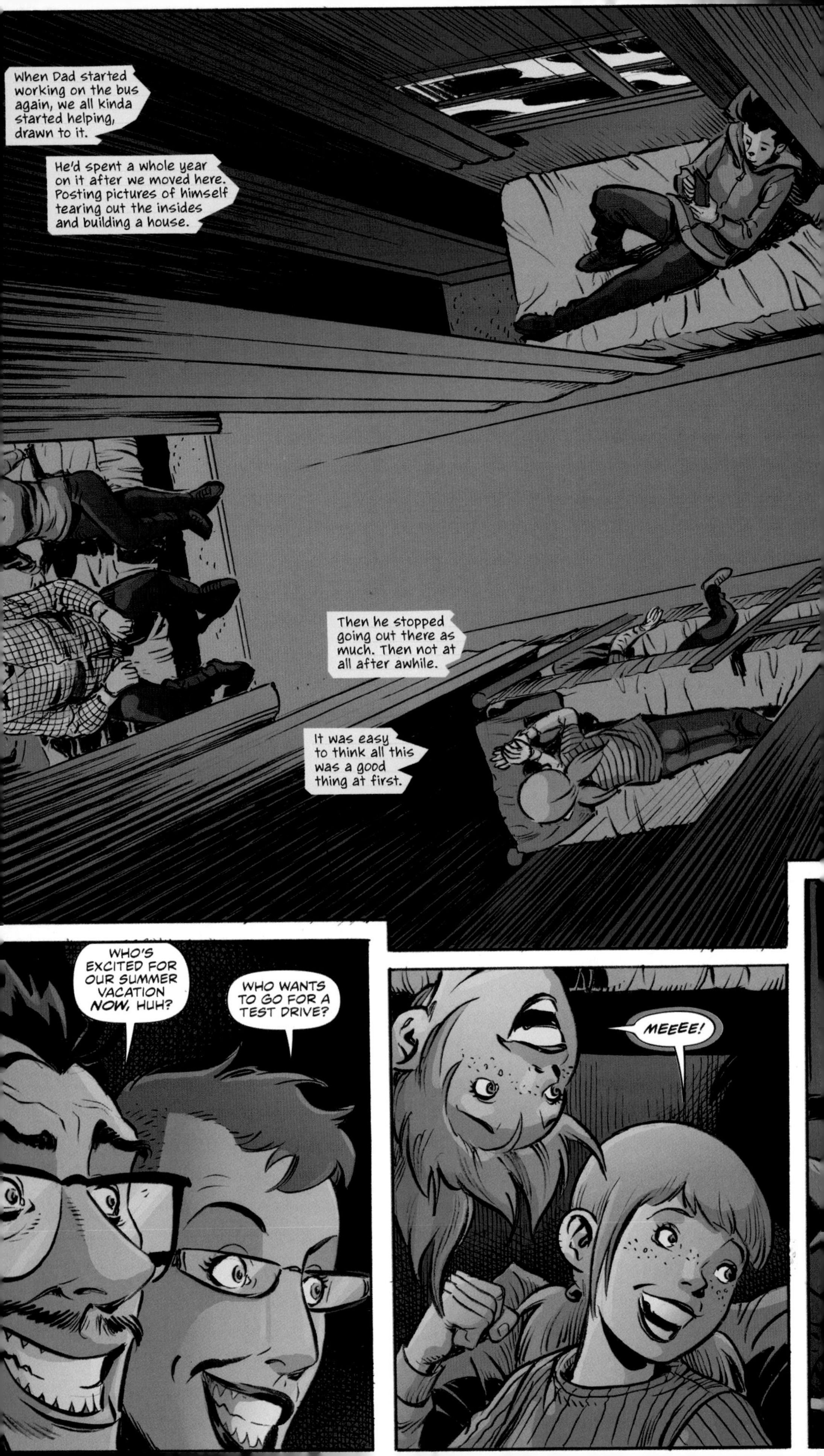

When Dad started working on the bus again, we all kinda started helping, drawn to it.
He'd spent a whole year on it after we moved here. Posting pictures of himself tearing out the insides and building a house.
Then he stopped going out there as much. Then not at all after awhile.
It was easy to think all this was a good thing at first.
WHO'S EXCITED FOR OUR SUMMER VACATION NOW, HUH?
WHO WANTS TO GO FOR A TEST DRIVE?
MEEEE!

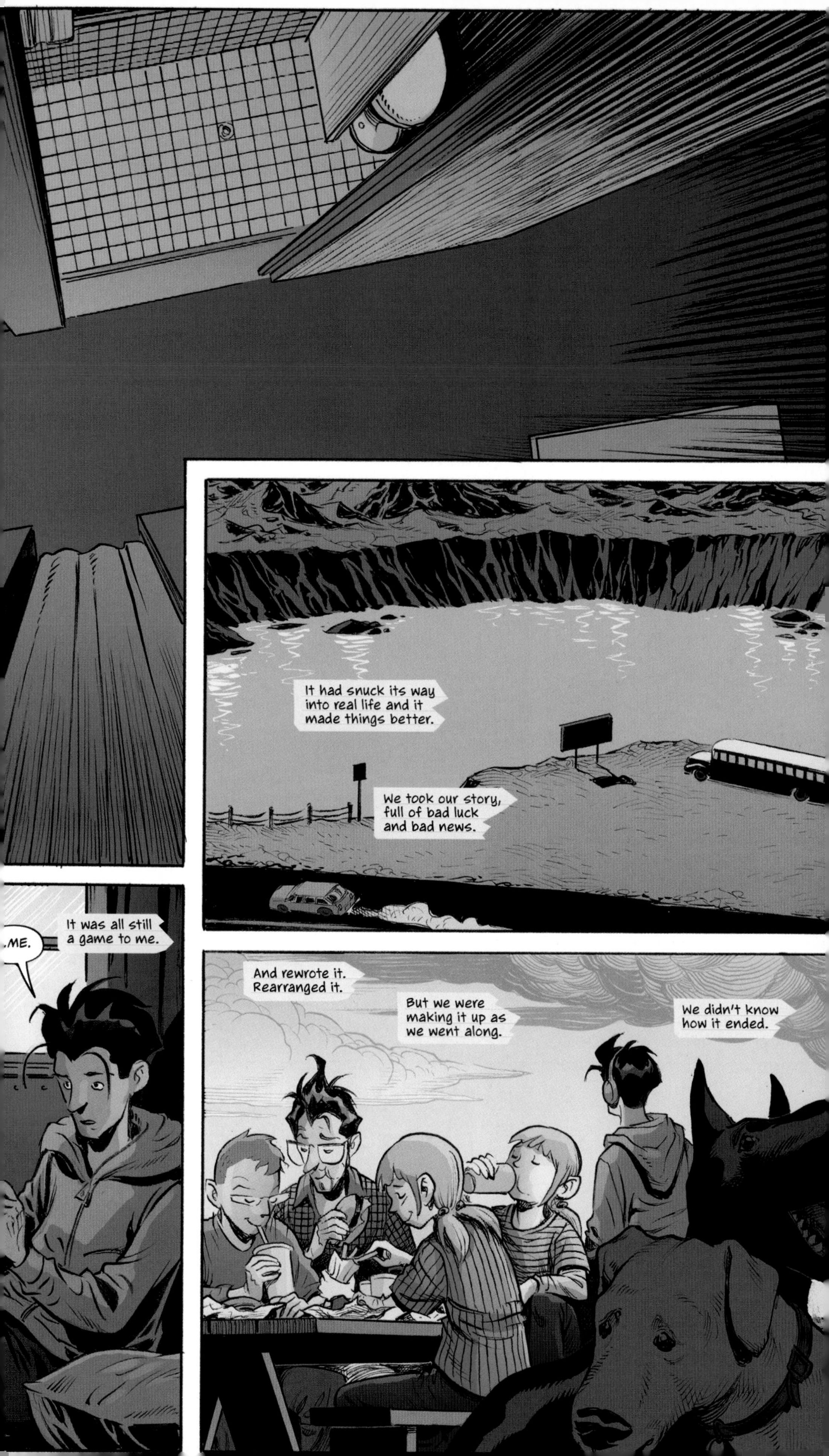
It had snuck its way into real life and it made things better.
We took our story, full of bad luck and bad news.
It was all still a game to me.
...ME.
And rewrote it. Rearranged it.
But we were making it up as we went along.
We didn't know how it ended.

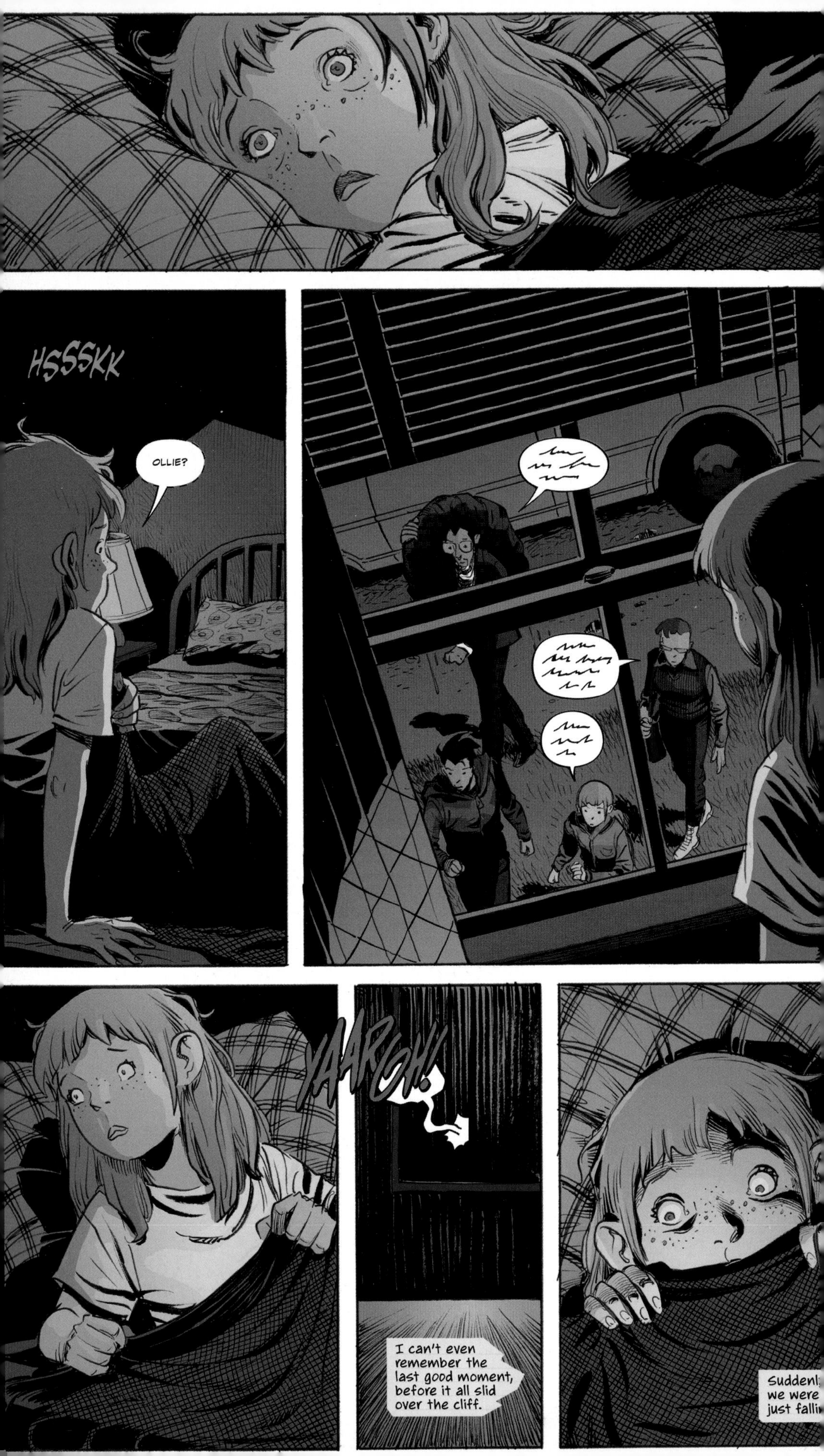
HSSSKK
OLLIE?
YAARGH!
I can't even remember the last good moment, before it all slid over the cliff.
Suddenl
we were
just falli

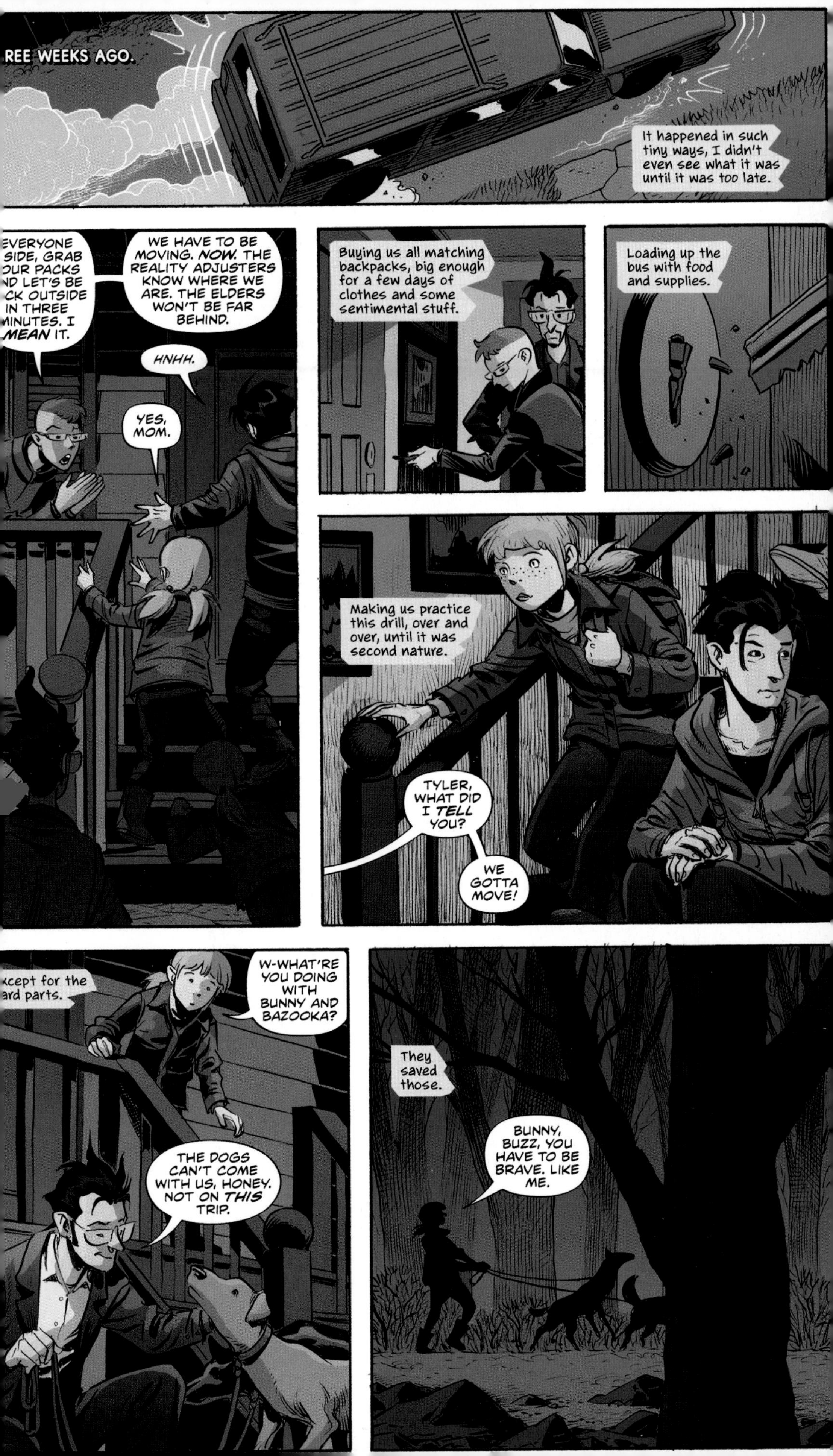

REE WEEKS AGO.
It happened in such tiny ways, I didn't even see what it was until it was too late.
EVERYONE SIDE, GRAB OUR PACKS ND LET'S BE CK OUTSIDE IN THREE MINUTES. I MEAN IT.
WE HAVE TO BE MOVING. NOW. THE REALITY ADJUSTERS KNOW WHERE WE ARE. THE ELDERS WON'T BE FAR BEHIND.
HNHH.
YES, MOM.
Buying us all matching backpacks, big enough for a few days of clothes and some sentimental stuff.
Loading up the bus with food and supplies.
Making us practice this drill, over and over, until it was second nature.
TYLER, WHAT DID I TELL YOU?
WE GOTTA MOVE!
xcept for the ard parts.
W-WHAT'RE YOU DOING WITH BUNNY AND BAZOOKA?
THE DOGS CAN'T COME WITH US, HONEY. NOT ON THIS TRIP.
They saved those.
BUNNY, BUZZ, YOU HAVE TO BE BRAVE. LIKE ME.

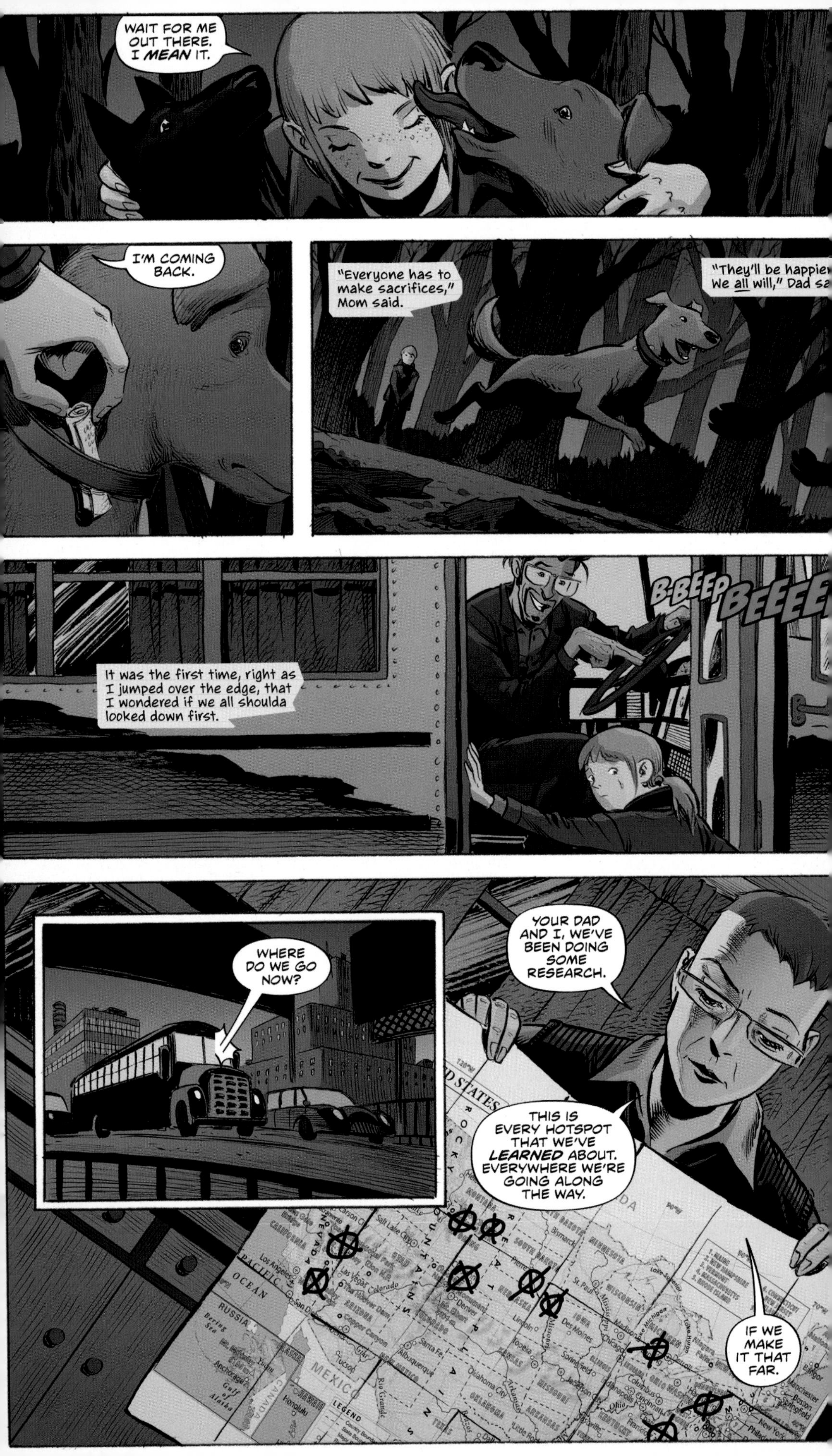
WAIT FOR ME OUT THERE. I MEAN IT.
I'M COMING BACK.
"Everyone has to make sacrifices," Mom said.
"They'll be happie We all will," Dad sa
It was the first time, right as I jumped over the edge, that I wondered if we all shoulda looked down first.
B-BEEP BEEEE
WHERE DO WE GO NOW?
YOUR DAD AND I, WE'VE BEEN DOING SOME RESEARCH.
THIS IS EVERY HOTSPOT THAT WE'VE LEARNED ABOUT. EVERYWHERE WE'RE GOING ALONG THE WAY.
IF WE MAKE IT THAT FAR.

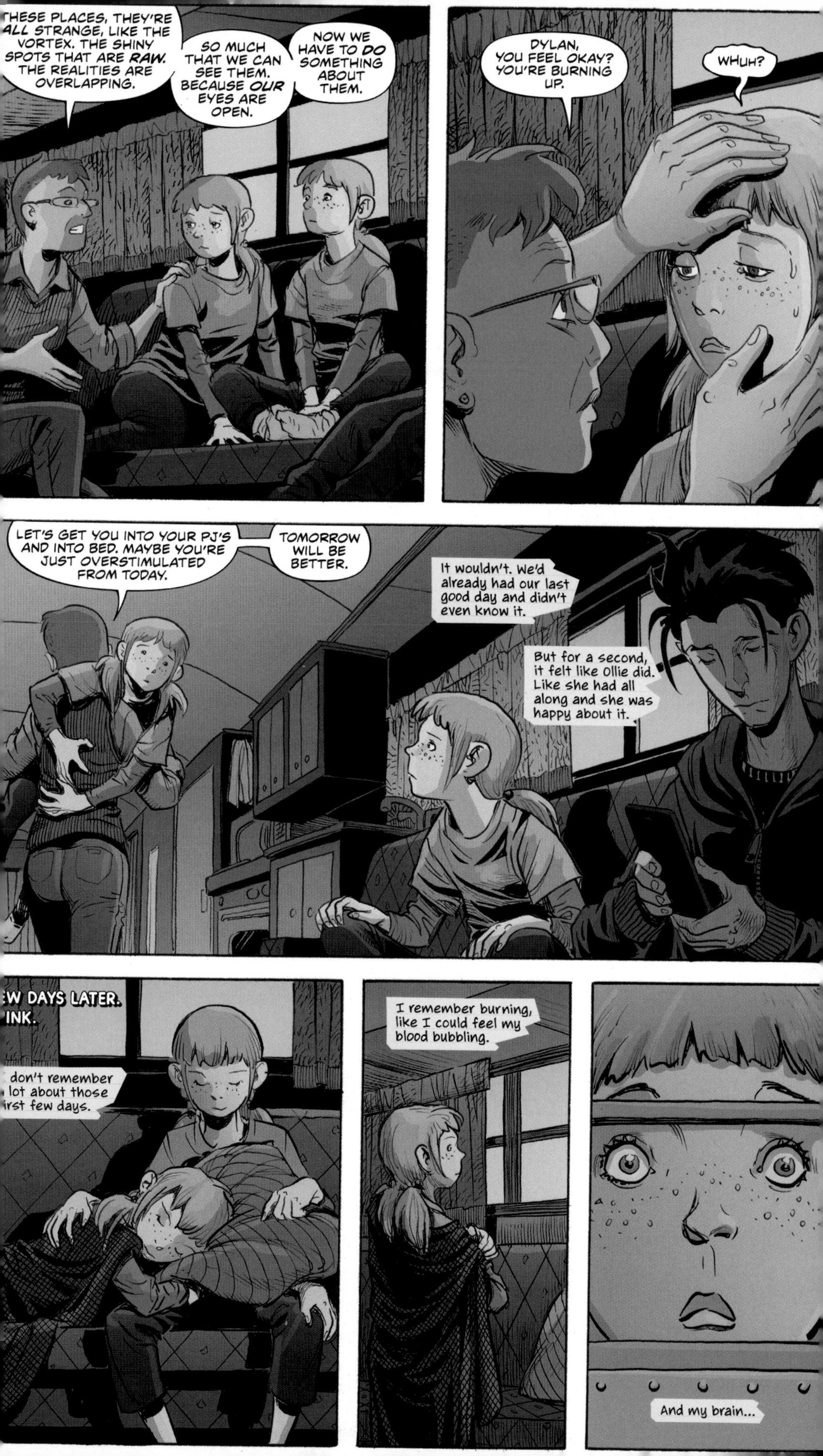

THESE PLACES, THEY'RE ALL STRANGE, LIKE THE VORTEX. THE SHINY SPOTS THAT ARE RAW. THE REALITIES ARE OVERLAPPING.
SO MUCH THAT WE CAN SEE THEM. BECAUSE OUR EYES ARE OPEN.
NOW WE HAVE TO DO SOMETHING ABOUT THEM.
DYLAN, YOU FEEL OKAY? YOU'RE BURNING UP.
WHUH?
LET'S GET YOU INTO YOUR PJ'S AND INTO BED. MAYBE YOU'RE JUST OVERSTIMULATED FROM TODAY.
TOMORROW WILL BE BETTER.
It wouldn't. We'd already had our last good day and didn't even know it.
But for a second, it felt like Ollie did. Like she had all along and she was happy about it.
EW DAYS LATER.
INK.
don't remember lot about those irst few days.
I remember burning, like I could feel my blood bubbling.
And my brain...

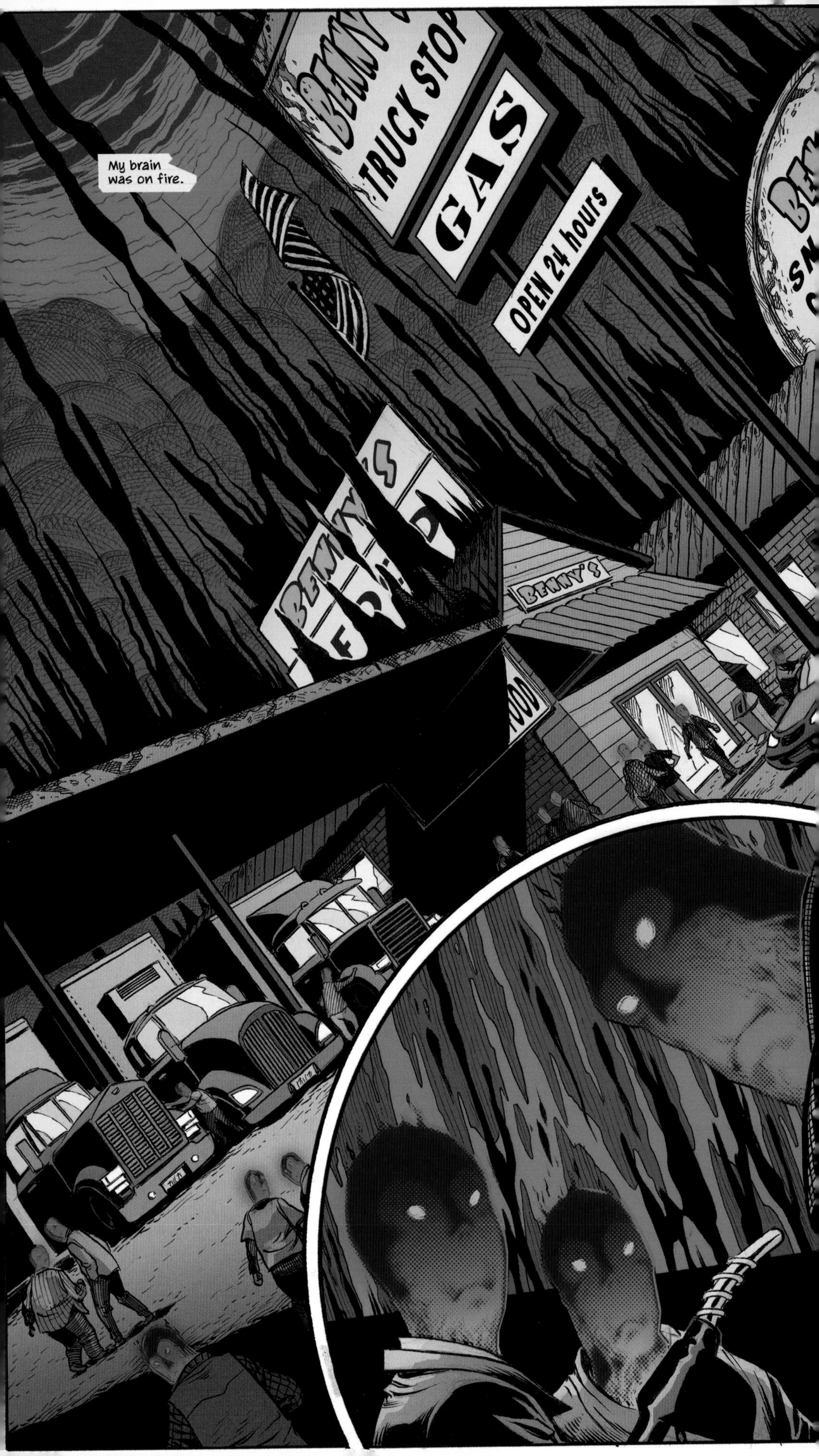
My brain was on fire.
TRUCK STOP
GAS
OPEN 24 hours
BENNY'S

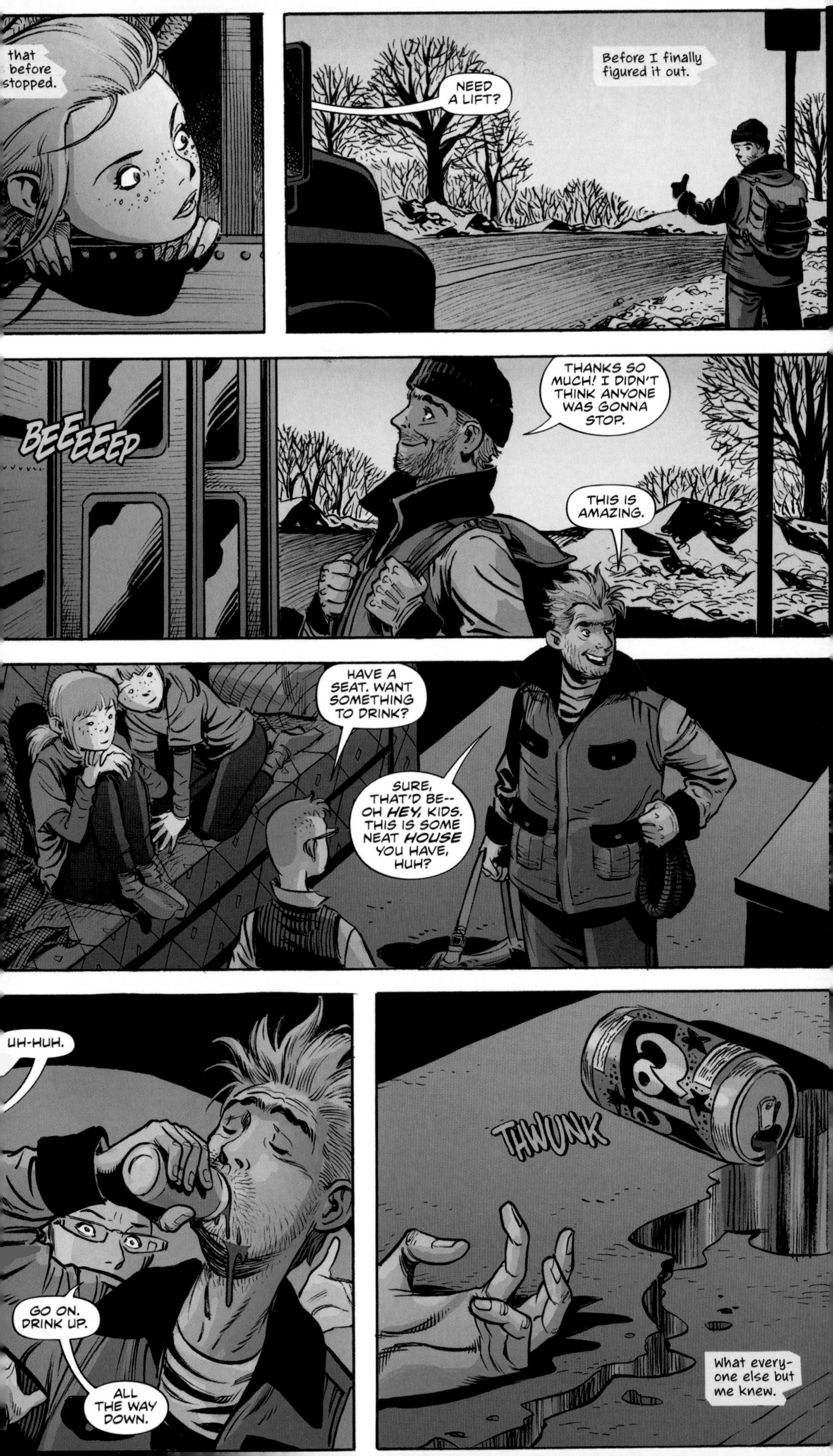
that before stopped.
NEED A LIFT?
Before I finally figured it out.
BEEEEEP
THANKS SO MUCH! I DIDN'T THINK ANYONE WAS GONNA STOP.
THIS IS AMAZING.
HAVE A SEAT. WANT SOMETHING TO DRINK?
SURE, THAT'D BE-- OH HEY, KIDS. THIS IS SOME NEAT HOUSE YOU HAVE, HUH?
UH-HUH.
GO ON. DRINK UP.
ALL THE WAY DOWN.
THWUNK
What every-one else but me knew.

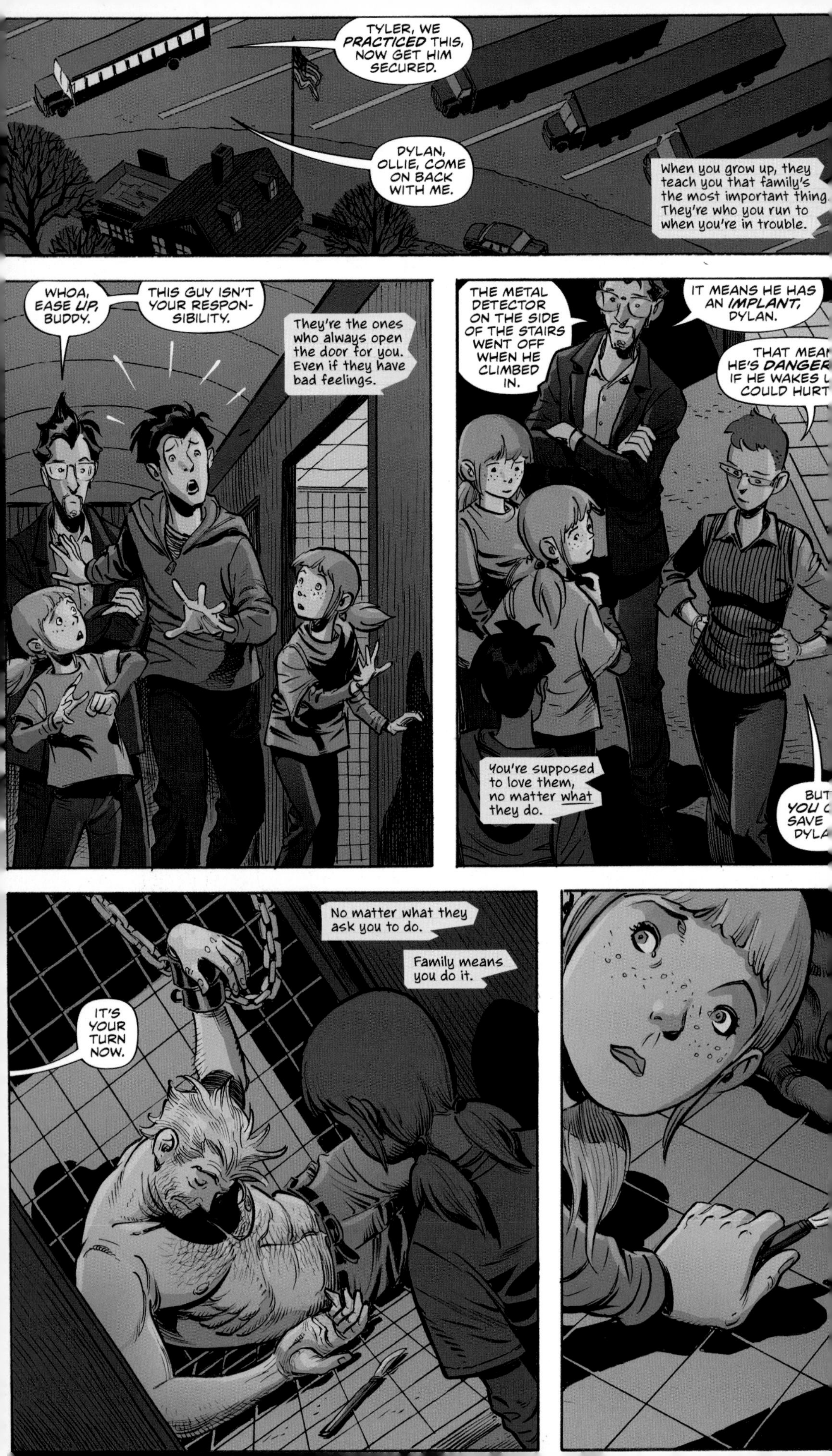
TYLER, WE PRACTICED THIS, NOW GET HIM SECURED.
DYLAN, OLLIE, COME ON BACK WITH ME.
When you grow up, they teach you that family's the most important thing. They're who you run to when you're in trouble.
WHOA, EASE UP, BUDDY.
THIS GUY ISN'T YOUR RESPONSIBILITY.
They're the ones who always open the door for you. Even if they have bad feelings.
THE METAL DETECTOR ON THE SIDE OF THE STAIRS WENT OFF WHEN HE CLIMBED IN.
IT MEANS HE HAS AN IMPLANT, DYLAN.
THAT MEAN HE'S DANGER IF HE WAKES U COULD HURT
You're supposed to love them, no matter what they do.
BUT YOU C SAVE DYLA
No matter what they ask you to do.
Family means you do it.
IT'S YOUR TURN NOW.

“We weren’t heroes. We weren’t saving anything. We were bad. Doing bad things.”

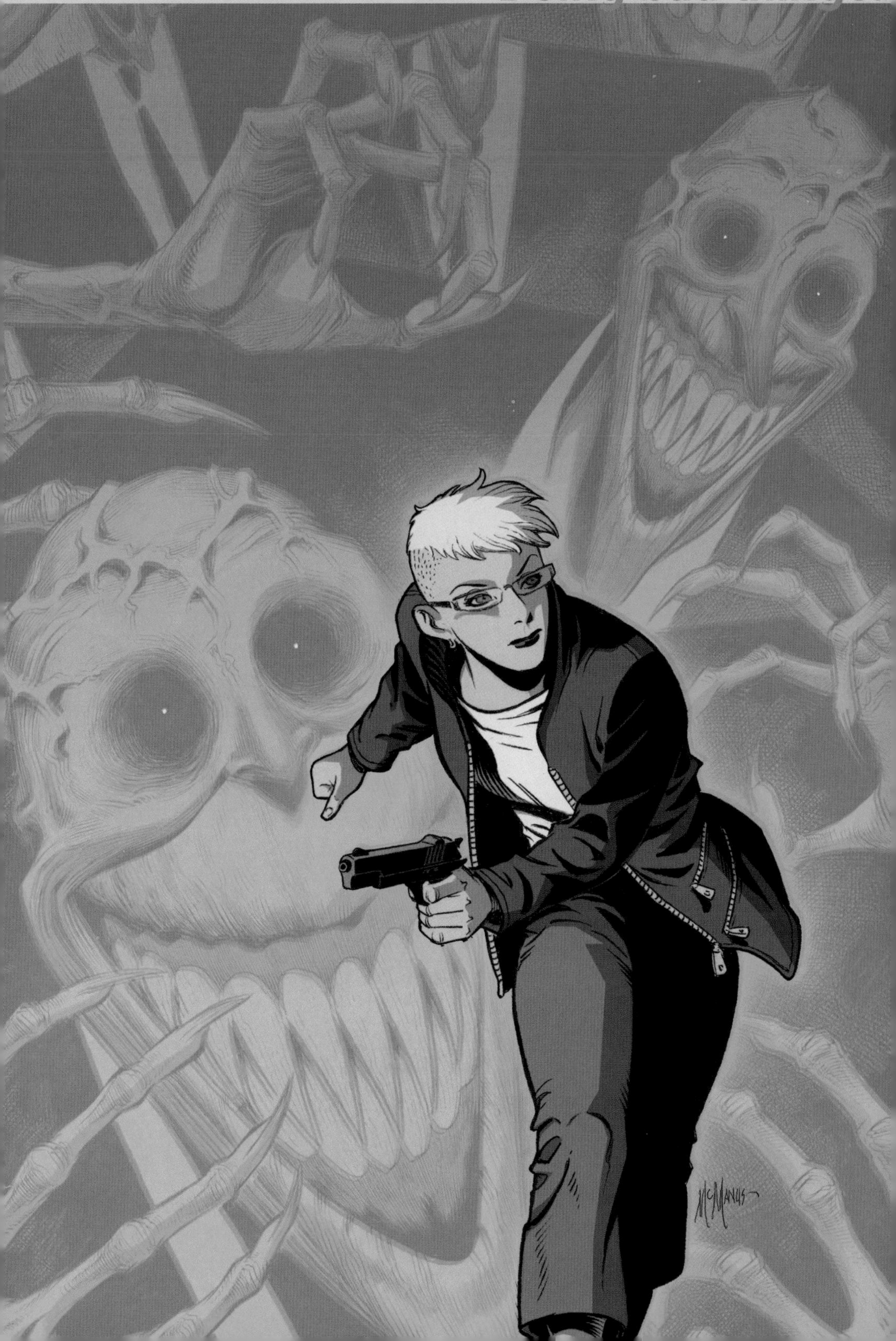

McManus

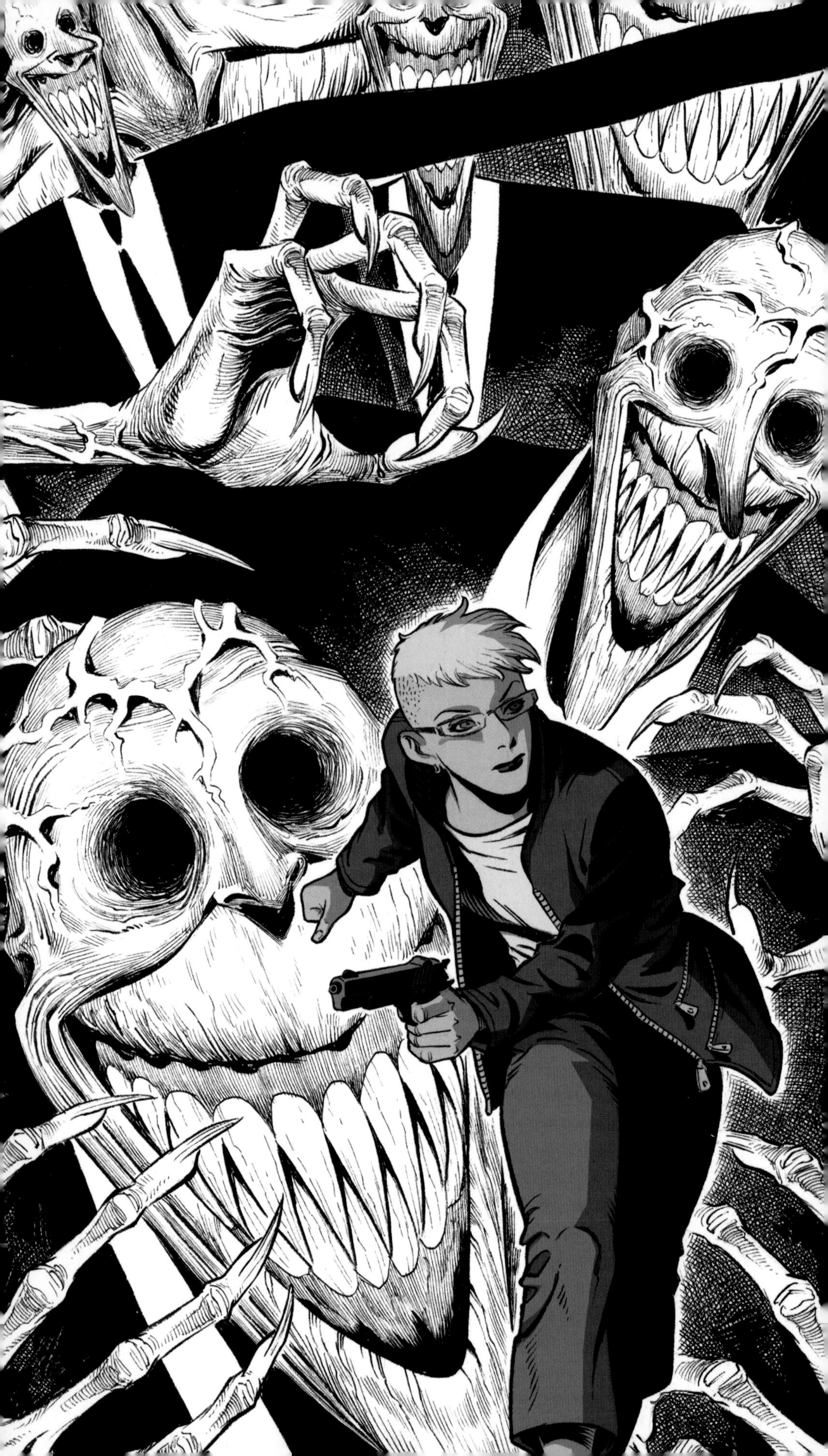

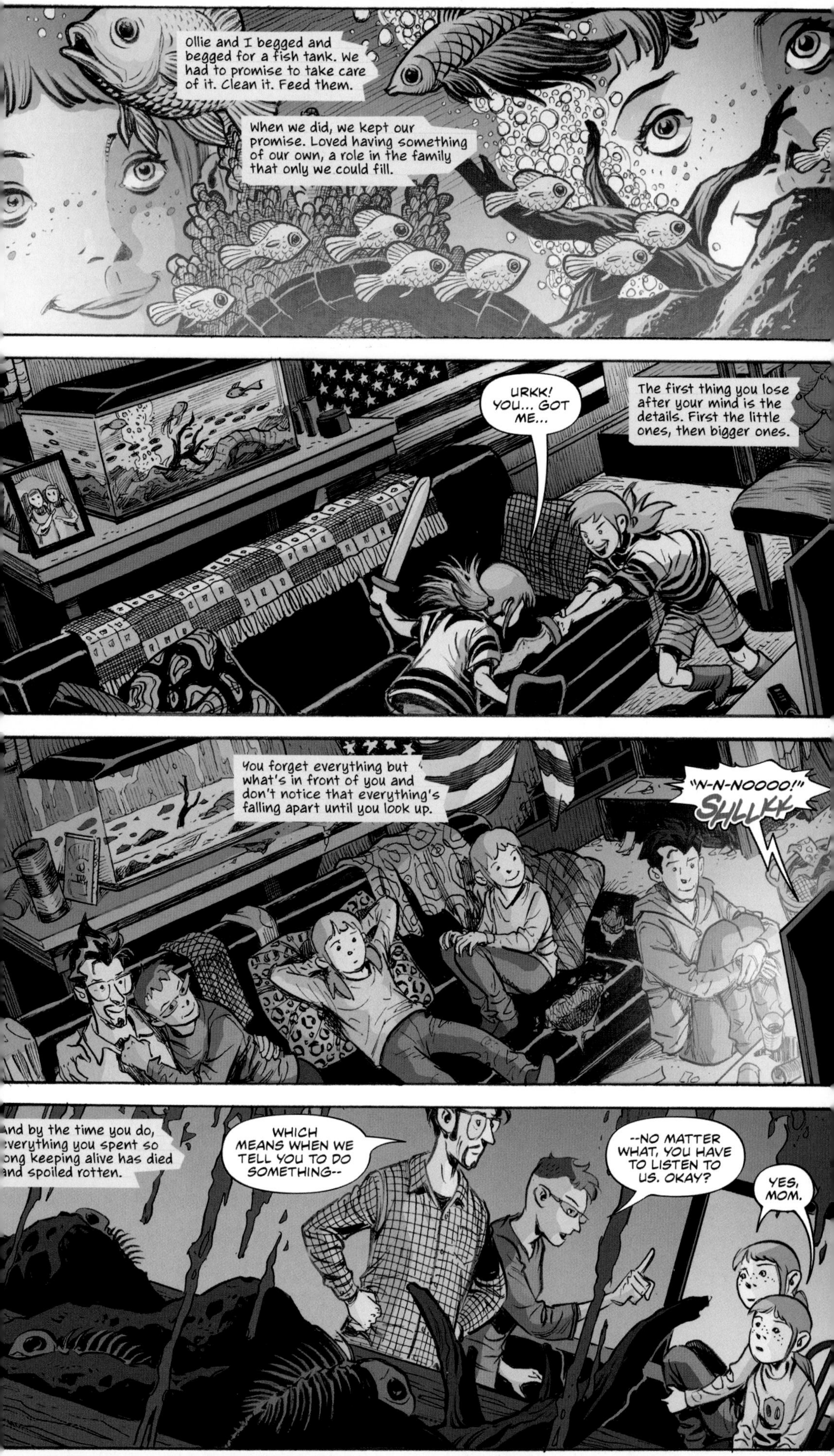

Ollie and I begged and begged for a fish tank. We had to promise to take care of it. Clean it. Feed them.
When we did, we kept our promise. Loved having something of our own, a role in the family that only we could fill.
URKK! YOU... GOT ME...
The first thing you lose after your mind is the details. First the little ones, then bigger ones.
You forget everything but what's in front of you and don't notice that everything's falling apart until you look up.
"N-N-NOOOO!"
SHLLKK
And by the time you do, everything you spent so long keeping alive has died and spoiled rotten.
WHICH MEANS WHEN WE TELL YOU TO DO SOMETHING--
--NO MATTER WHAT, YOU HAVE TO LISTEN TO US. OKAY?
YES, MOM.

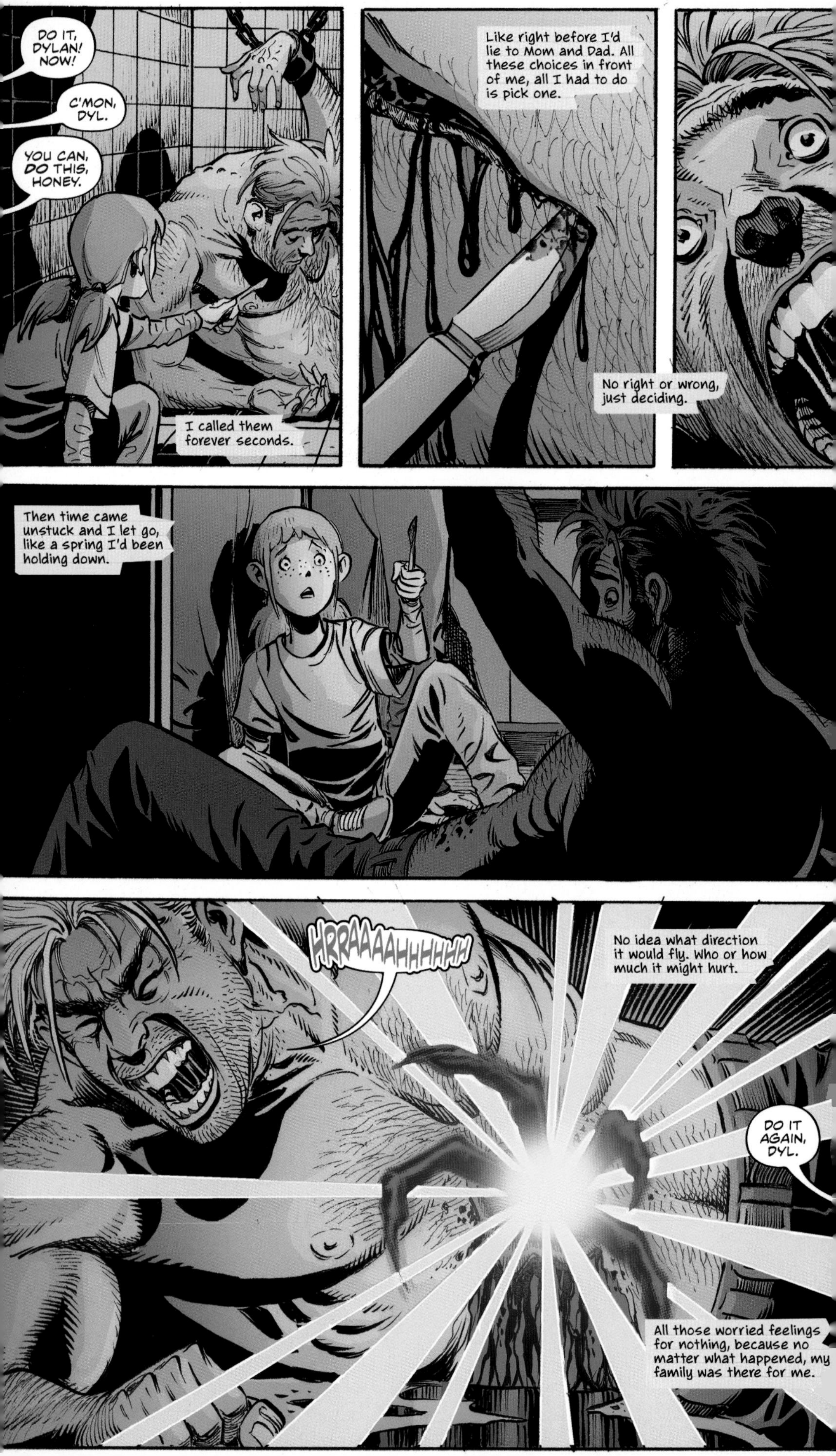
DO IT, DYLAN! NOW!
C'MON, DYL.
YOU CAN, DO THIS, HONEY.
I called them forever seconds.
Like right before I'd lie to Mom and Dad. All these choices in front of me, all I had to do is pick one.
No right or wrong, just deciding.
Then time came unstuck and I let go, like a spring I'd been holding down.
HRRAAAAAHHHHHH
No idea what direction it would fly. Who or how much it might hurt.
DO IT AGAIN, DYL.
All those worried feelings for nothing, because no matter what happened, my family was there for me.

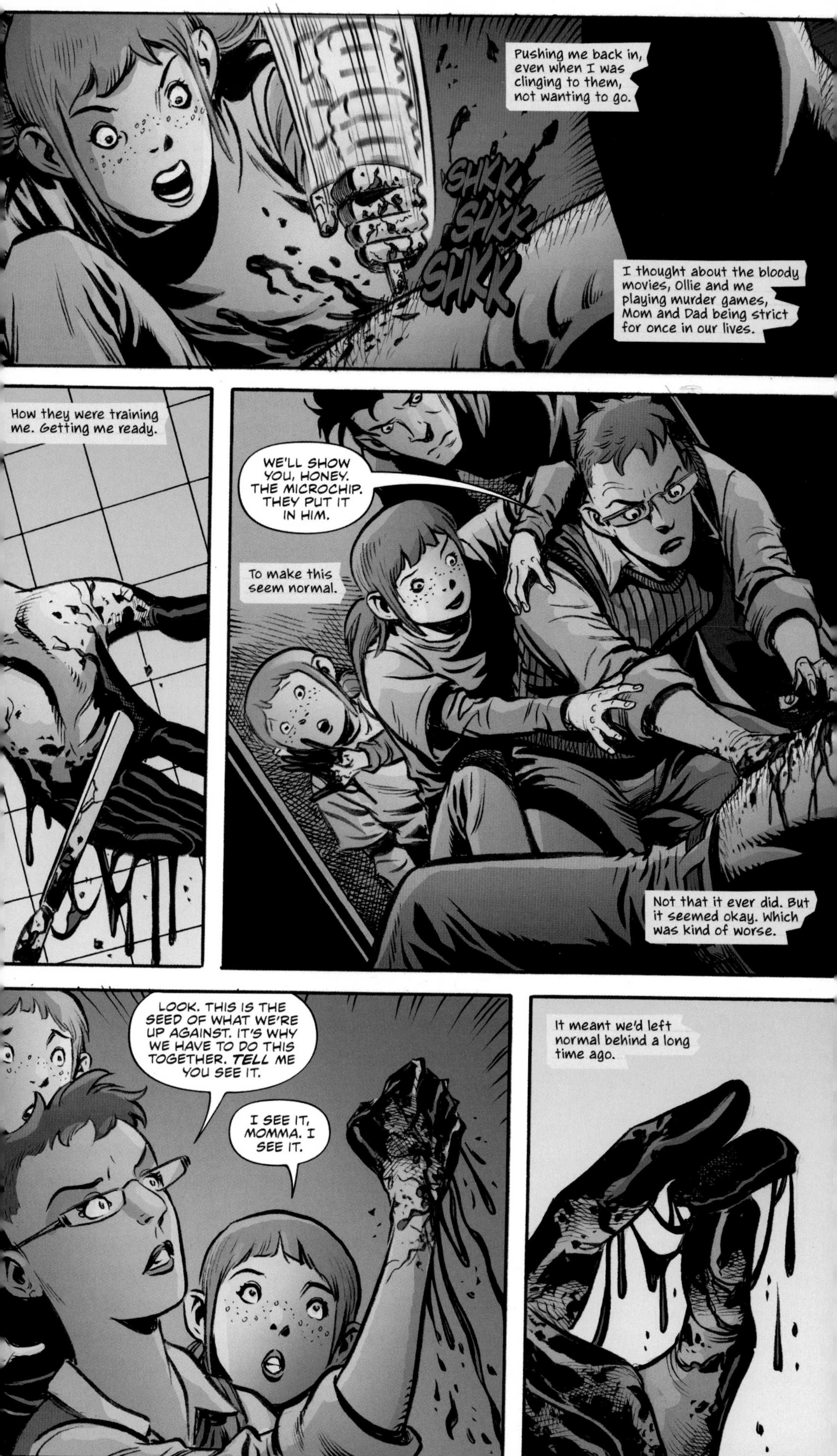
Pushing me back in, even when I was clinging to them, not wanting to go.
SHKK SHKK SHKK
I thought about the bloody movies, Ollie and me playing murder games, Mom and Dad being strict for once in our lives.
How they were training me. Getting me ready.
WE'LL SHOW YOU, HONEY. THE MICROCHIP. THEY PUT IT IN HIM.
To make this seem normal.
Not that it ever did. But it seemed okay. Which was kind of worse.
LOOK. THIS IS THE SEED OF WHAT WE'RE UP AGAINST. IT'S WHY WE HAVE TO DO THIS TOGETHER. TELL ME YOU SEE IT.
I SEE IT, MOMMA. I SEE IT.
It meant we'd left normal behind a long time ago.

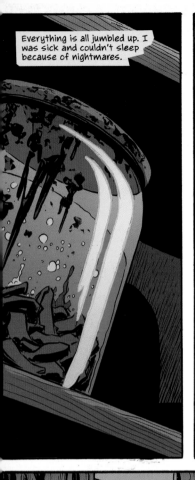

Everything is all jumbled up. I was sick and couldn't sleep because of nightmares.

And Dad said we still had to prepare for war.

One of them was named Tom. That's all he said before he fell asleep. I tried so hard to remember.

I thought someone should.

We stayed away from highways. Always driving through the middle of nowhere. Where it was safe.

But otherwise it was like any oth vacation.

We learned all kindsa new things.

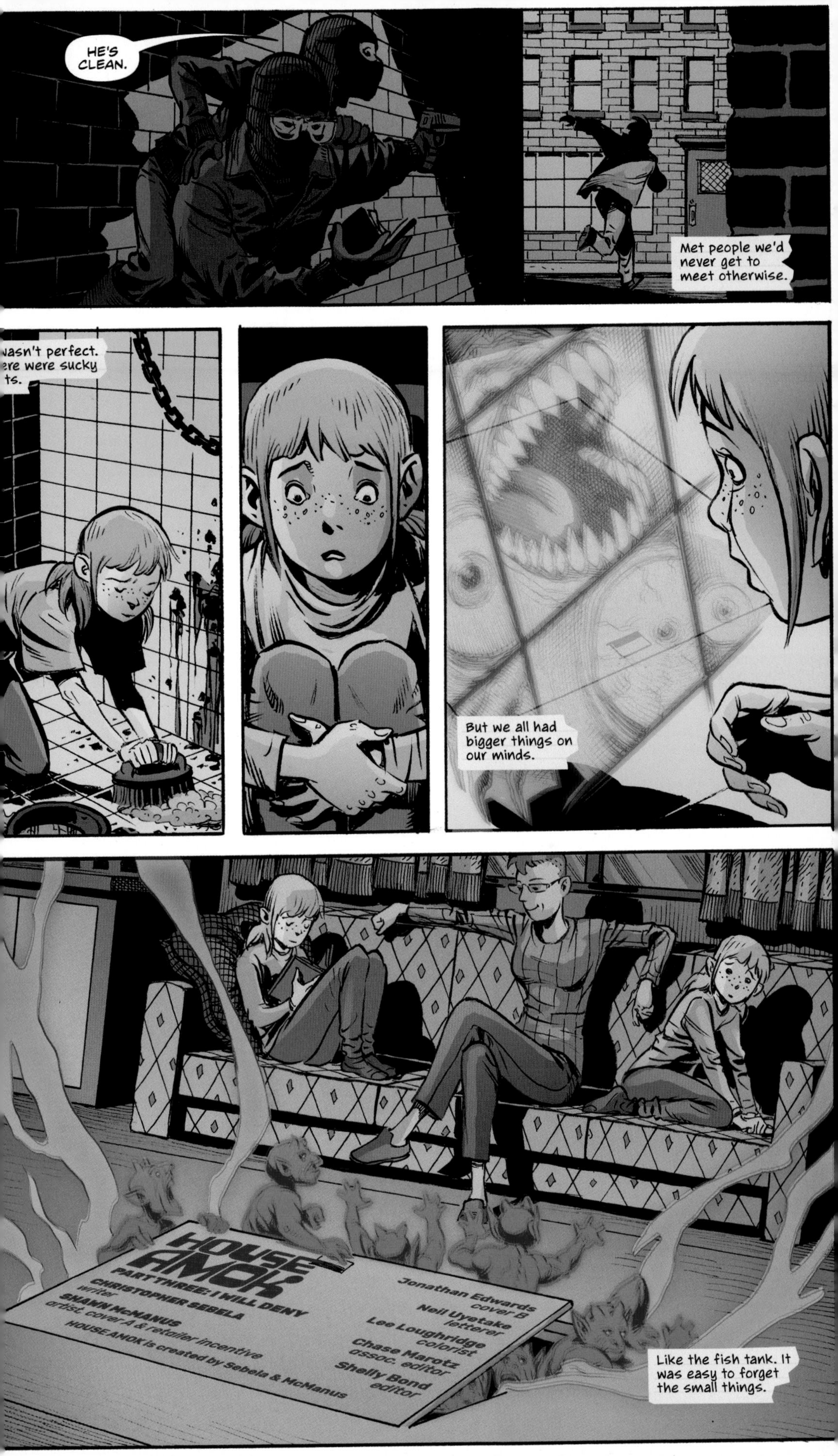
HE'S CLEAN.
Met people we'd never get to meet otherwise.
wasn't perfect. ere were sucky ts.
But we all had bigger things on our minds.
HOUSE AMOK
PART THREE: I WILL DENY
CHRISTOPHER SEBELA
writer
SHAWN McMANUS
artist, cover A & retailer incentive
HOUSE AMOK is created by Sebela & McManus
Jonathan Edwards
cover B
Neil Uyetake
letterer
Lee Loughridge
colorist
Chase Marotz
assoc. editor
Shelly Bond
editor
Like the fish tank. It was easy to forget the small things.

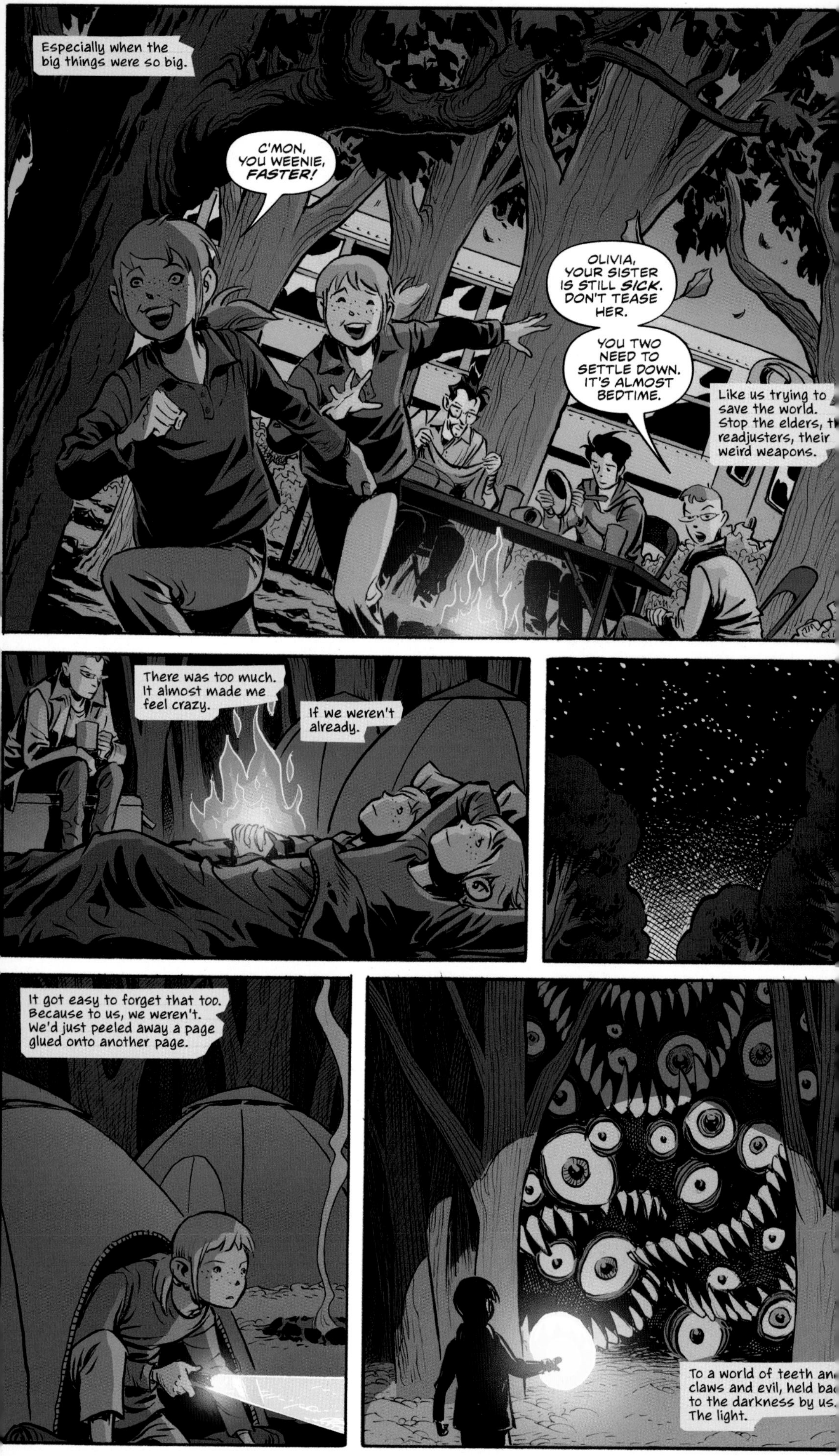
Especially when the big things were so big.
C'MON, YOU WEENIE, *FASTER!*
OLIVIA, YOUR SISTER IS STILL *SICK*. DON'T TEASE HER.
YOU TWO NEED TO SETTLE DOWN. IT'S ALMOST BEDTIME.
Like us trying to save the world. Stop the elders, t readjusters, their weird weapons.
There was too much. It almost made me feel crazy.
If we weren't already.
It got easy to forget that too. Because to us, we weren't. We'd just peeled away a page glued onto another page.
To a world of teeth an claws and evil, held ba to the darkness by us. The light.

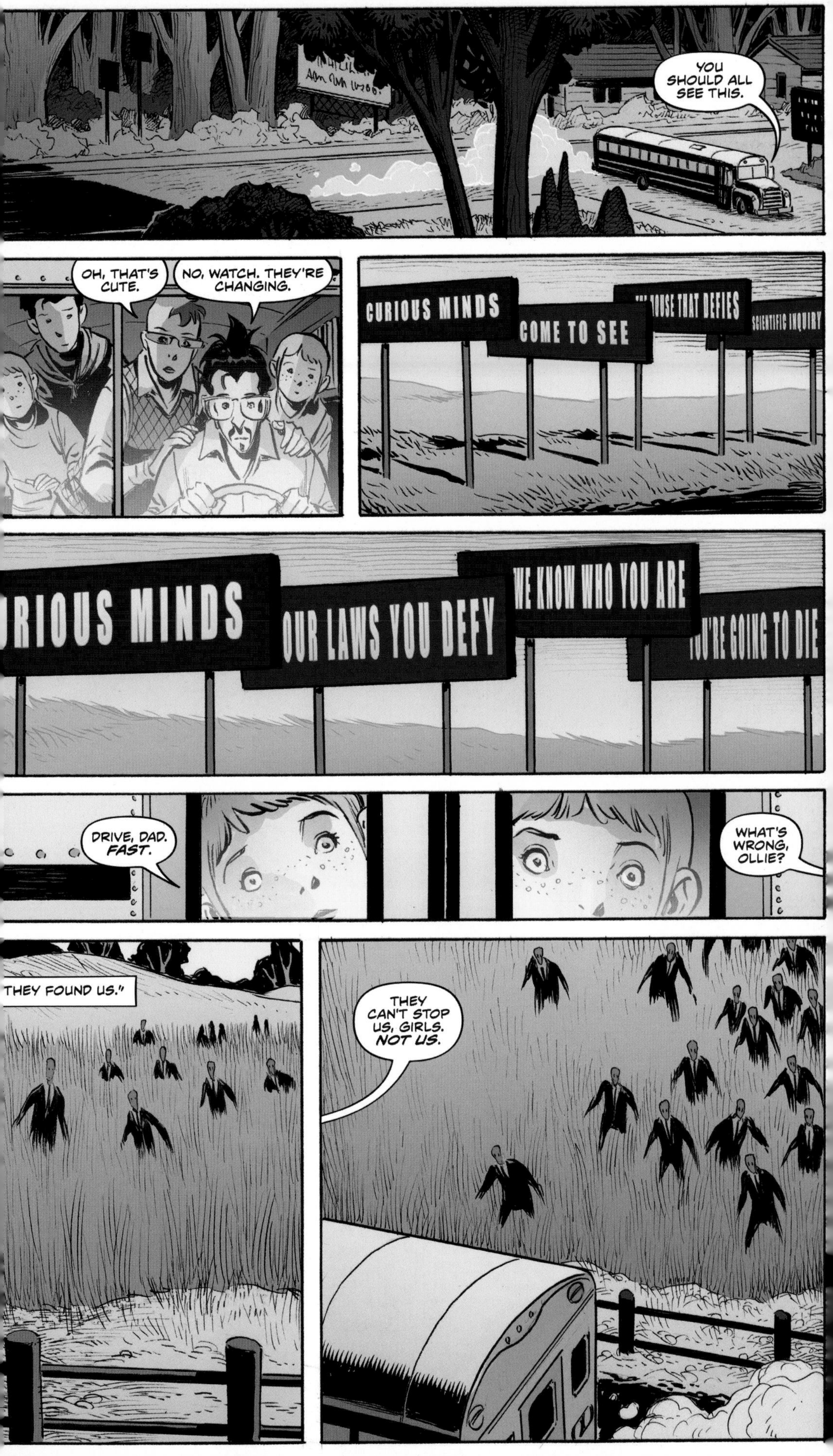

YOU SHOULD ALL SEE THIS.
OH, THAT'S CUTE.
NO, WATCH. THEY'RE CHANGING.
CURIOUS MINDS
COME TO SEE
HOUSE THAT DEFIES
SCIENTIFIC INQUIRY
RIOUS MINDS
OUR LAWS YOU DEFY
WE KNOW WHO YOU ARE
YOU'RE GOING TO DIE
DRIVE, DAD. *FAST.*
WHAT'S WRONG, OLLIE?
THEY FOUND US."
THEY CAN'T STOP US, GIRLS. *NOT US.*

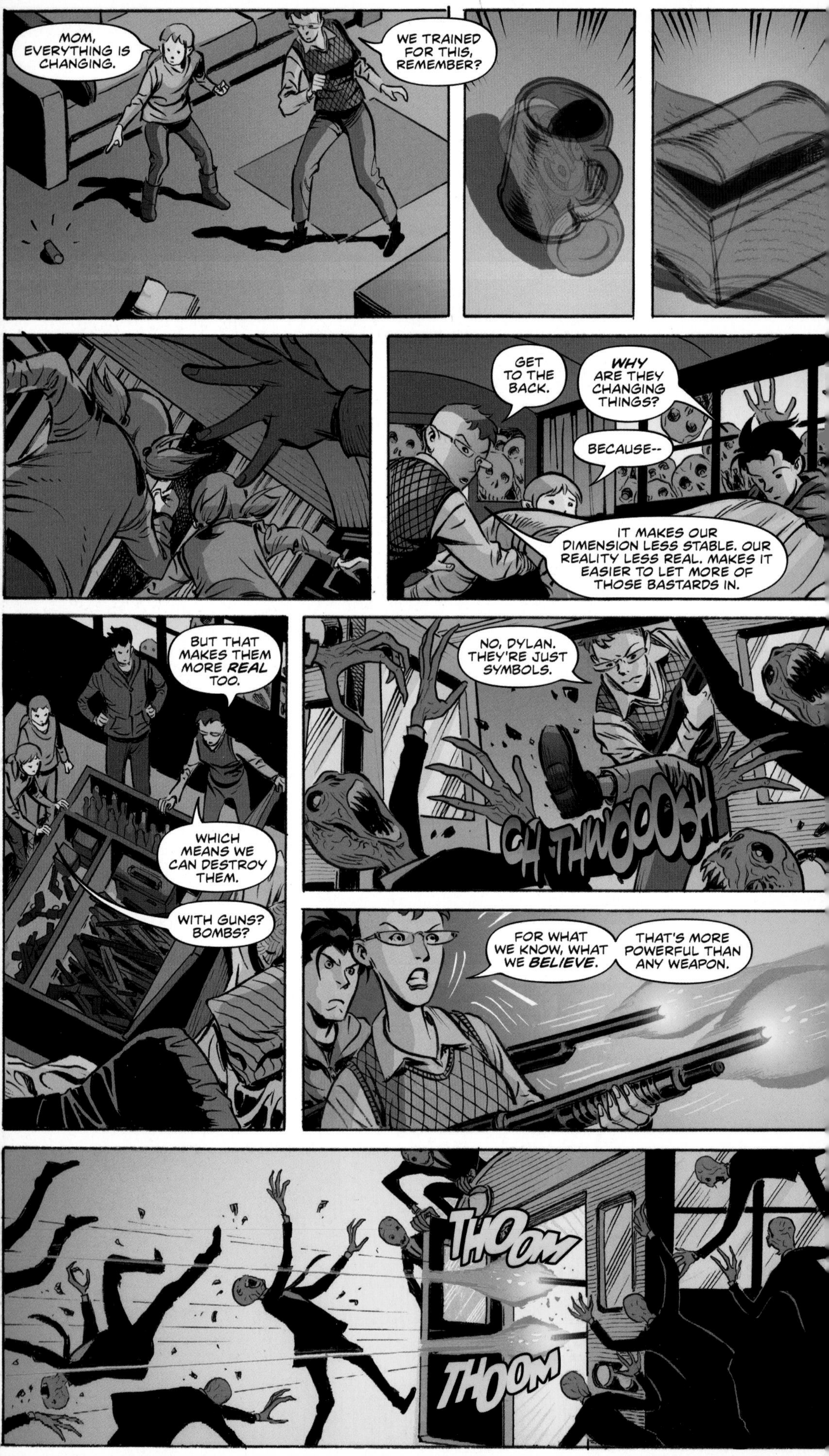
MOM, EVERYTHING IS CHANGING.
WE TRAINED FOR THIS, REMEMBER?
GET TO THE BACK.
WHY ARE THEY CHANGING THINGS?
BECAUSE--
IT MAKES OUR DIMENSION LESS STABLE. OUR REALITY LESS REAL. MAKES IT EASIER TO LET MORE OF THOSE BASTARDS IN.
BUT THAT MAKES THEM MORE REAL TOO.
WHICH MEANS WE CAN DESTROY THEM.
WITH GUNS? BOMBS?
NO, DYLAN. THEY'RE JUST SYMBOLS.
CH THWOOOSH
FOR WHAT WE KNOW, WHAT WE BELIEVE.
THAT'S MORE POWERFUL THAN ANY WEAPON.
THOOM
THOOM

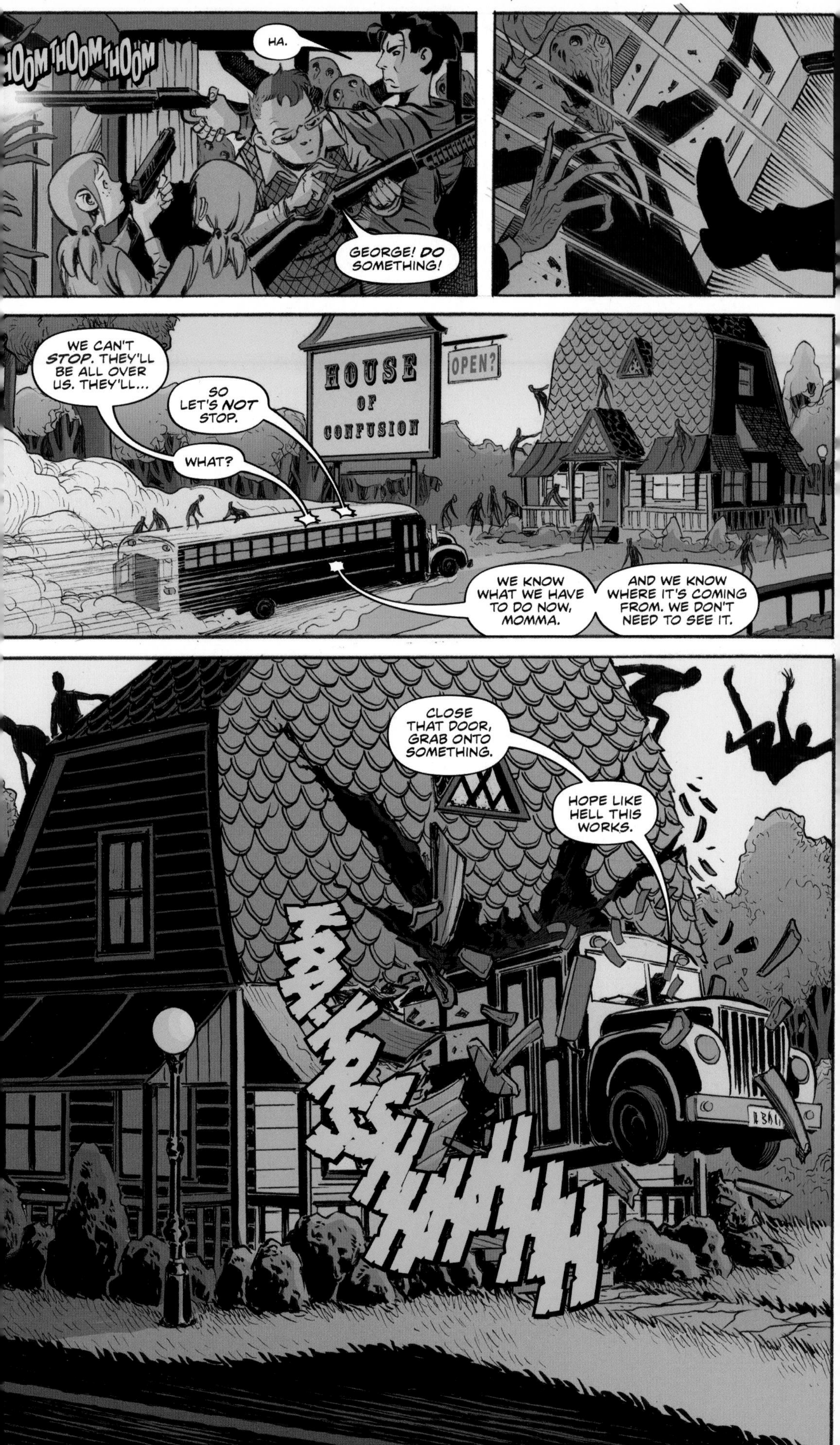

THOOM THOOM THOOM
HA.
GEORGE! DO SOMETHING!
HOUSE OF CONFUSION
OPEN?
WE CAN'T STOP. THEY'LL BE ALL OVER US. THEY'LL...
SO LET'S NOT STOP.
WHAT?
WE KNOW WHAT WE HAVE TO DO NOW, MOMMA.
AND WE KNOW WHERE IT'S COMING FROM. WE DON'T NEED TO SEE IT.
CLOSE THAT DOOR, GRAB ONTO SOMETHING.
HOPE LIKE HELL THIS WORKS.

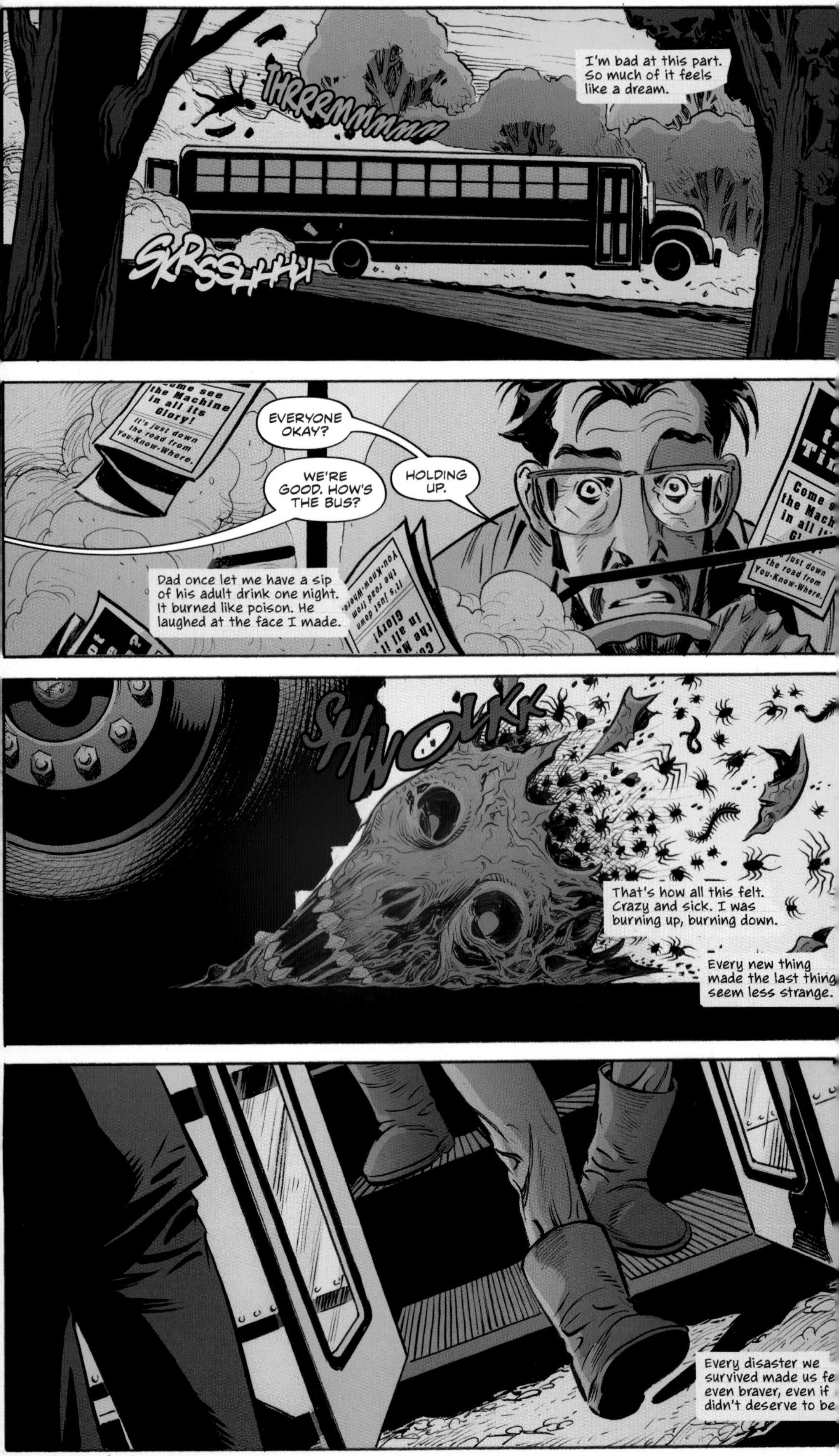
I'm bad at this part. So much of it feels like a dream.
THRRRMMMmmm
SKRSSHHH
ome see the Machine in all its Glory! It's just down the road from You-Know-Where.
EVERYONE OKAY?
WE'RE GOOD. HOW'S THE BUS?
HOLDING UP.
Dad once let me have a sip of his adult drink one night. It burned like poison. He laughed at the face I made.
SHWOKK
That's how all this felt. Crazy and sick. I was burning up, burning down.
Every new thing made the last thing seem less strange.
Every disaster we survived made us fe
even braver, even if
didn't deserve to be

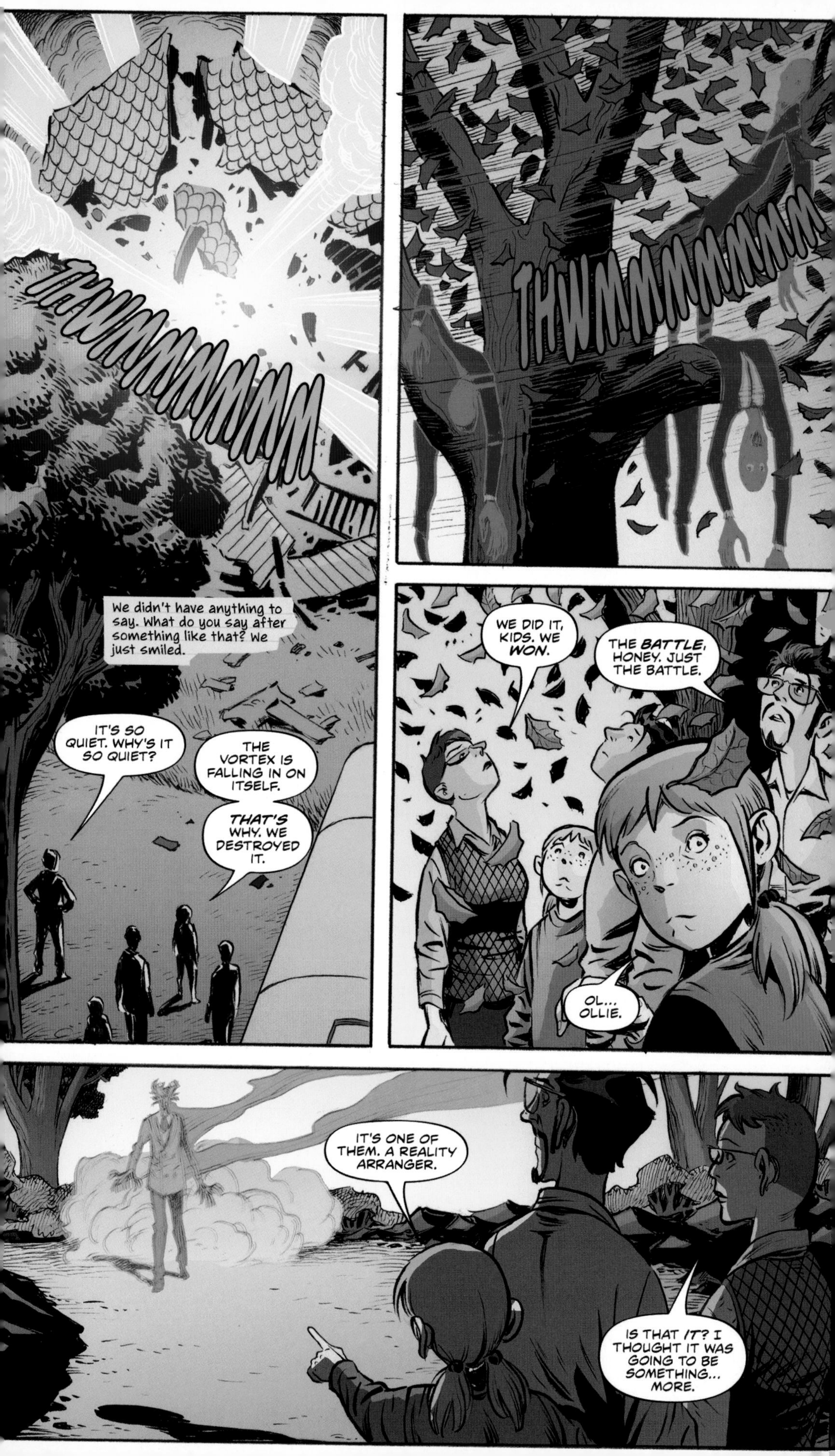
THWMMMMMMM
THWMMMMMMM
We didn't have anything to say. What do you say after something like that? We just smiled.
IT'S SO QUIET. WHY'S IT SO QUIET?
THE VORTEX IS FALLING IN ON ITSELF.
THAT'S WHY. WE DESTROYED IT.
WE DID IT, KIDS. WE WON.
THE BATTLE, HONEY. JUST THE BATTLE.
OL... OLLIE.
IT'S ONE OF THEM. A REALITY ARRANGER.
IS THAT IT? I THOUGHT IT WAS GOING TO BE SOMETHING... MORE.

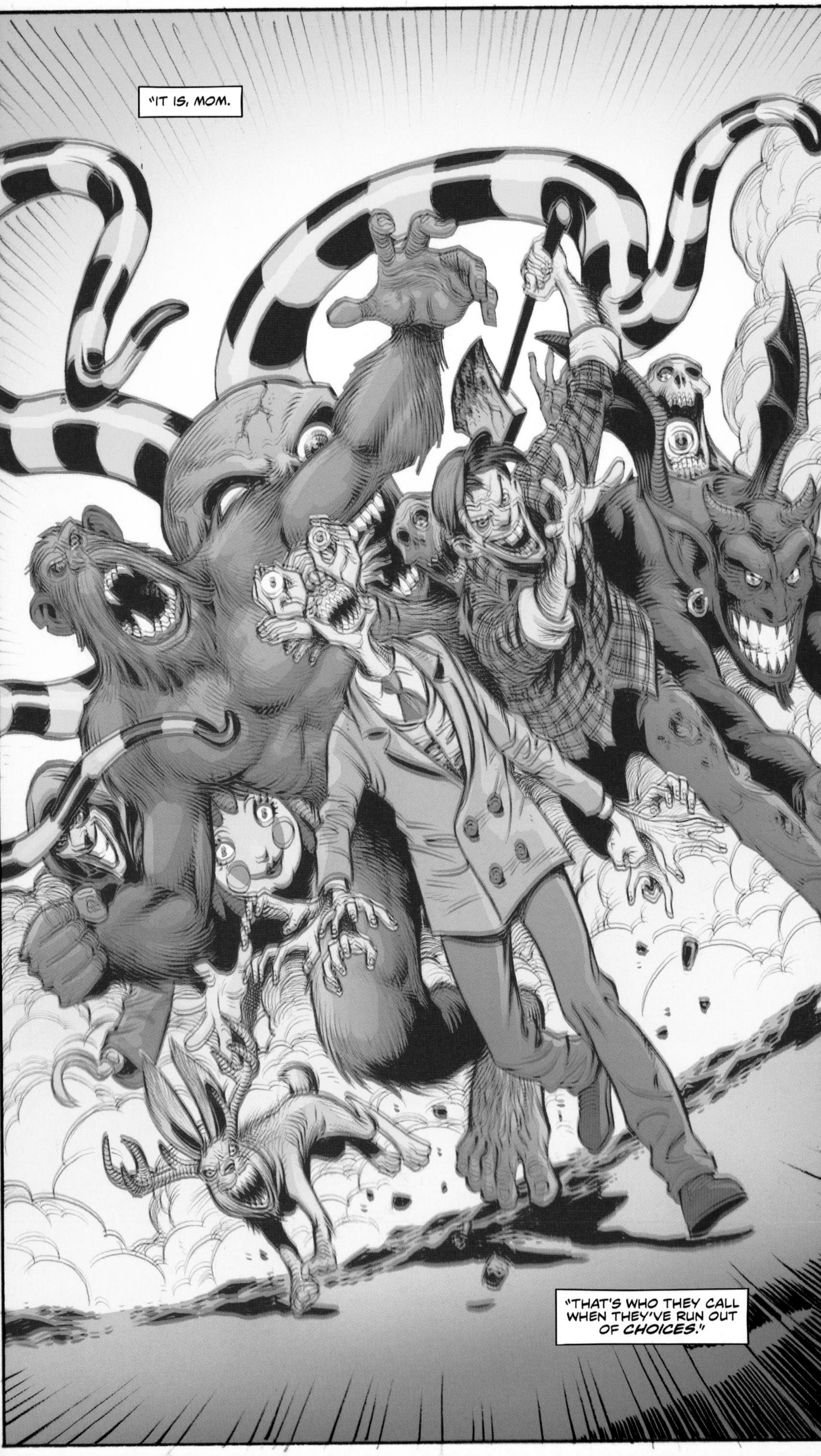
"IT IS, MOM.
"THAT'S WHO THEY CALL WHEN THEY'VE RUN OUT OF *CHOICES*."

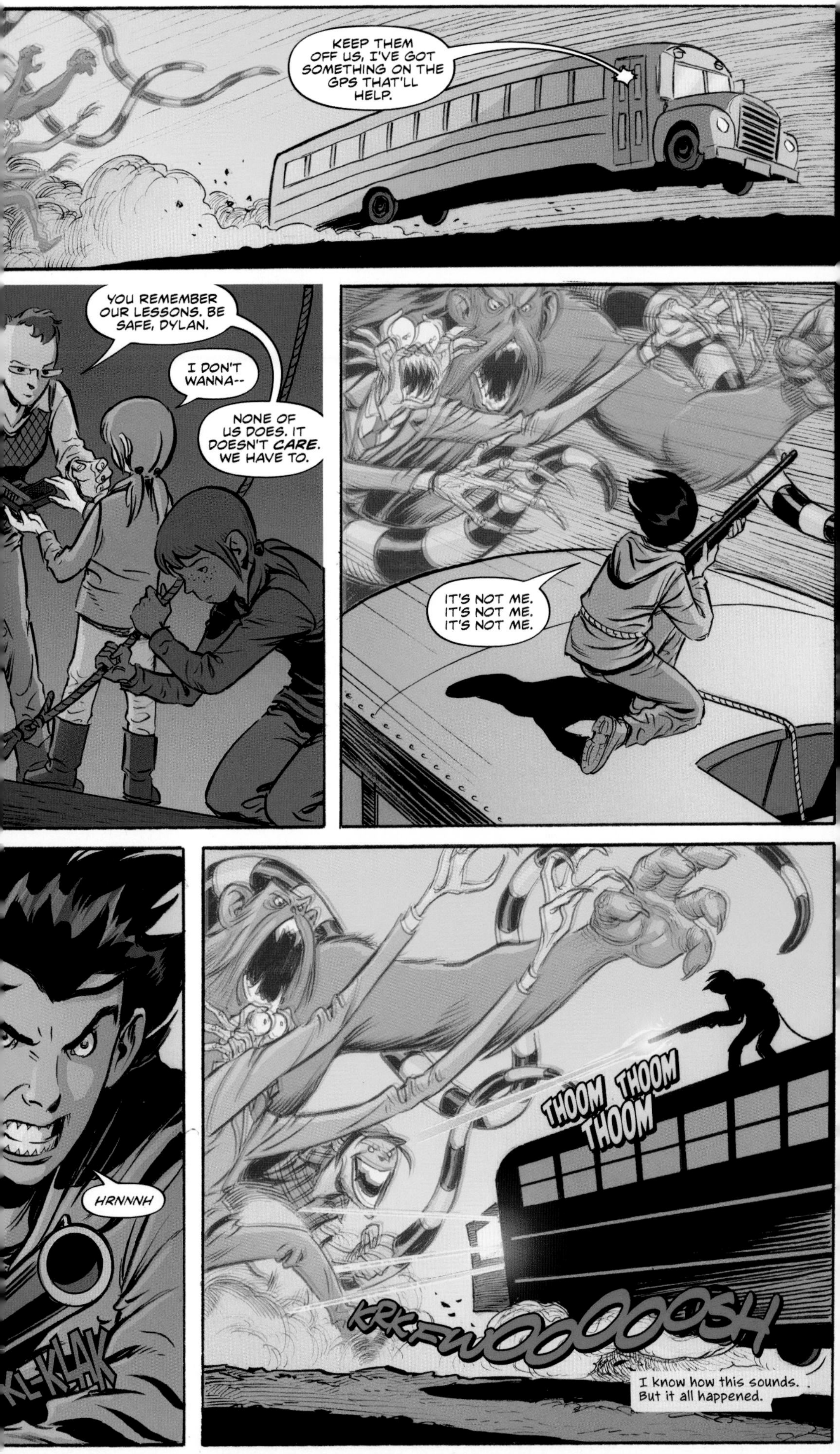
KEEP THEM OFF US, I'VE GOT SOMETHING ON THE GPS THAT'LL HELP.
YOU REMEMBER OUR LESSONS. BE SAFE, DYLAN.
I DON'T WANNA--
NONE OF US DOES. IT DOESN'T CARE. WE HAVE TO.
IT'S NOT ME. IT'S NOT ME. IT'S NOT ME.
HRNNNH
KL-KLAK
THOOM THOOM THOOM
KRK-FWOOOOOOSH
I know how this sounds. But it all happened.

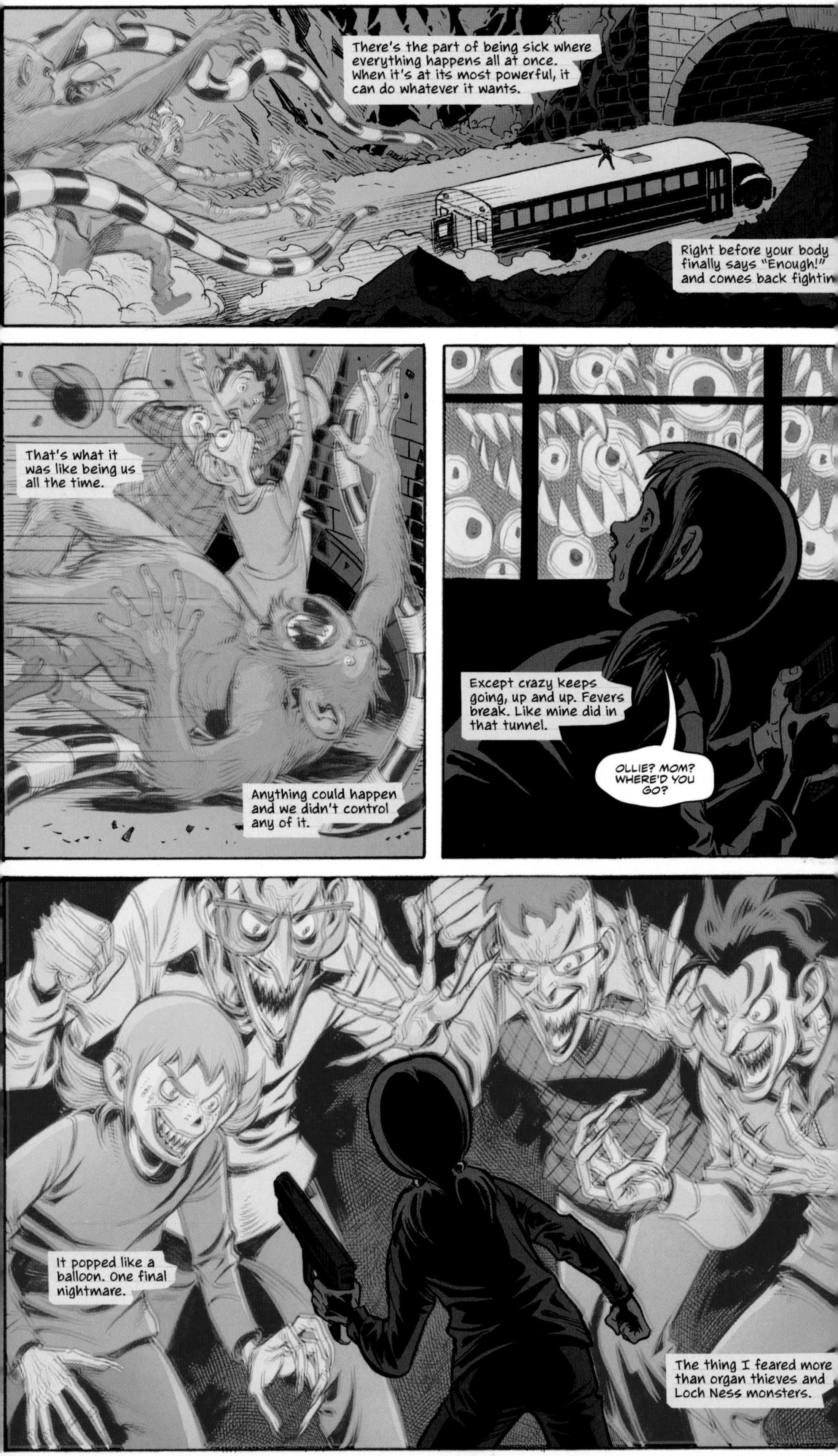
There's the part of being sick where everything happens all at once. When it's at its most powerful, it can do whatever it wants.
Right before your body finally says "Enough!" and comes back fightin
That's what it was like being us all the time.
Anything could happen and we didn't control any of it.
Except crazy keeps going, up and up. Fevers break. Like mine did in that tunnel.
OLLIE? MOM? WHERE'D YOU GO?
It popped like a balloon. One final nightmare.
The thing I feared more than organ thieves and Loch Ness monsters.

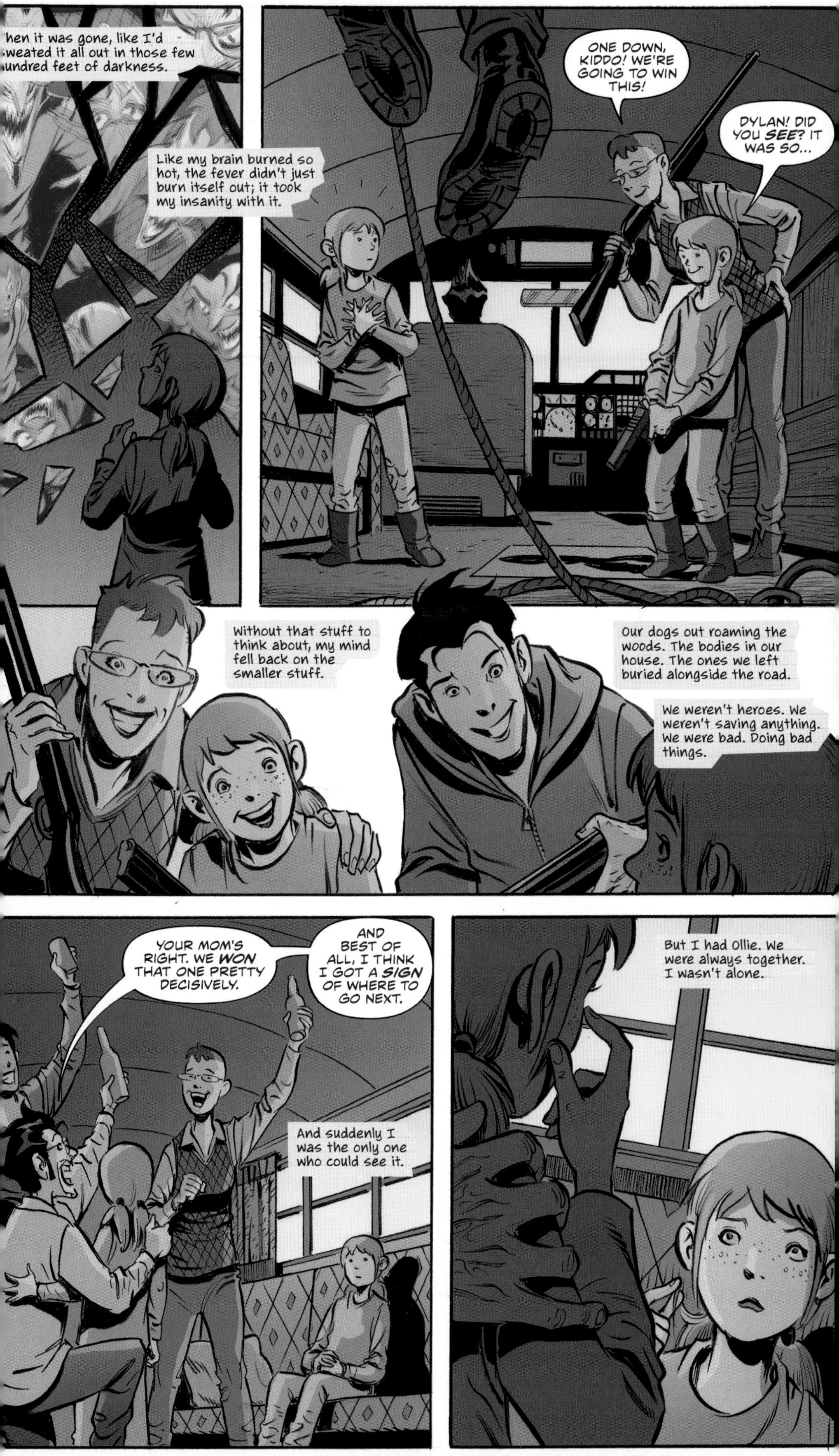
hen it was gone, like I'd
weated it all out in those few
undred feet of darkness.
Like my brain burned so hot, the fever didn't just burn itself out; it took my insanity with it.
ONE DOWN, KIDDO! WE'RE GOING TO WIN THIS!
DYLAN! DID YOU SEE? IT WAS SO...
Without that stuff to think about, my mind fell back on the smaller stuff.
Our dogs out roaming the woods. The bodies in our house. The ones we left buried alongside the road.
We weren't heroes. We weren't saving anything. We were bad. Doing bad things.
YOUR MOM'S RIGHT. WE WON THAT ONE PRETTY DECISIVELY.
AND BEST OF ALL, I THINK I GOT A SIGN OF WHERE TO GO NEXT.
And suddenly I was the only one who could see it.
But I had Ollie. We were always together. I wasn't alone.

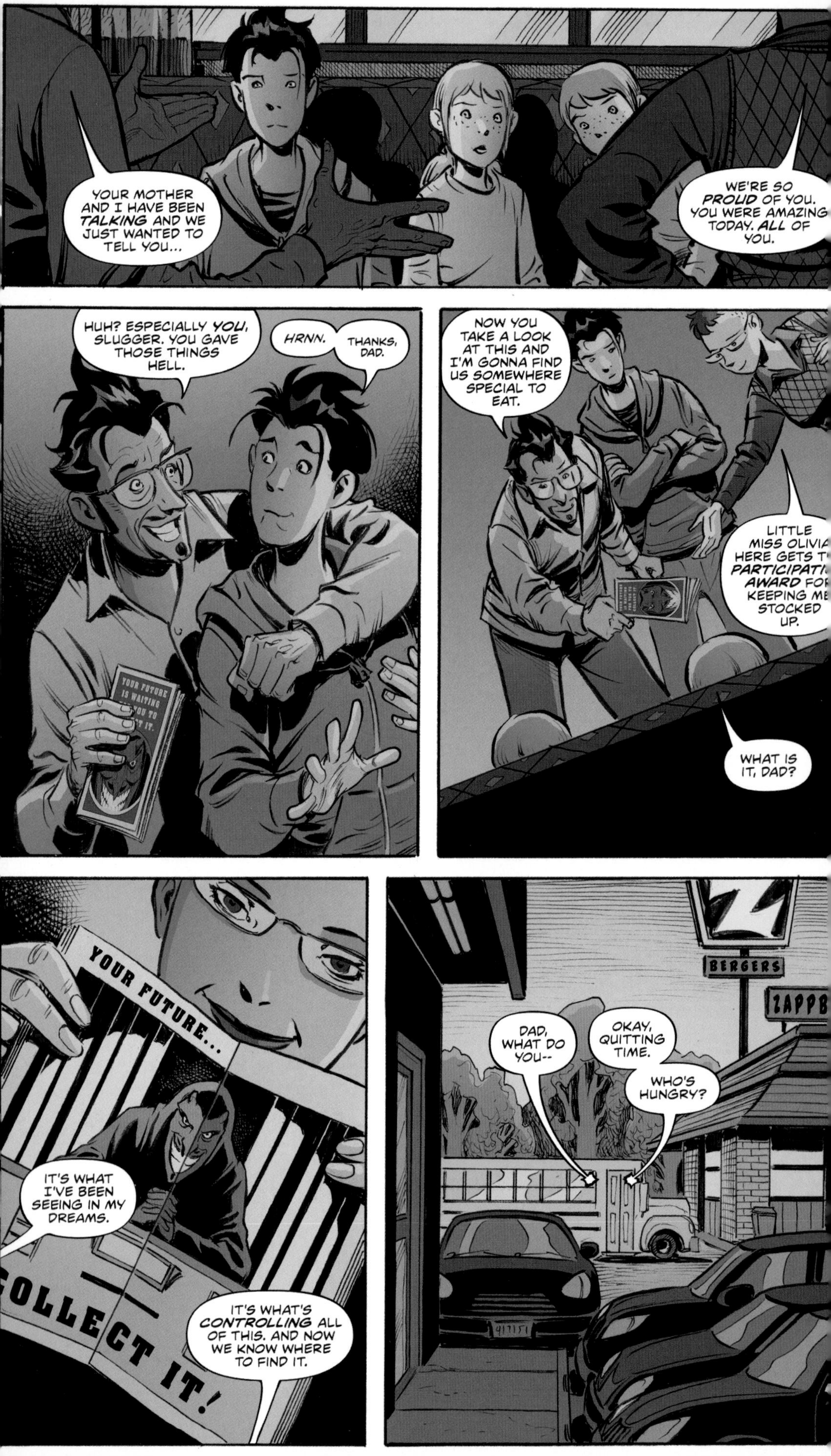

YOUR MOTHER AND I HAVE BEEN *TALKING* AND WE JUST WANTED TO TELL YOU...
WE'RE SO *PROUD* OF YOU. YOU WERE AMAZING TODAY. *ALL* OF YOU.
HUH? ESPECIALLY *YOU*, SLUGGER. YOU GAVE THOSE THINGS HELL.
HRNN.
THANKS, DAD.
NOW YOU TAKE A LOOK AT THIS AND I'M GONNA FIND US SOMEWHERE SPECIAL TO EAT.
LITTLE MISS OLIVIA HERE GETS T *PARTICIPATI AWARD* FO KEEPING ME STOCKED UP.
WHAT IS IT, DAD?
YOUR FUTURE...
COLLECT IT!
IT'S WHAT I'VE BEEN SEEING IN MY DREAMS.
IT'S WHAT'S *CONTROLLING* ALL OF THIS. AND NOW WE KNOW WHERE TO FIND IT.
BERGERS
DAD, WHAT DO YOU--
OKAY, QUITTING TIME.
WHO'S HUNGRY?

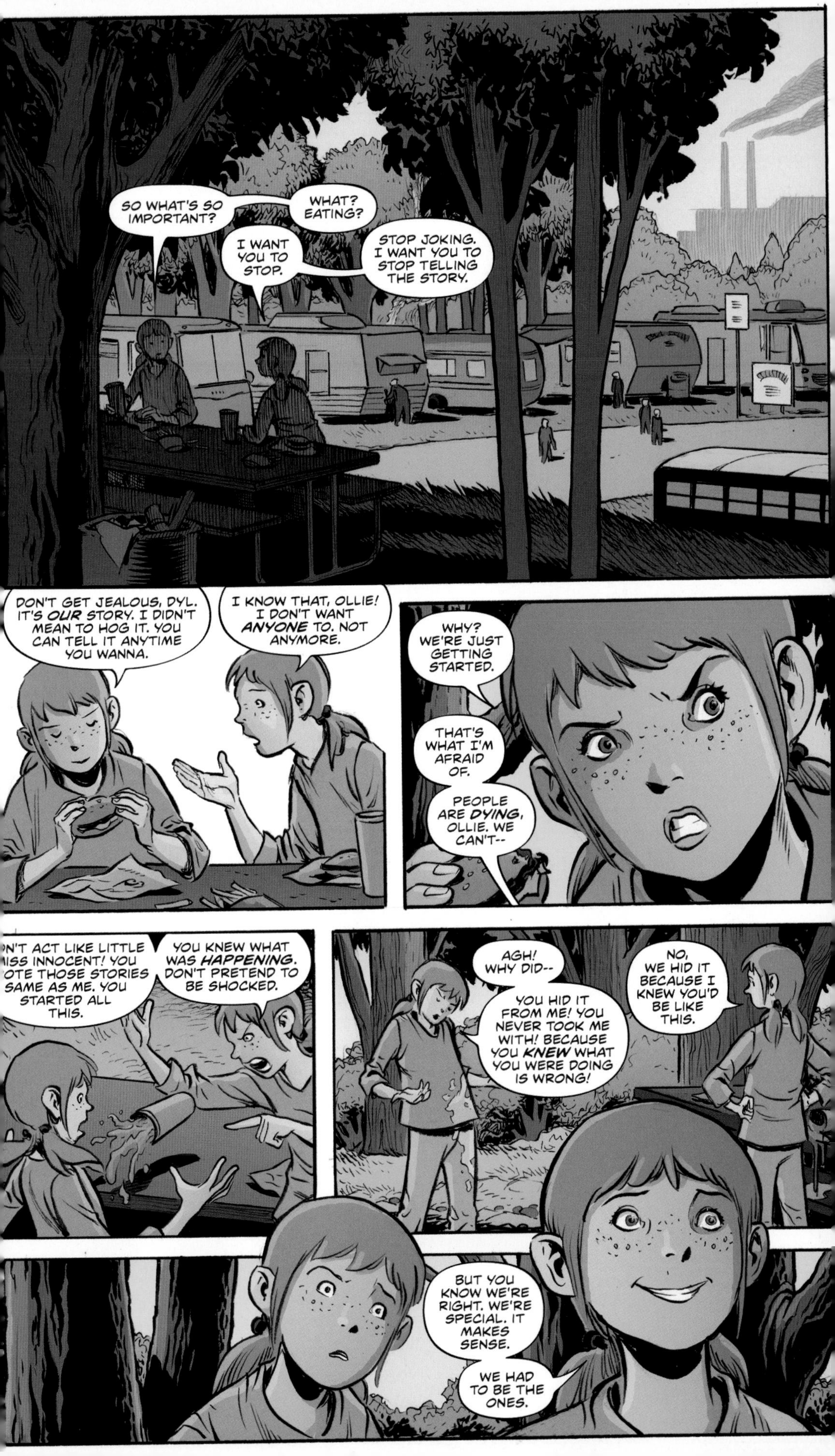
SO WHAT'S SO IMPORTANT?
WHAT? EATING?
I WANT YOU TO STOP.
STOP JOKING. I WANT YOU TO STOP TELLING THE STORY.
DON'T GET JEALOUS, DYL. IT'S OUR STORY. I DIDN'T MEAN TO HOG IT. YOU CAN TELL IT ANYTIME YOU WANNA.
I KNOW THAT, OLLIE! I DON'T WANT ANYONE TO. NOT ANYMORE.
WHY? WE'RE JUST GETTING STARTED.
THAT'S WHAT I'M AFRAID OF.
PEOPLE ARE DYING, OLLIE. WE CAN'T--
N'T ACT LIKE LITTLE ISS INNOCENT! YOU OTE THOSE STORIES SAME AS ME. YOU STARTED ALL THIS.
YOU KNEW WHAT WAS HAPPENING. DON'T PRETEND TO BE SHOCKED.
AGH! WHY DID--
YOU HID IT FROM ME! YOU NEVER TOOK ME WITH! BECAUSE YOU KNEW WHAT YOU WERE DOING IS WRONG!
NO, WE HID IT BECAUSE I KNEW YOU'D BE LIKE THIS.
BUT YOU KNOW WE'RE RIGHT. WE'RE SPECIAL. IT MAKES SENSE.
WE HAD TO BE THE ONES.

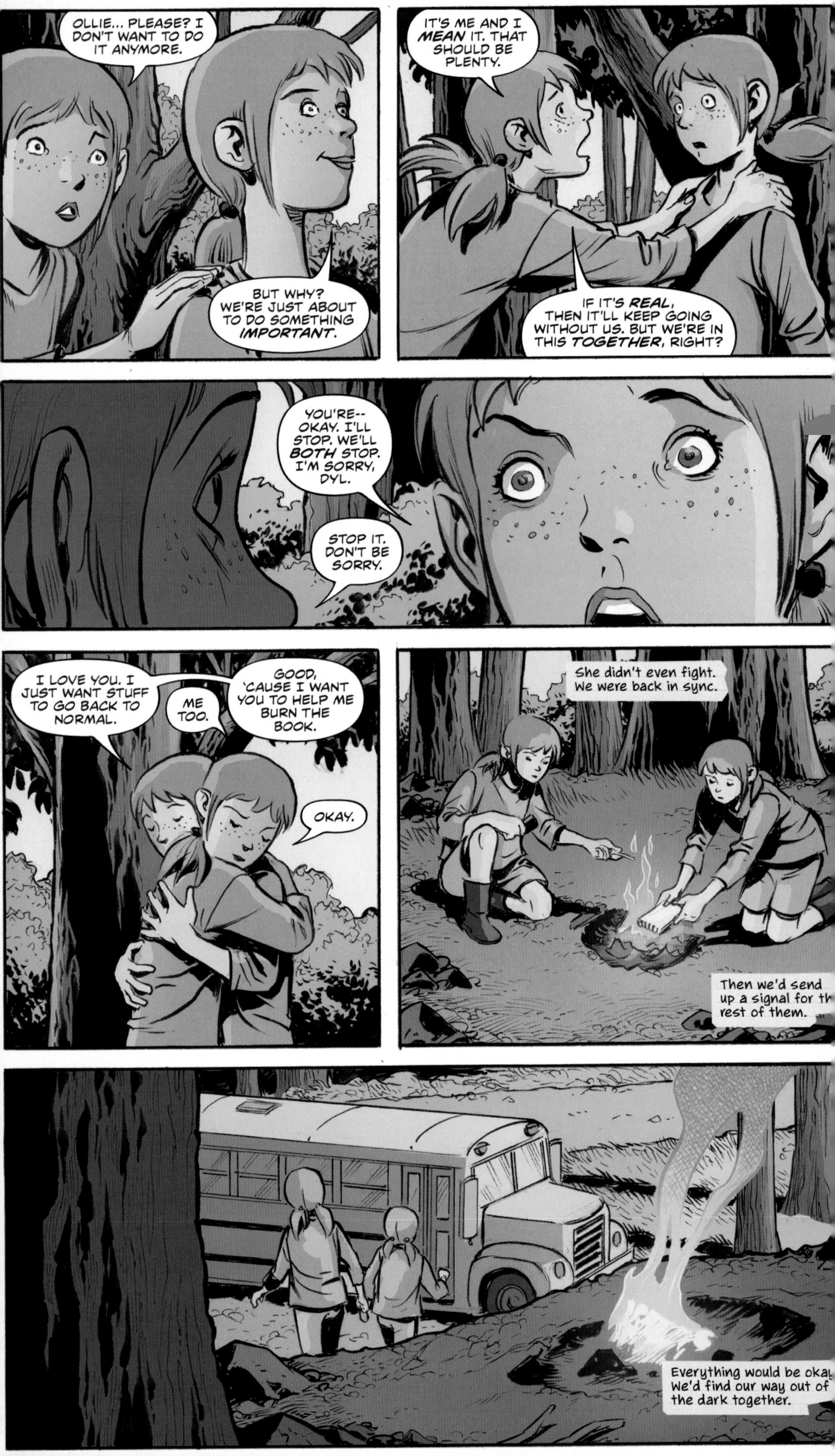
OLLIE... PLEASE? I DON'T WANT TO DO IT ANYMORE.
BUT WHY? WE'RE JUST ABOUT TO DO SOMETHING IMPORTANT.
IT'S ME AND I MEAN IT. THAT SHOULD BE PLENTY.
IF IT'S REAL, THEN IT'LL KEEP GOING WITHOUT US. BUT WE'RE IN THIS TOGETHER, RIGHT?
YOU'RE-- OKAY. I'LL STOP. WE'LL BOTH STOP. I'M SORRY, DYL.
STOP IT. DON'T BE SORRY.
I LOVE YOU. I JUST WANT STUFF TO GO BACK TO NORMAL.
ME TOO.
GOOD, 'CAUSE I WANT YOU TO HELP ME BURN THE BOOK.
OKAY.
She didn't even fight. We were back in sync.
Then we'd send up a signal for th rest of them.
Everything would be oka We'd find our way out of the dark together.

Everyone slept in the next morning. No one was in a rush to get anywhere. We had cereal and watched cartoons.

Dad didn't talk about machines. Mom didn't mention rearrangers. They stayed in bed.

I went for walk, found a store. Things felt calm again.

Like my fever had gotten all of us sick and when it broke, it carried us all to safety.

I could breathe again. My thoughts felt like my own.

Even though I could fall right back in if I wanted to.

It felt like a darkness behind me, the way my family always was. I wanted to fall back into them, but that meant losing myself to it.

But I wouldn't have to decide.

Things were gonna be better.

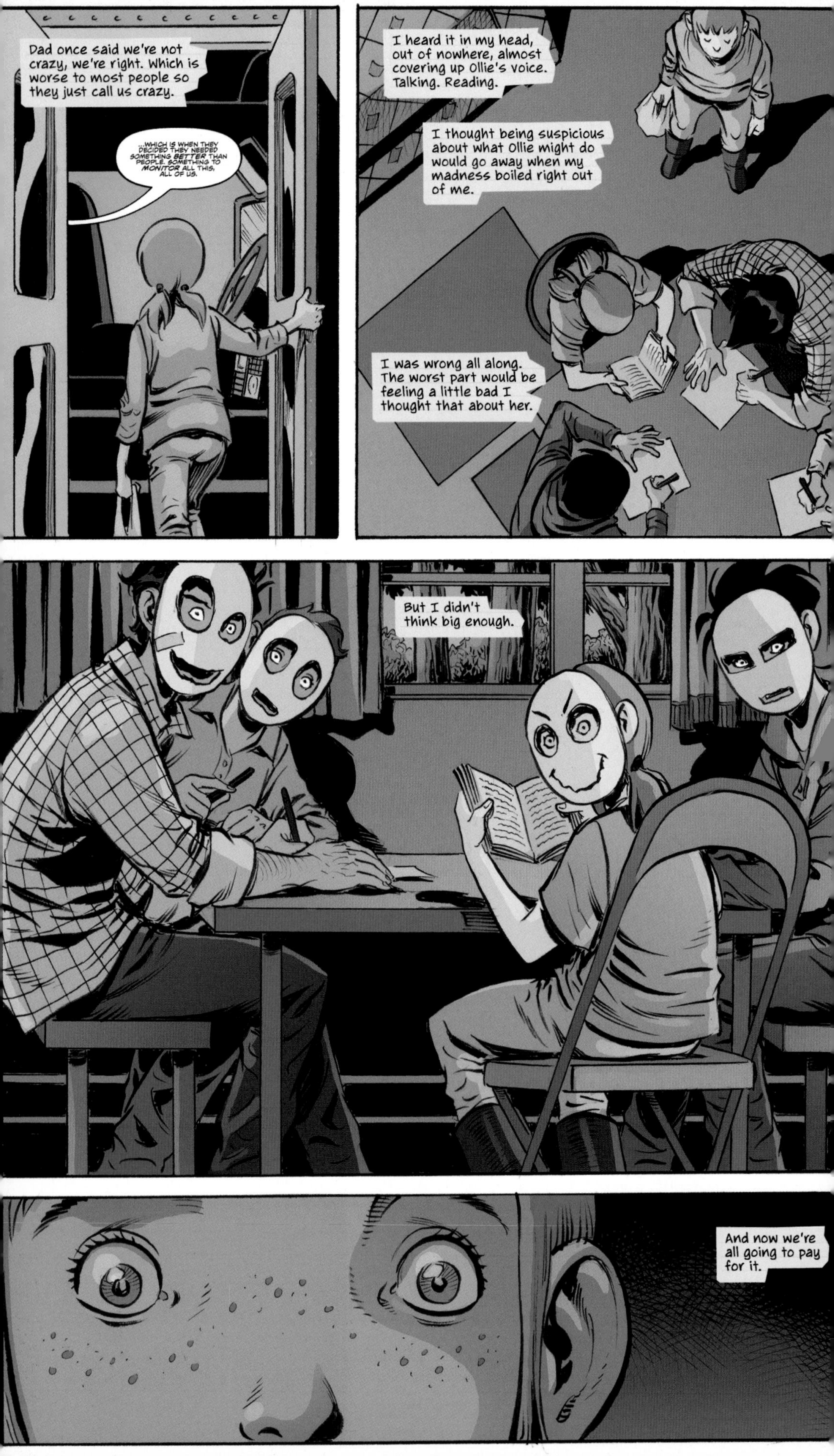

Dad once said we're not crazy, we're right. Which is worse to most people so they just call us crazy.
...WHICH IS WHEN THEY DECIDED THEY NEEDED SOMETHING *BETTER* THAN PEOPLE. SOMETHING TO *MONITOR* ALL THIS, ALL OF US.
I heard it in my head, out of nowhere, almost covering up Ollie's voice. Talking. Reading.
I thought being suspicious about what Ollie might do would go away when my madness boiled right out of me.
I was wrong all along. The worst part would be feeling a little bad I thought that about her.
But I didn't think big enough.
And now we're all going to pay for it.

“Maybe deep down I wanted this to happen.”

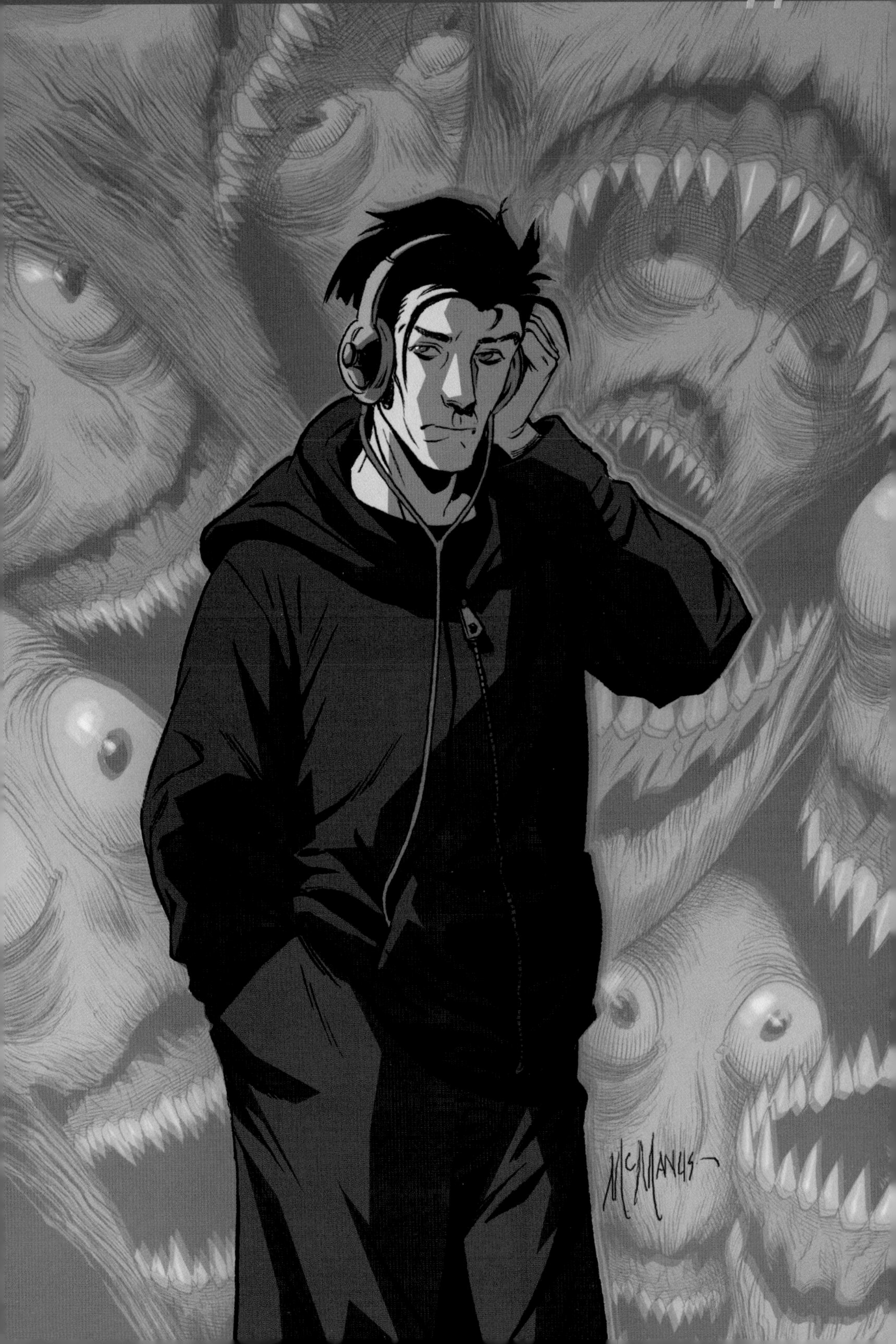
McMANUS

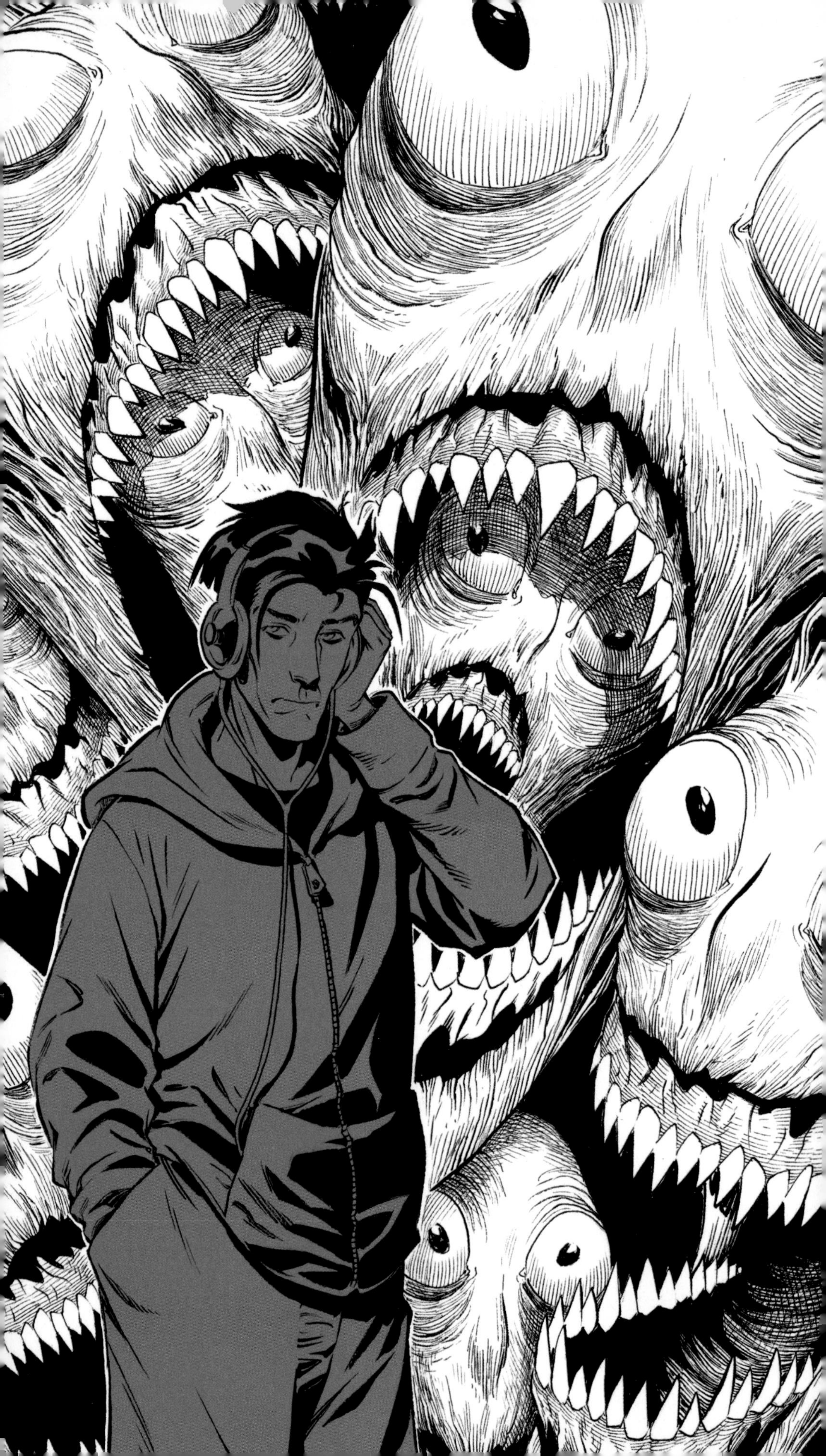

used to love
ts and crafts.

Everything about school, the real world, it all came to a stop and went away for this.

A jumble of things all around you and you could put them together to make anything.

r was as close to ood witch magic s I ever got.

Even if I was never good at it.

hands were ways too clumsy make the stuff my head real.

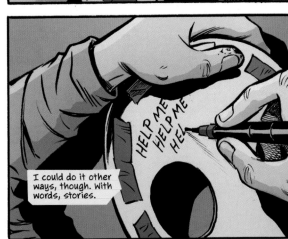

I could do it other ways, though. With words, stories.

HELP ME HELP ME HE!

crets. Even cret from Ollie.

HELP ME HELP ME HEL

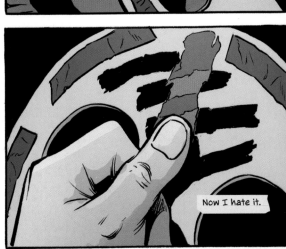

Now I hate it.

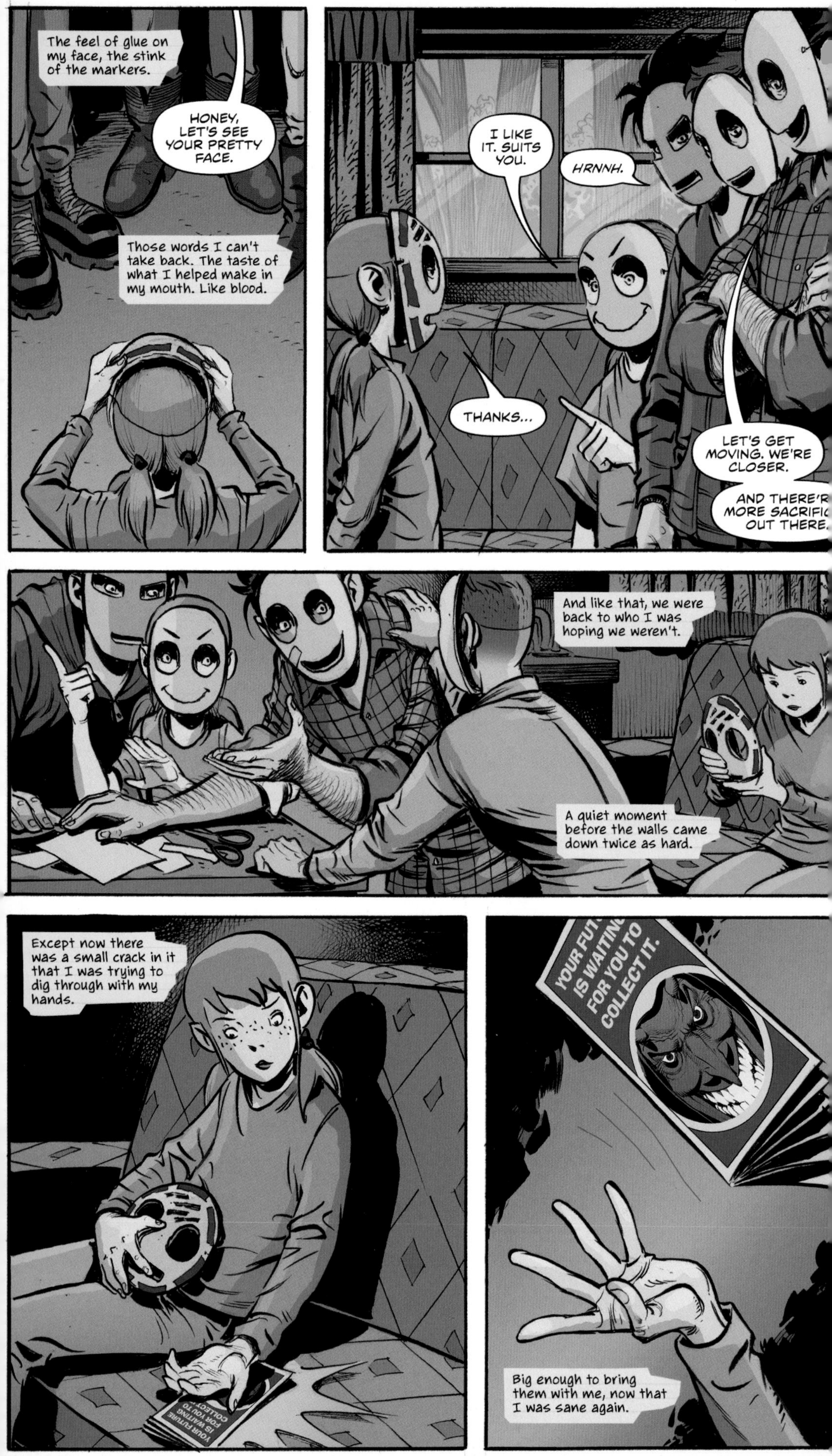
The feel of glue on my face, the stink of the markers.
HONEY, LET'S SEE YOUR PRETTY FACE.
Those words I can't take back. The taste of what I helped make in my mouth. Like blood.
I LIKE IT. SUITS YOU.
HRNNH.
THANKS...
LET'S GET MOVING. WE'RE CLOSER.
AND THERE'R MORE SACRIFIC OUT THERE.
And like that, we were back to who I was hoping we weren't.
A quiet moment before the walls came down twice as hard.
Except now there was a small crack in it that I was trying to dig through with my hands.
YOUR FUTU IS WAITIN FOR YOU TO COLLECT IT.
Big enough to bring them with me, now that I was sane again.

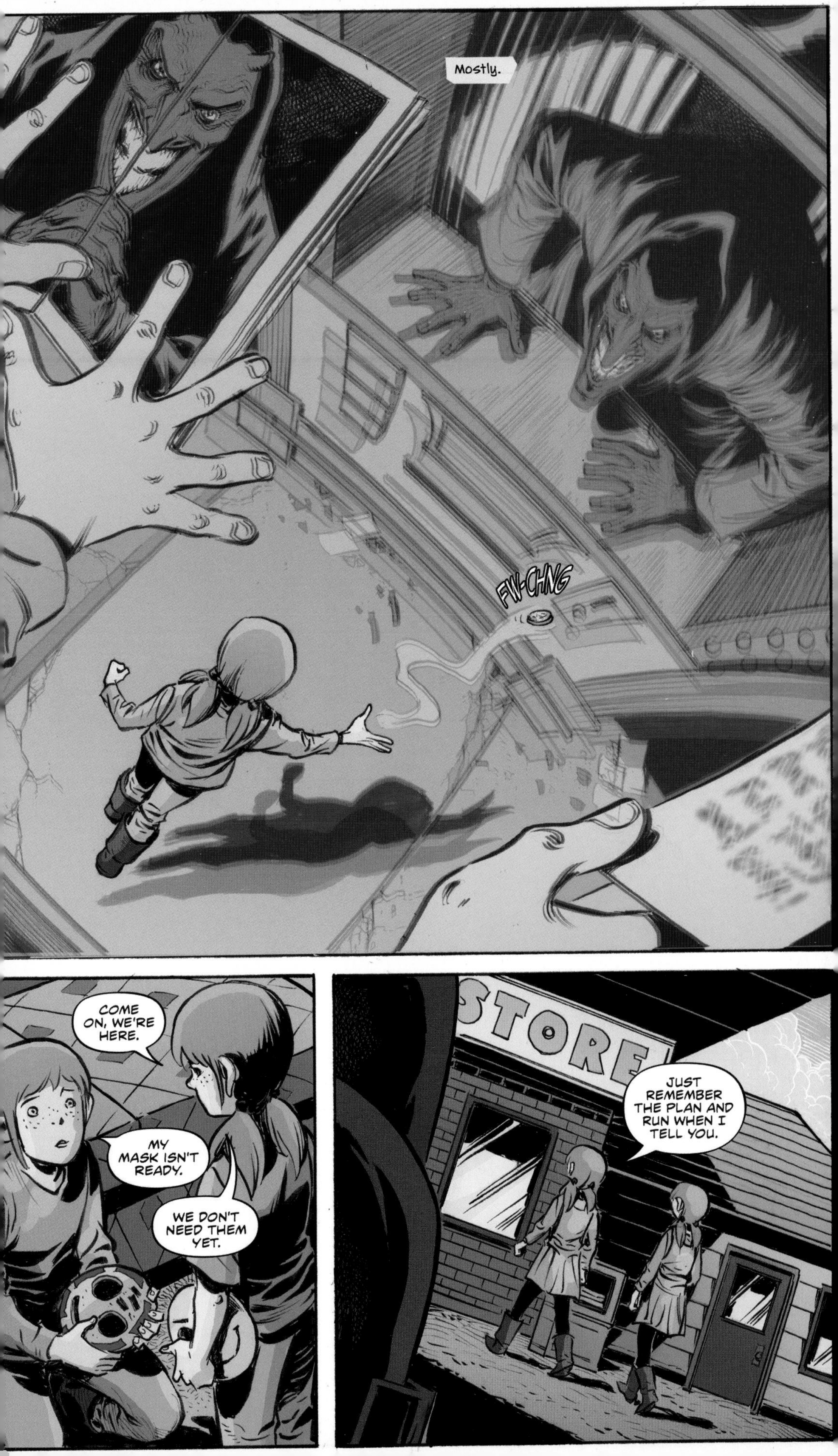
Mostly.
FW-CHNG
COME ON, WE'RE HERE.
MY MASK ISN'T READY.
WE DON'T NEED THEM YET.
STORE
JUST REMEMBER THE PLAN AND RUN WHEN I TELL YOU.

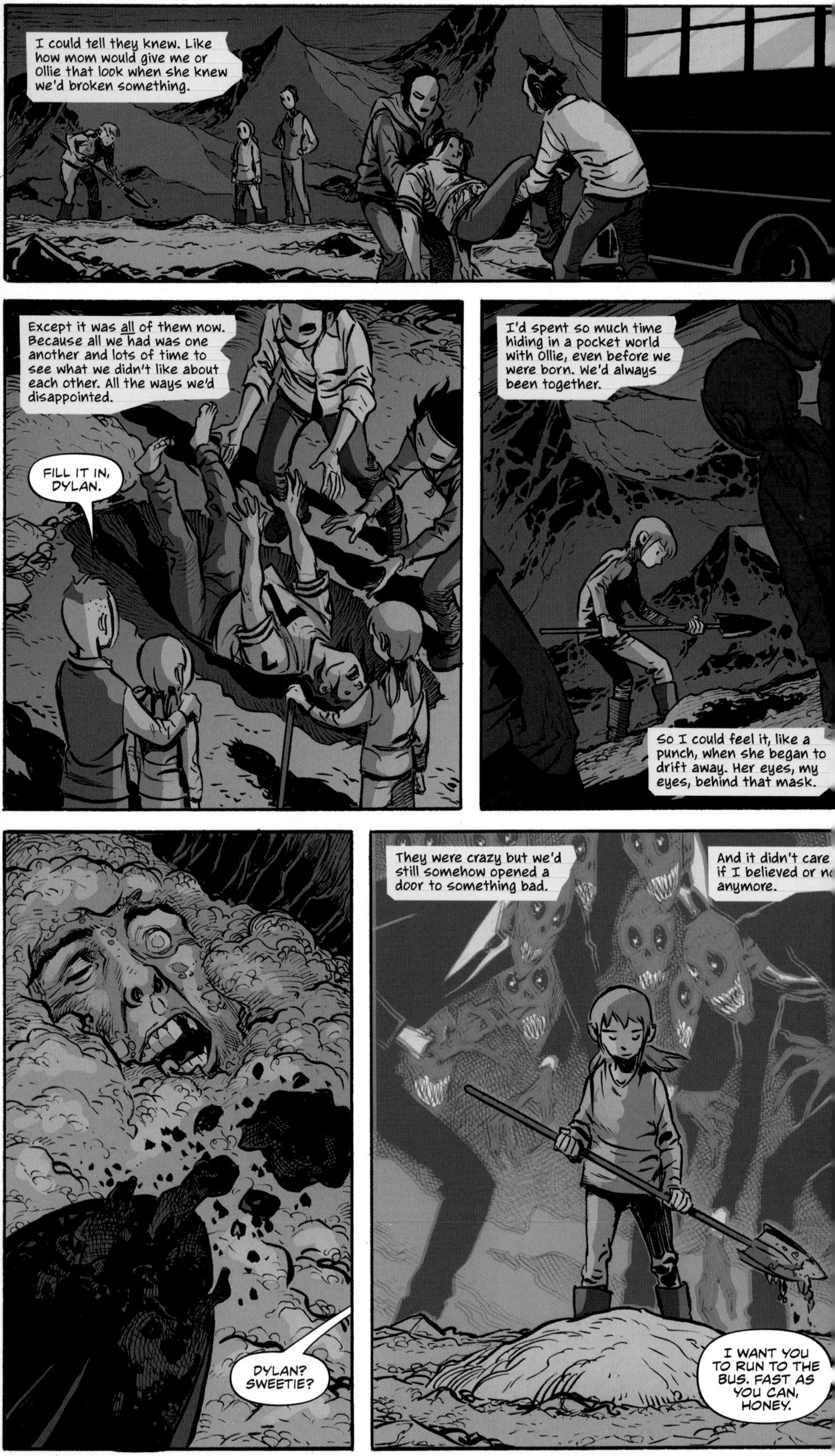
I could tell they knew. Like how mom would give me or Ollie that look when she knew we'd broken something.
Except it was all of them now. Because all we had was one another and lots of time to see what we didn't like about each other. All the ways we'd disappointed.
FILL IT IN, DYLAN.
I'd spent so much time hiding in a pocket world with Ollie, even before we were born. We'd always been together.
So I could feel it, like a punch, when she began to drift away. Her eyes, my eyes, behind that mask.
DYLAN? SWEETIE?
They were crazy but we'd still somehow opened a door to something bad.
And it didn't care if I believed or no anymore.
I WANT YOU TO RUN TO THE BUS. FAST AS YOU CAN, HONEY.

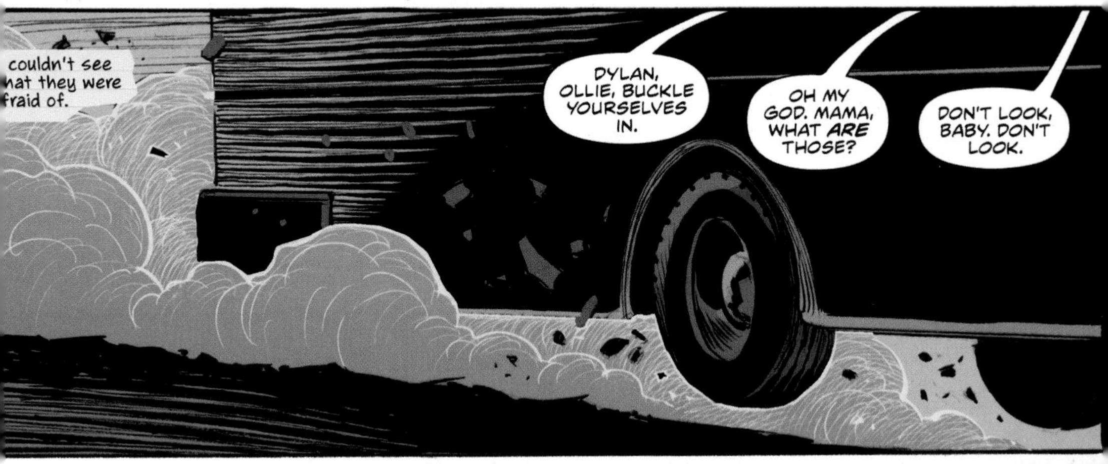
couldn't see
hat they were
fraid of.
DYLAN, OLLIE, BUCKLE YOURSELVES IN.
OH MY GOD. MAMA, WHAT ARE THOSE?
DON'T LOOK, BABY. DON'T LOOK.

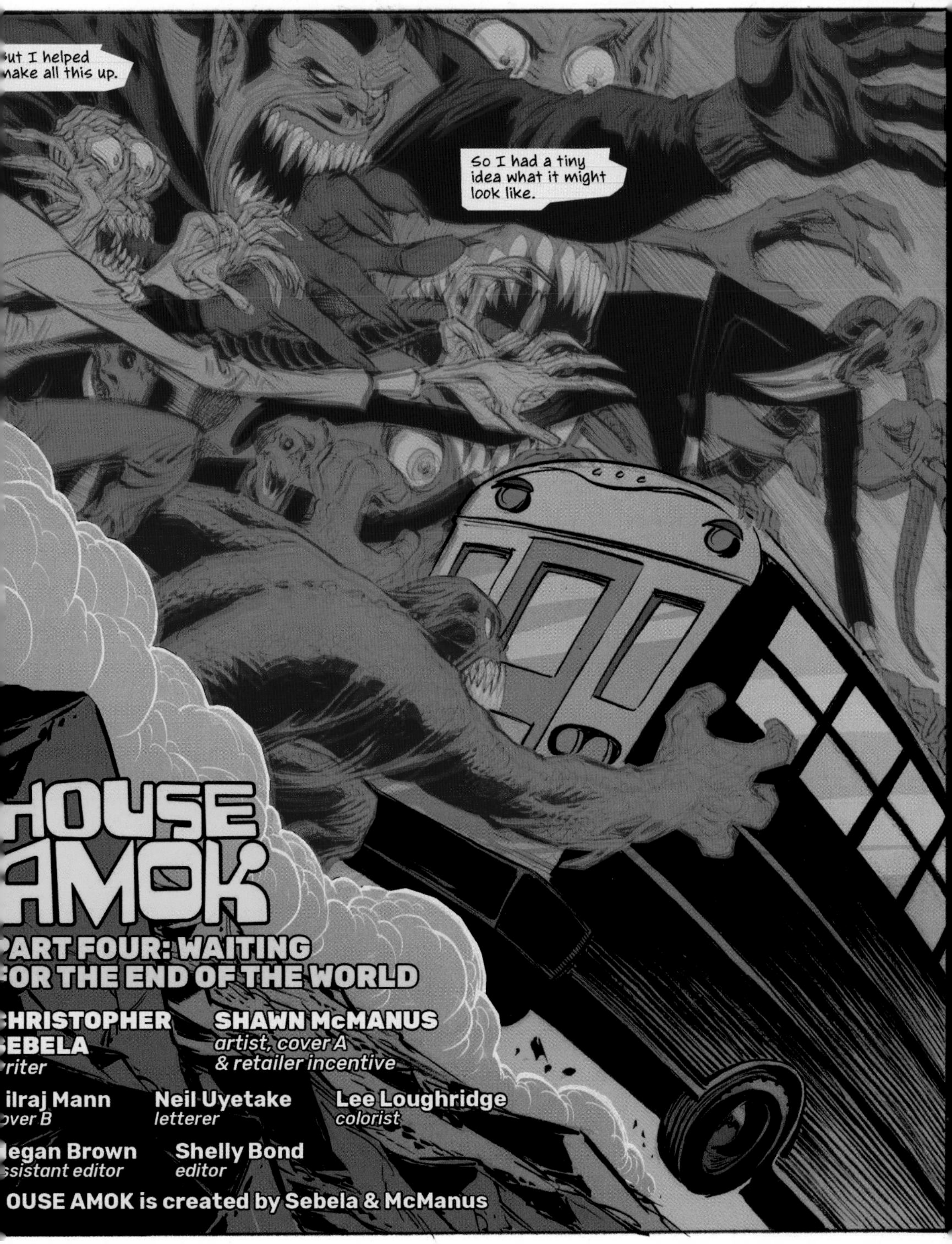
ut I helped
nake all this up.
So I had a tiny idea what it might look like.
HOUSE AMOK
ART FOUR: WAITING FOR THE END OF THE WORLD
HRISTOPHER EBELA
riter
SHAWN McMANUS
artist, cover A & retailer incentive
ilraj Mann
over B
Neil Uyetake
letterer
Lee Loughridge
colorist
legan Brown
ssistant editor
Shelly Bond
editor
OUSE AMOK is created by Sebela & McManus

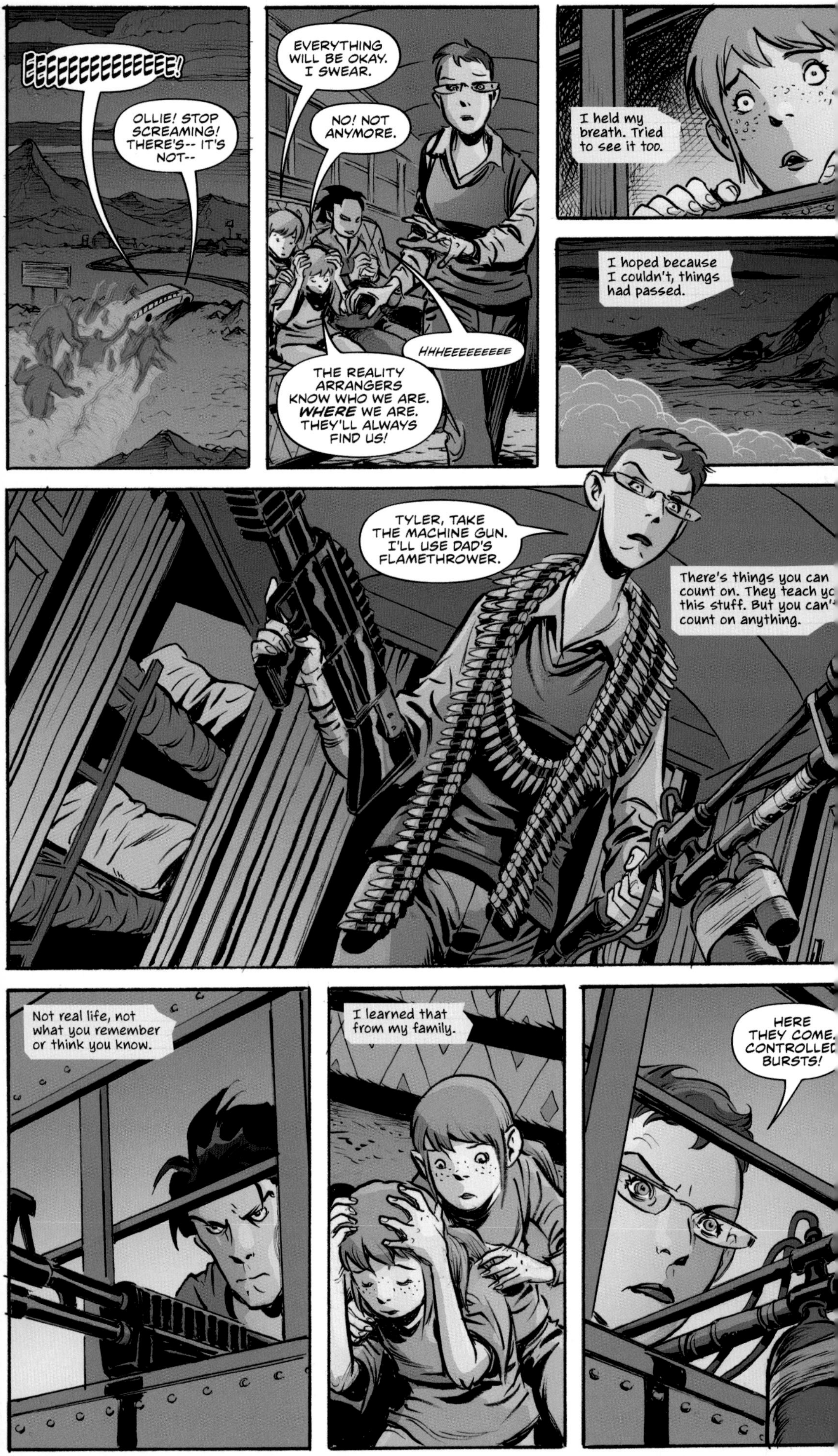
EEEEEEEEEEEEEE!
OLLIE! STOP SCREAMING! THERE'S-- IT'S NOT--
EVERYTHING WILL BE OKAY. I SWEAR.
NO! NOT ANYMORE.
HHHEEEEEEEEE
THE REALITY ARRANGERS KNOW WHO WE ARE. *WHERE* WE ARE. THEY'LL ALWAYS FIND US!
I held my breath. Tried to see it too.
I hoped because I couldn't, things had passed.
TYLER, TAKE THE MACHINE GUN. I'LL USE DAD'S FLAMETHROWER.
There's things you can count on. They teach yo this stuff. But you can' count on anything.
Not real life, not what you remember or think you know.
I learned that from my family.
HERE THEY COME. CONTROLLEI BURSTS!

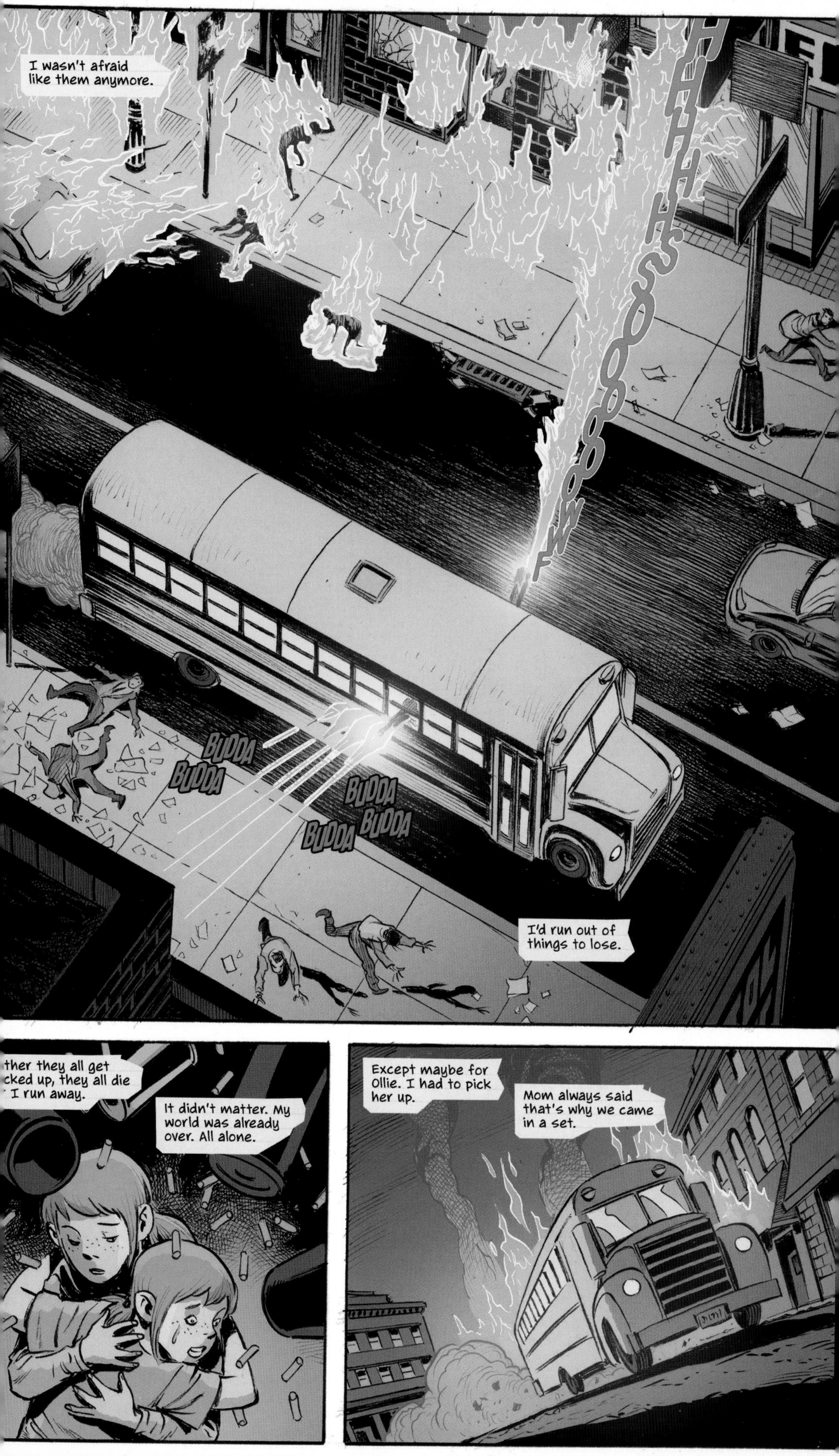
I wasn't afraid like them anymore.
FWOOOOOOSSHHHHHHH
BUDDA BUDDA
BUDDA BUDDA
BUDDA
I'd run out of things to lose.
ther they all get
cked up, they all die
I run away.
It didn't matter. My world was already over. All alone.
Except maybe for Ollie. I had to pick her up.
Mom always said that's why we came in a set.

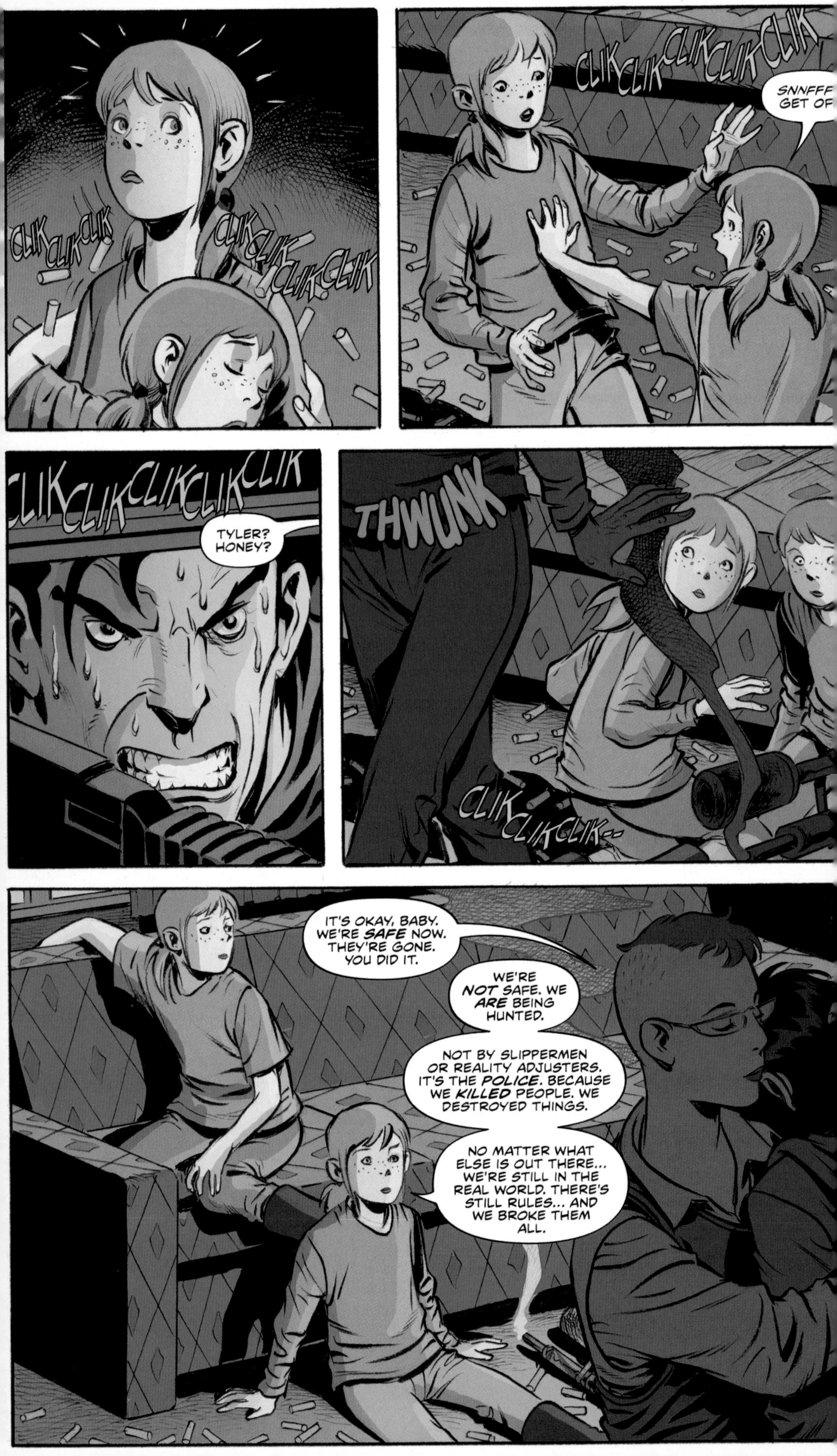
CLIK CLIK CLIK
CLIK CLIK CLIK CLIK
CLIK CLIK CLIK CLIK CLIK
SNNFFF GET OF
CLIK CLIK CLIK CLIK CLIK
TYLER? HONEY?
THWUNK
CLIK CLIK CLIK--
IT'S OKAY, BABY. WE'RE *SAFE* NOW. THEY'RE GONE. YOU DID IT.
WE'RE *NOT* SAFE. WE *ARE* BEING HUNTED.
NOT BY SLIPPERMEN OR REALITY ADJUSTERS. IT'S THE *POLICE*. BECAUSE WE *KILLED* PEOPLE. WE DESTROYED THINGS.
NO MATTER WHAT ELSE IS OUT THERE... WE'RE STILL IN THE REAL WORLD. THERE'S STILL RULES... AND WE BROKE THEM ALL.

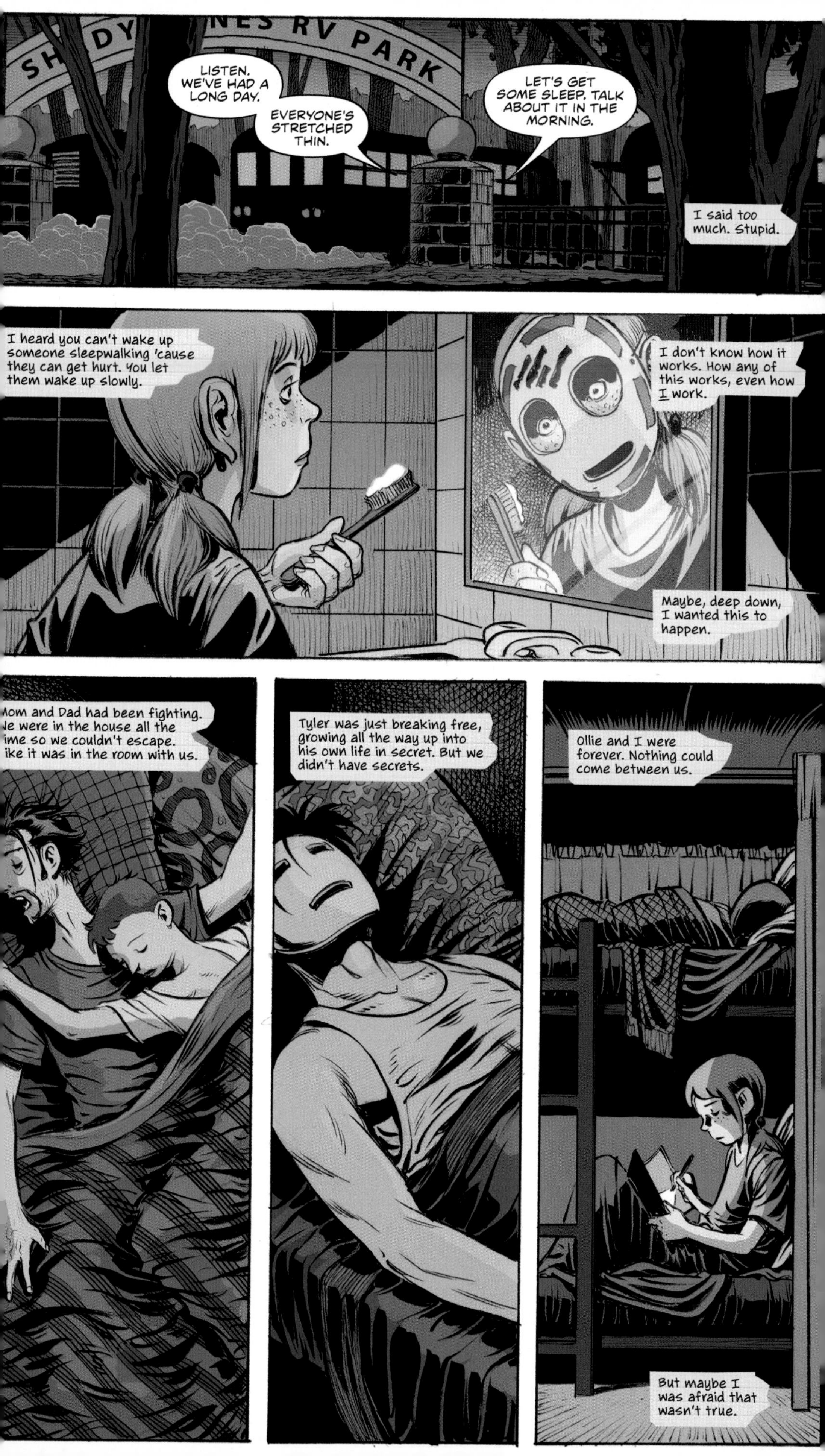
RV PARK
LISTEN. WE'VE HAD A LONG DAY.
EVERYONE'S STRETCHED THIN.
LET'S GET SOME SLEEP. TALK ABOUT IT IN THE MORNING.
I said too much. Stupid.
I heard you can't wake up someone sleepwalking 'cause they can get hurt. You let them wake up slowly.
I don't know how it works. How any of this works, even how I work.
Maybe, deep down, I wanted this to happen.
om and Dad had been fighting. e were in the house all the ime so we couldn't escape. ike it was in the room with us.
Tyler was just breaking free, growing all the way up into his own life in secret. But we didn't have secrets.
Ollie and I were forever. Nothing could come between us.
But maybe I was afraid that wasn't true.

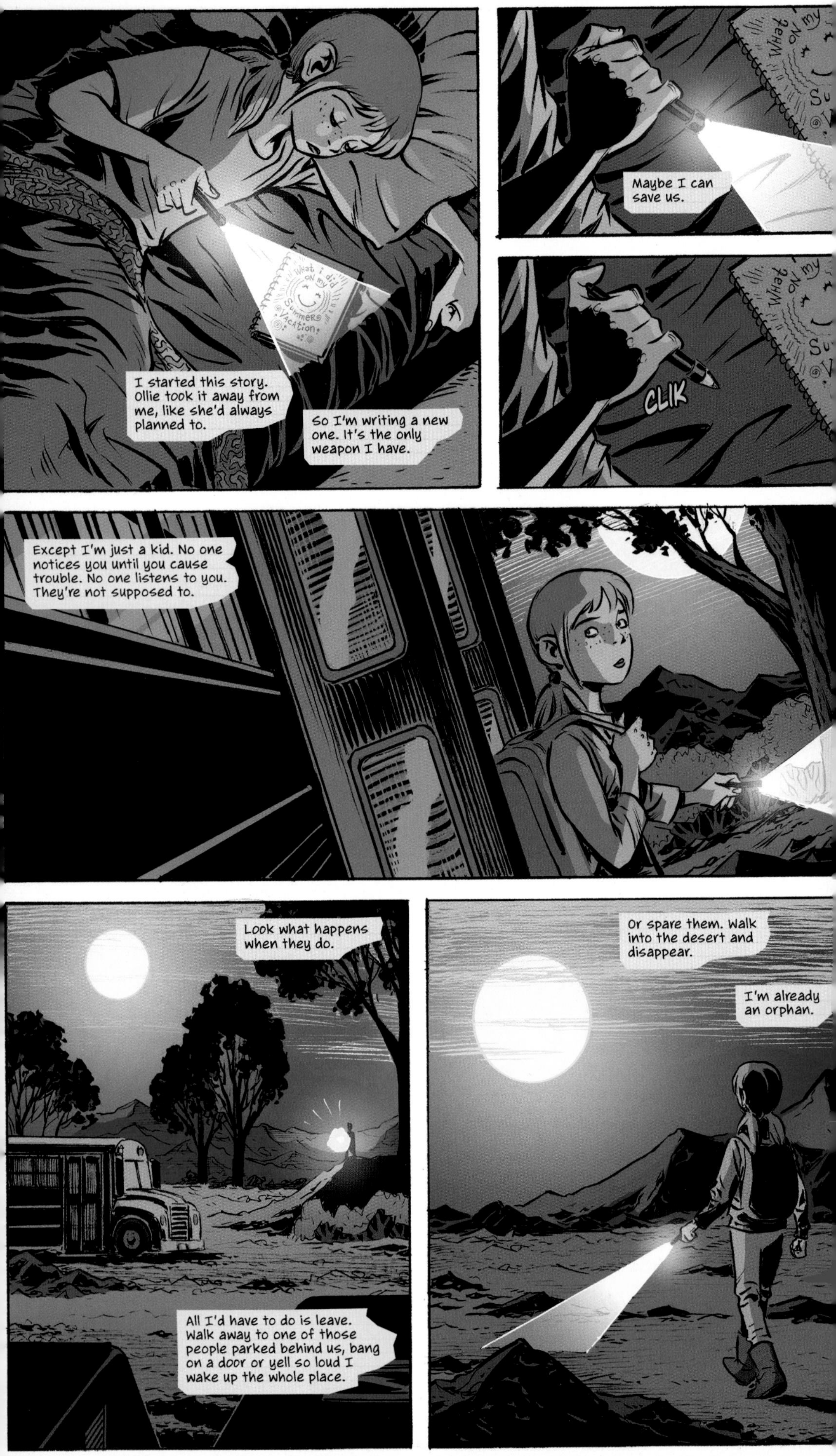

What I did on my Summer Vacation!
I started this story. Ollie took it away from me, like she'd always planned to.
So I'm writing a new one. It's the only weapon I have.
Maybe I can save us.
CLIK
Except I'm just a kid. No one notices you until you cause trouble. No one listens to you. They're not supposed to.
Look what happens when they do.
All I'd have to do is leave. Walk away to one of those people parked behind us, bang on a door or yell so loud I wake up the whole place.
Or spare them. Walk into the desert and disappear.
I'm already an orphan.

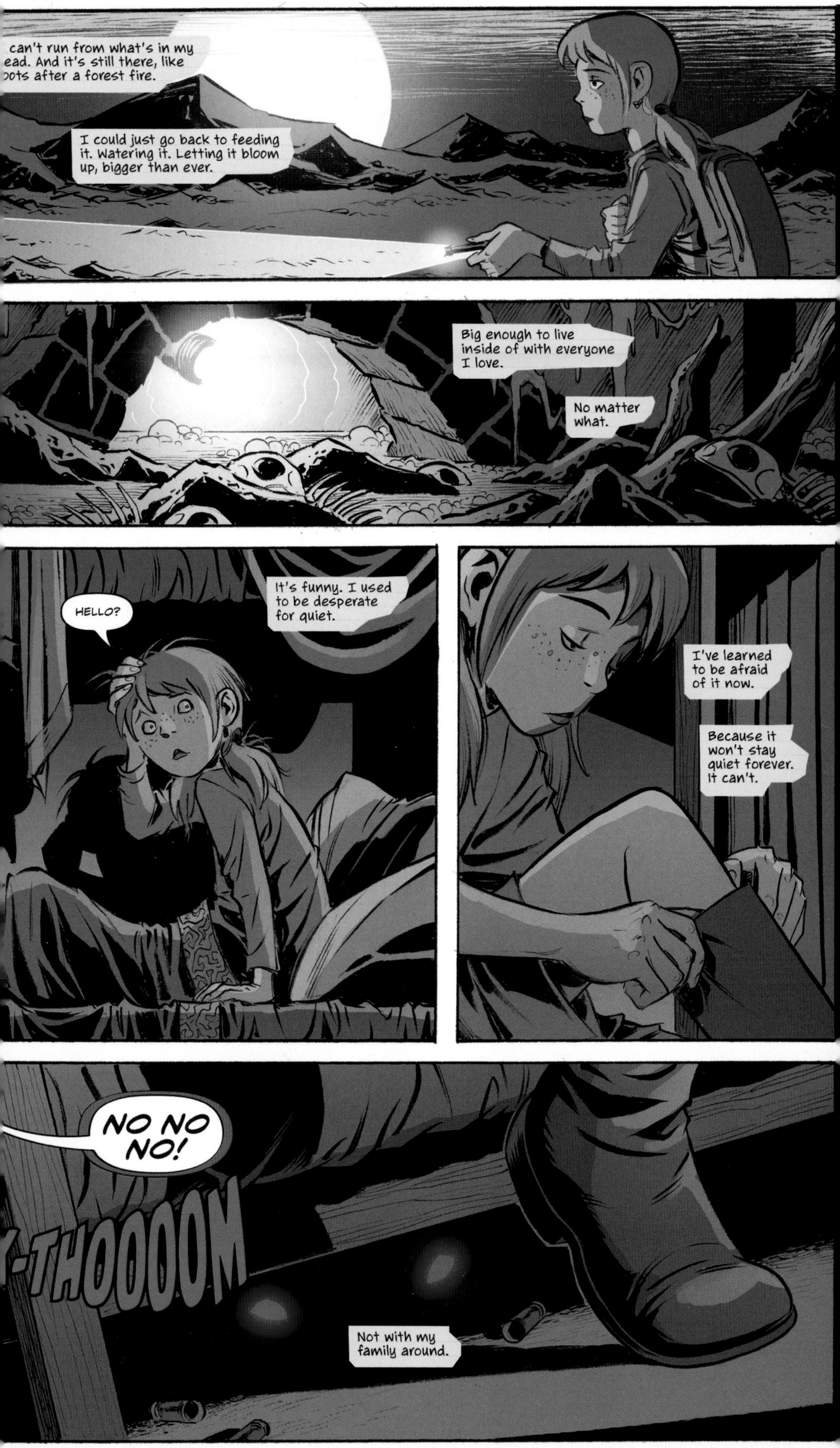

can't run from what's in my ead. And it's still there, like oots after a forest fire.
I could just go back to feeding it. Watering it. Letting it bloom up, bigger than ever.
Big enough to live inside of with everyone I love.
No matter what.
HELLO?
It's funny. I used to be desperate for quiet.
I've learned to be afraid of it now.
Because it won't stay quiet forever. It can't.
NO NO NO!
-THOOOOM
Not with my family around.

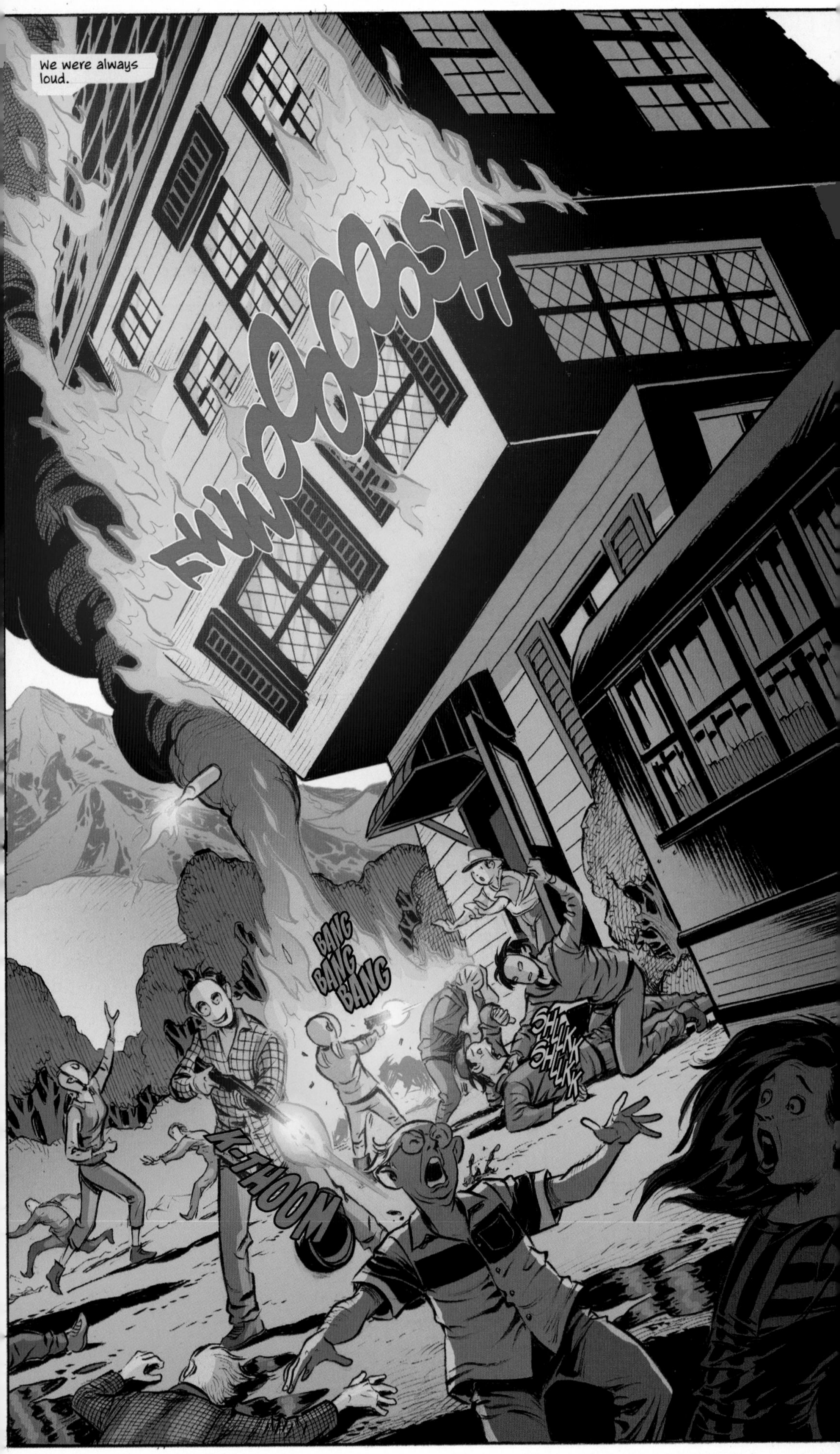
We were always loud.
FWOOOOOOSH
BANG
BANG
BANG
SHLUNK
SHLUNK
K-THOOOM

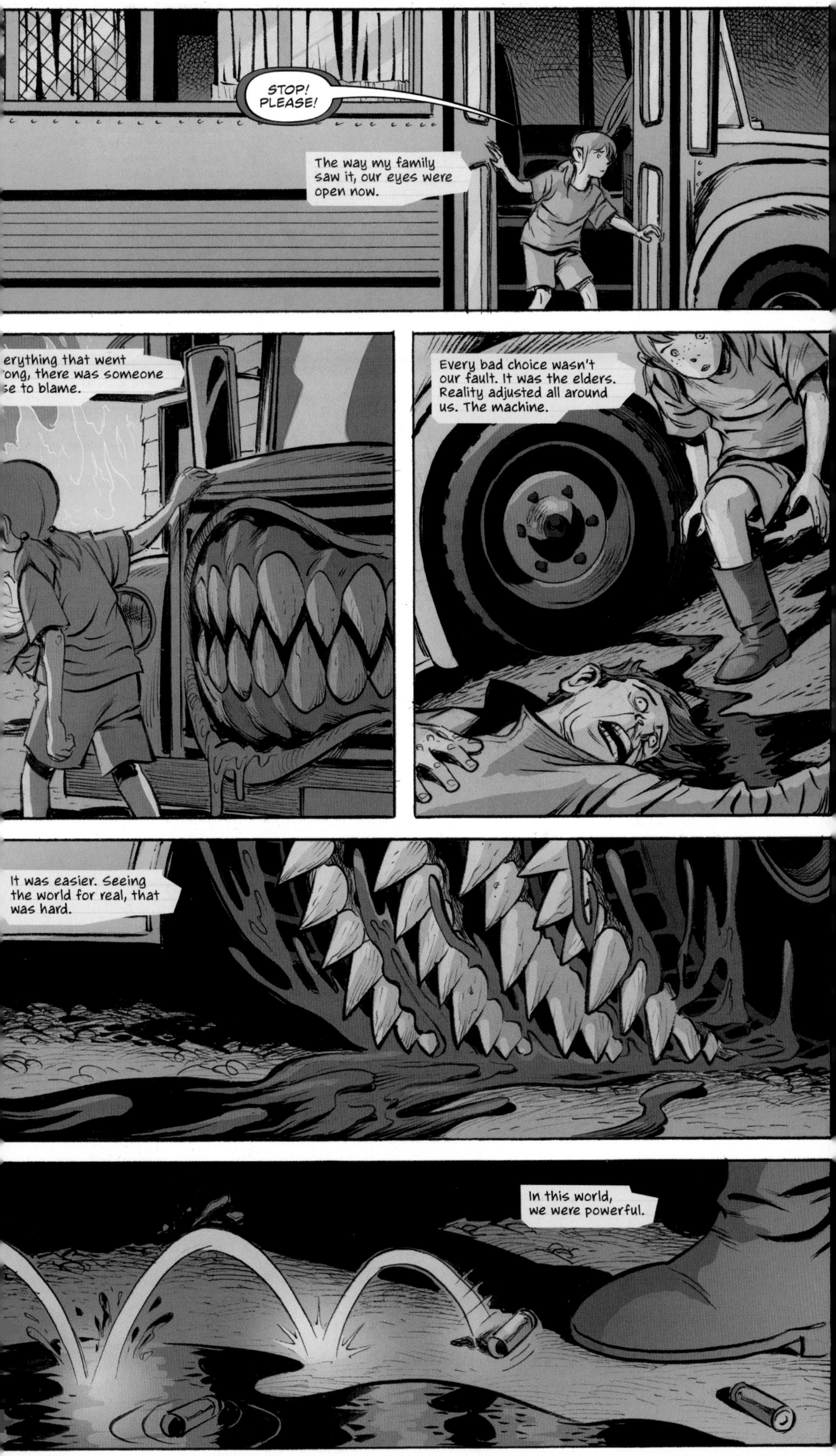
STOP! PLEASE!
The way my family saw it, our eyes were open now.
erything that went
ong, there was someone
se to blame.
Every bad choice wasn't our fault. It was the elders. Reality adjusted all around us. The machine.
It was easier. Seeing the world for real, that was hard.
In this world, we were powerful.

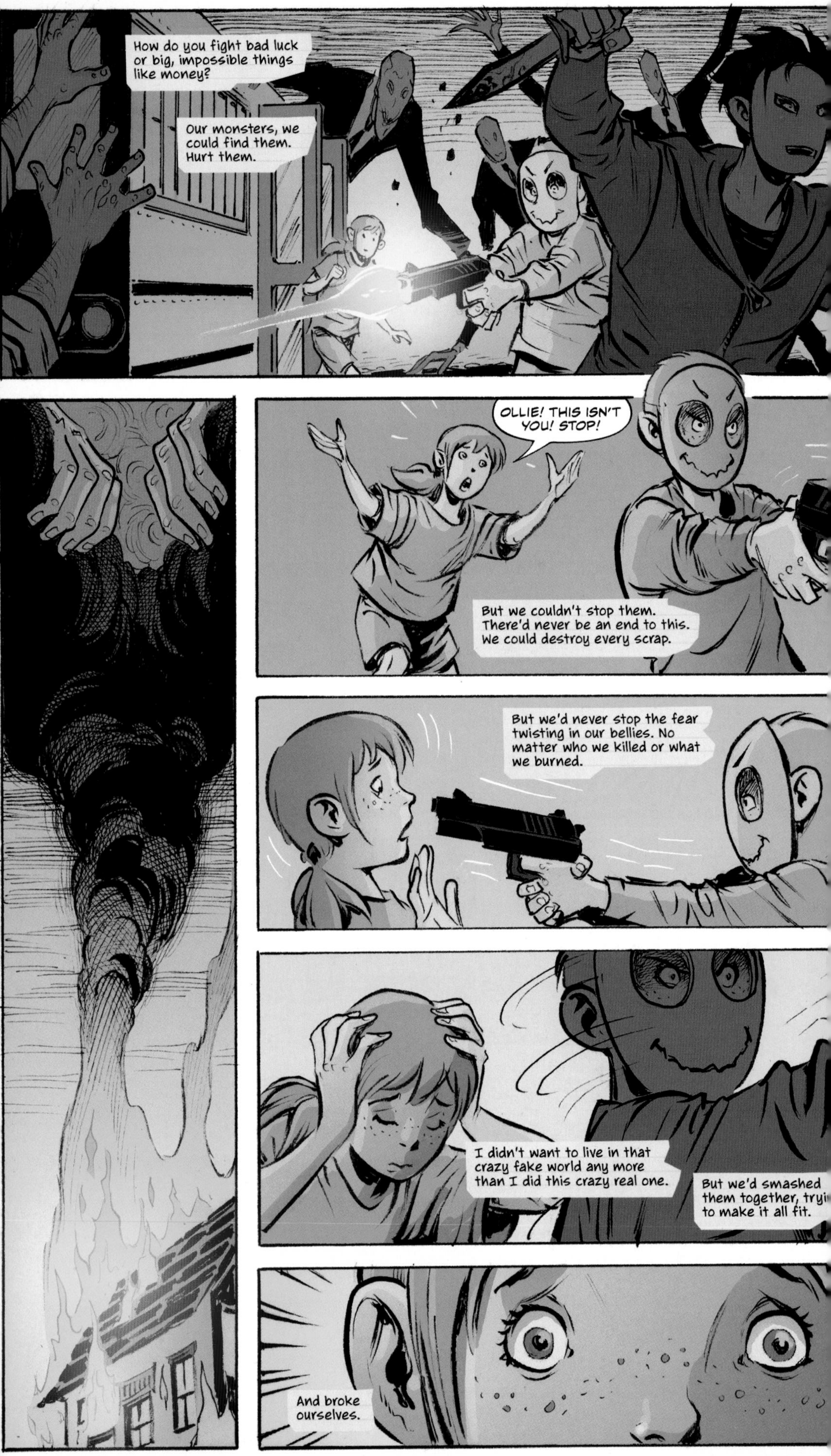
How do you fight bad luck or big, impossible things like money?
Our monsters, we could find them. Hurt them.
OLLIE! THIS ISN'T YOU! STOP!
But we couldn't stop them. There'd never be an end to this. We could destroy every scrap.
But we'd never stop the fear twisting in our bellies. No matter who we killed or what we burned.
I didn't want to live in that crazy fake world any more than I did this crazy real one.
And broke ourselves.

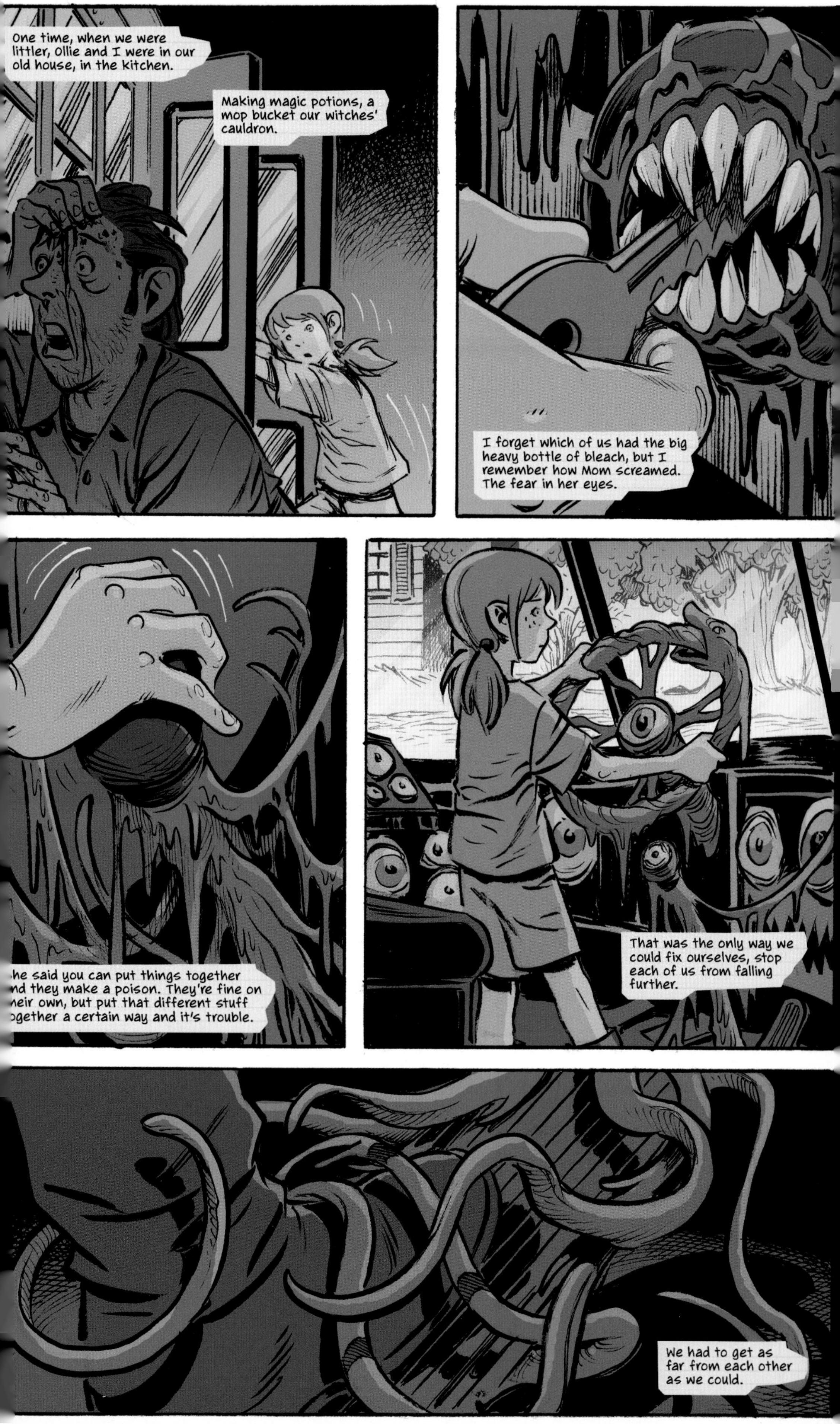
One time, when we were littler, Ollie and I were in our old house, in the kitchen.
Making magic potions, a mop bucket our witches' cauldron.
I forget which of us had the big heavy bottle of bleach, but I remember how Mom screamed. The fear in her eyes.
he said you can put things together nd they make a poison. They're fine on neir own, but put that different stuff ogether a certain way and it's trouble.
That was the only way we could fix ourselves, stop each of us from falling further.
We had to get as far from each other as we could.

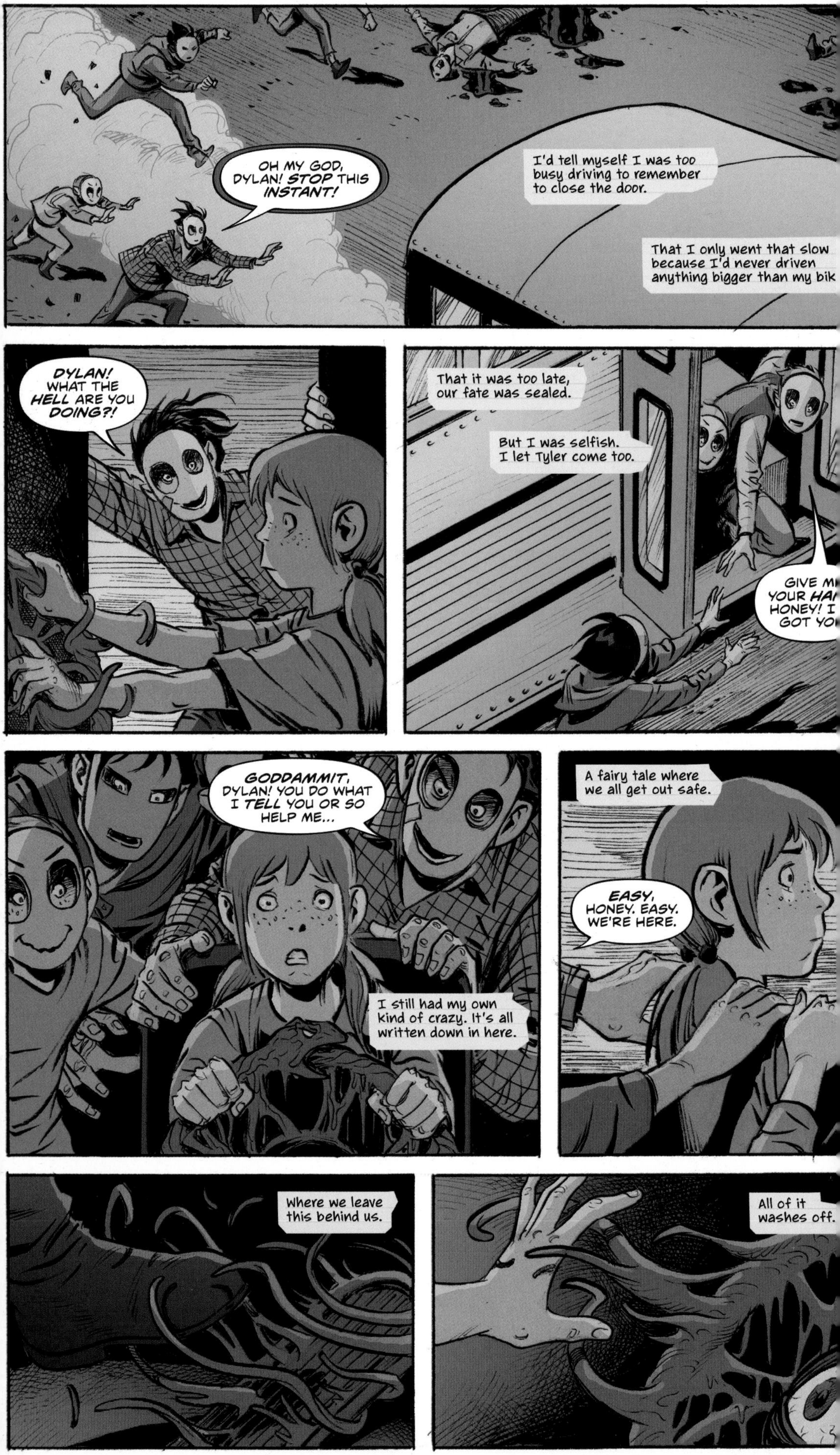
OH MY GOD, DYLAN! STOP THIS INSTANT!
I'd tell myself I was too busy driving to remember to close the door.
That I only went that slow because I'd never driven anything bigger than my bik
DYLAN! WHAT THE HELL ARE YOU DOING?!
That it was too late, our fate was sealed.
But I was selfish. I let Tyler come too.
GIVE M YOUR HA HONEY! I GOT YO
GODDAMMIT, DYLAN! YOU DO WHAT I TELL YOU OR SO HELP ME...
I still had my own kind of crazy. It's all written down in here.
A fairy tale where we all get out safe.
EASY, HONEY. EASY. WE'RE HERE.
Where we leave this behind us.
All of it washes off.

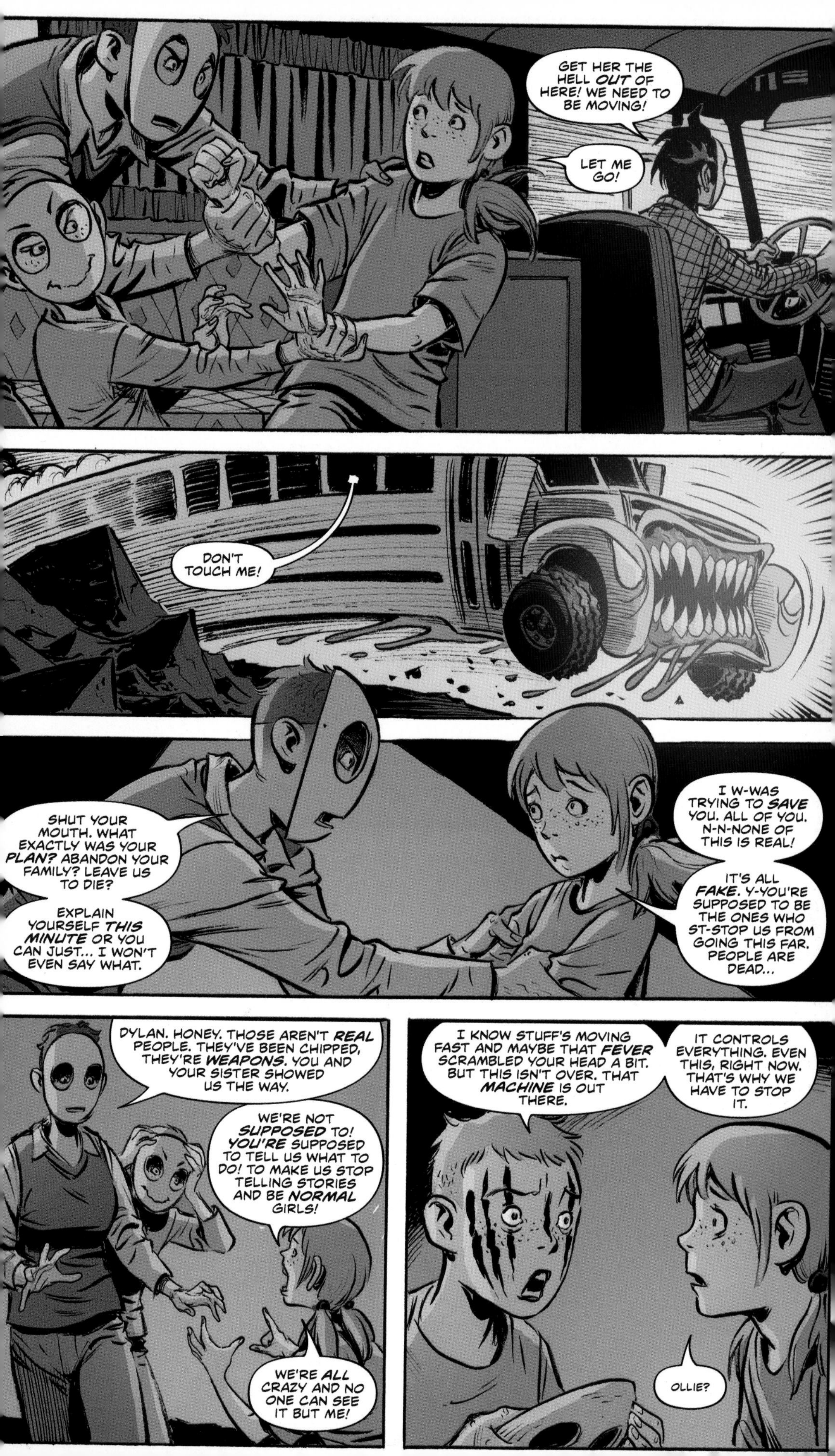

GET HER THE HELL OUT OF HERE! WE NEED TO BE MOVING!
LET ME GO!
DON'T TOUCH ME!
SHUT YOUR MOUTH. WHAT EXACTLY WAS YOUR PLAN? ABANDON YOUR FAMILY? LEAVE US TO DIE?
EXPLAIN YOURSELF THIS MINUTE OR YOU CAN JUST... I WON'T EVEN SAY WHAT.
I W-WAS TRYING TO SAVE YOU. ALL OF YOU. N-N-NONE OF THIS IS REAL!
IT'S ALL FAKE. Y-YOU'RE SUPPOSED TO BE THE ONES WHO ST-STOP US FROM GOING THIS FAR. PEOPLE ARE DEAD...
DYLAN. HONEY. THOSE AREN'T REAL PEOPLE. THEY'VE BEEN CHIPPED, THEY'RE WEAPONS. YOU AND YOUR SISTER SHOWED US THE WAY.
WE'RE NOT SUPPOSED TO! YOU'RE SUPPOSED TO TELL US WHAT TO DO! TO MAKE US STOP TELLING STORIES AND BE NORMAL GIRLS!
WE'RE ALL CRAZY AND NO ONE CAN SEE IT BUT ME!
I KNOW STUFF'S MOVING FAST AND MAYBE THAT FEVER SCRAMBLED YOUR HEAD A BIT. BUT THIS ISN'T OVER. THAT MACHINE IS OUT THERE.
IT CONTROLS EVERYTHING. EVEN THIS, RIGHT NOW. THAT'S WHY WE HAVE TO STOP IT.
OLLIE?

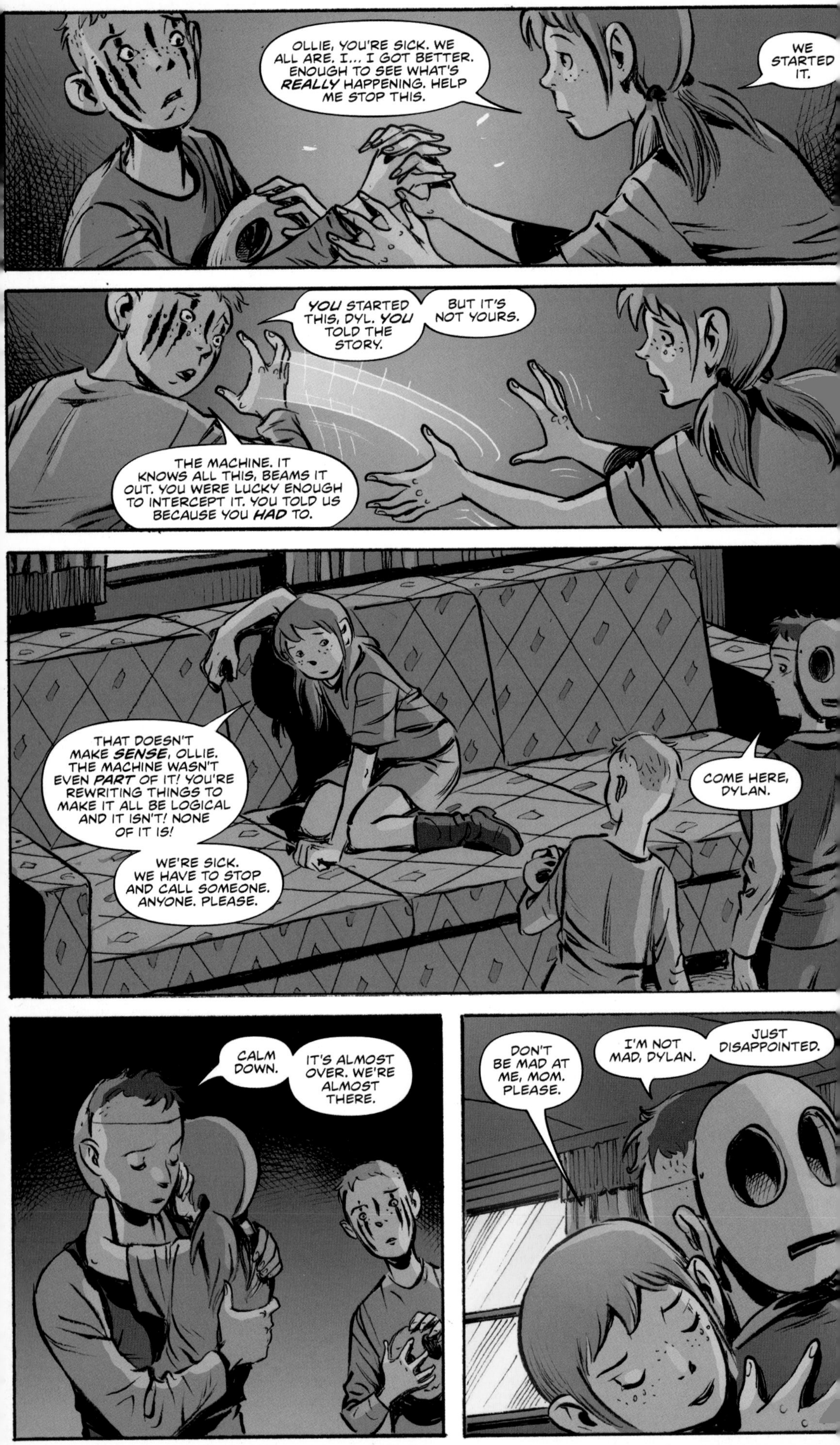
OLLIE, YOU'RE SICK. WE ALL ARE. I... I GOT BETTER. ENOUGH TO SEE WHAT'S REALLY HAPPENING. HELP ME STOP THIS.
WE STARTED IT.
YOU STARTED THIS, DYL. YOU TOLD THE STORY.
BUT IT'S NOT YOURS.
THE MACHINE. IT KNOWS ALL THIS, BEAMS IT OUT. YOU WERE LUCKY ENOUGH TO INTERCEPT IT. YOU TOLD US BECAUSE YOU HAD TO.
THAT DOESN'T MAKE SENSE, OLLIE. THE MACHINE WASN'T EVEN PART OF IT! YOU'RE REWRITING THINGS TO MAKE IT ALL BE LOGICAL AND IT ISN'T! NONE OF IT IS!
WE'RE SICK. WE HAVE TO STOP AND CALL SOMEONE. ANYONE. PLEASE.
COME HERE, DYLAN.
CALM DOWN.
IT'S ALMOST OVER. WE'RE ALMOST THERE.
DON'T BE MAD AT ME, MOM. PLEASE.
I'M NOT MAD, DYLAN.
JUST DISAPPOINTED.

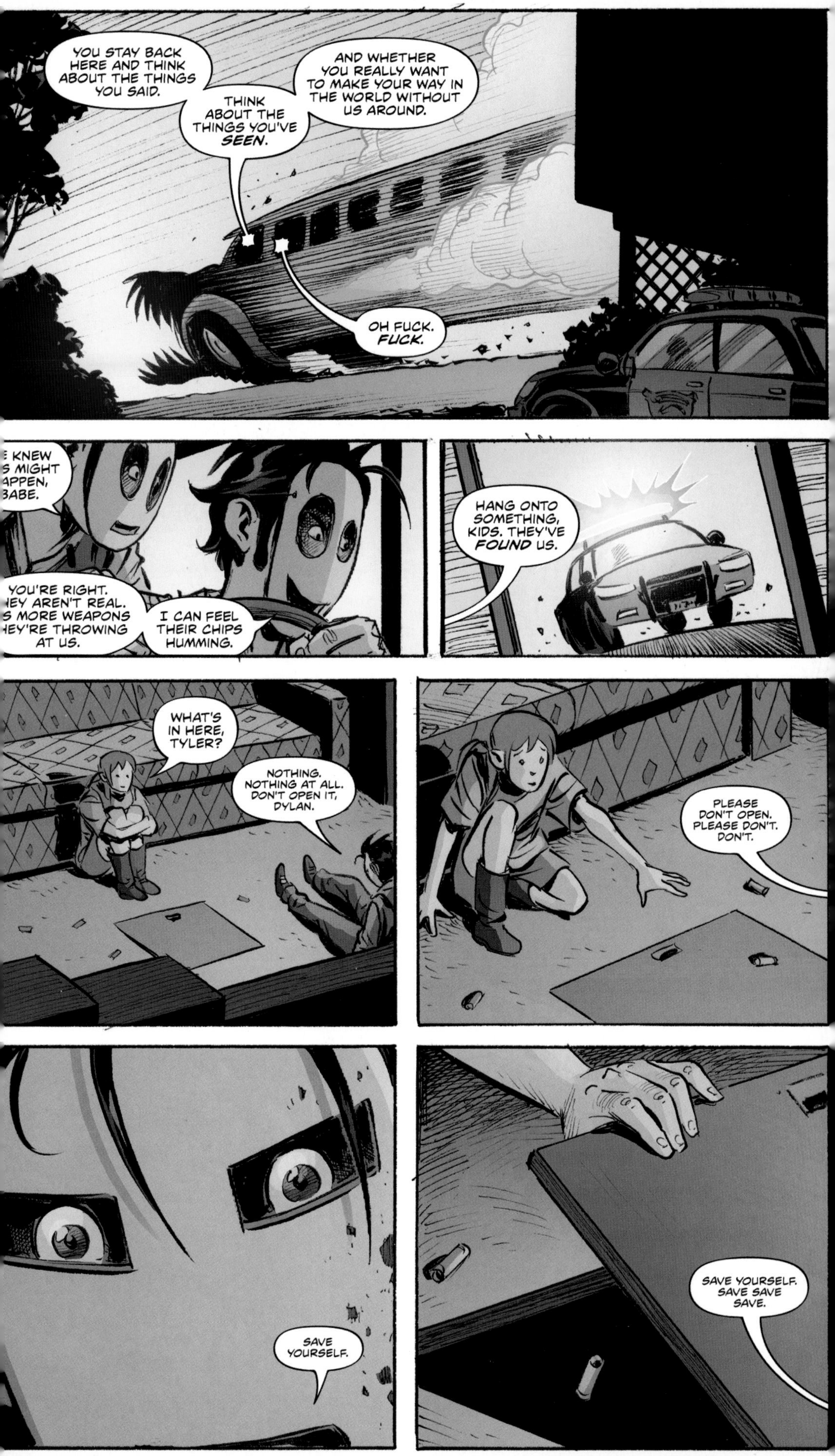
YOU STAY BACK HERE AND THINK ABOUT THE THINGS YOU SAID.
THINK ABOUT THE THINGS YOU'VE SEEN.
AND WHETHER YOU REALLY WANT TO MAKE YOUR WAY IN THE WORLD WITHOUT US AROUND.
OH FUCK. FUCK.
E KNEW S MIGHT APPEN, BABE.
YOU'RE RIGHT. HEY AREN'T REAL. S MORE WEAPONS HEY'RE THROWING AT US.
I CAN FEEL THEIR CHIPS HUMMING.
HANG ONTO SOMETHING, KIDS. THEY'VE FOUND US.
WHAT'S IN HERE, TYLER?
NOTHING. NOTHING AT ALL. DON'T OPEN IT, DYLAN.
PLEASE DON'T OPEN. PLEASE DON'T. DON'T.
SAVE YOURSELF.
SAVE YOURSELF. SAVE SAVE SAVE.

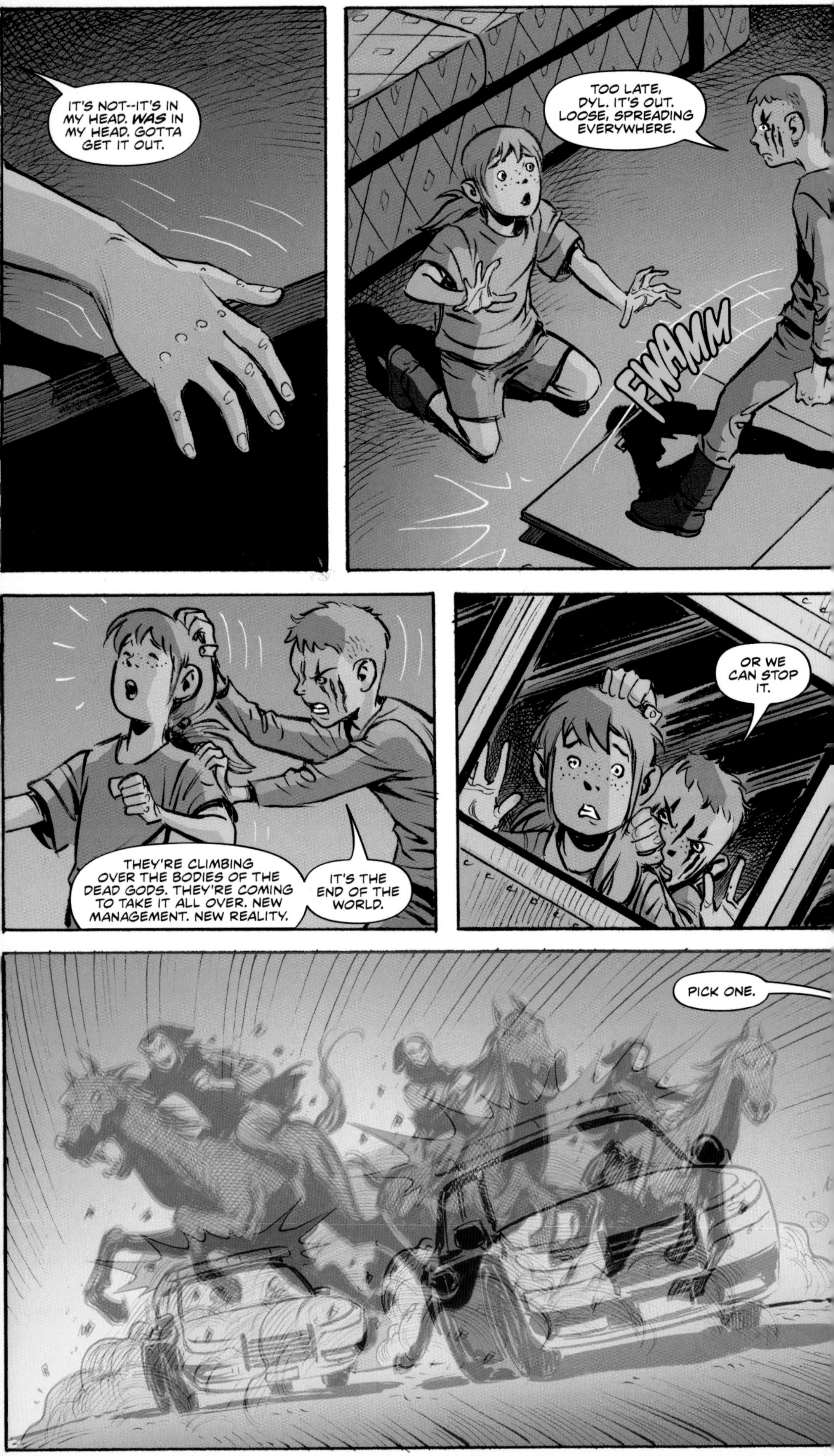
IT'S NOT--IT'S IN MY HEAD. **WAS** IN MY HEAD. GOTTA GET IT OUT.
TOO LATE, DYL. IT'S OUT. LOOSE, SPREADING EVERYWHERE.
FWAMM
THEY'RE CLIMBING OVER THE BODIES OF THE DEAD GODS. THEY'RE COMING TO TAKE IT ALL OVER. NEW MANAGEMENT. NEW REALITY.
IT'S THE END OF THE WORLD.
OR WE CAN STOP IT.
PICK ONE.

“Words, screams, thoughts
It ate everything.”

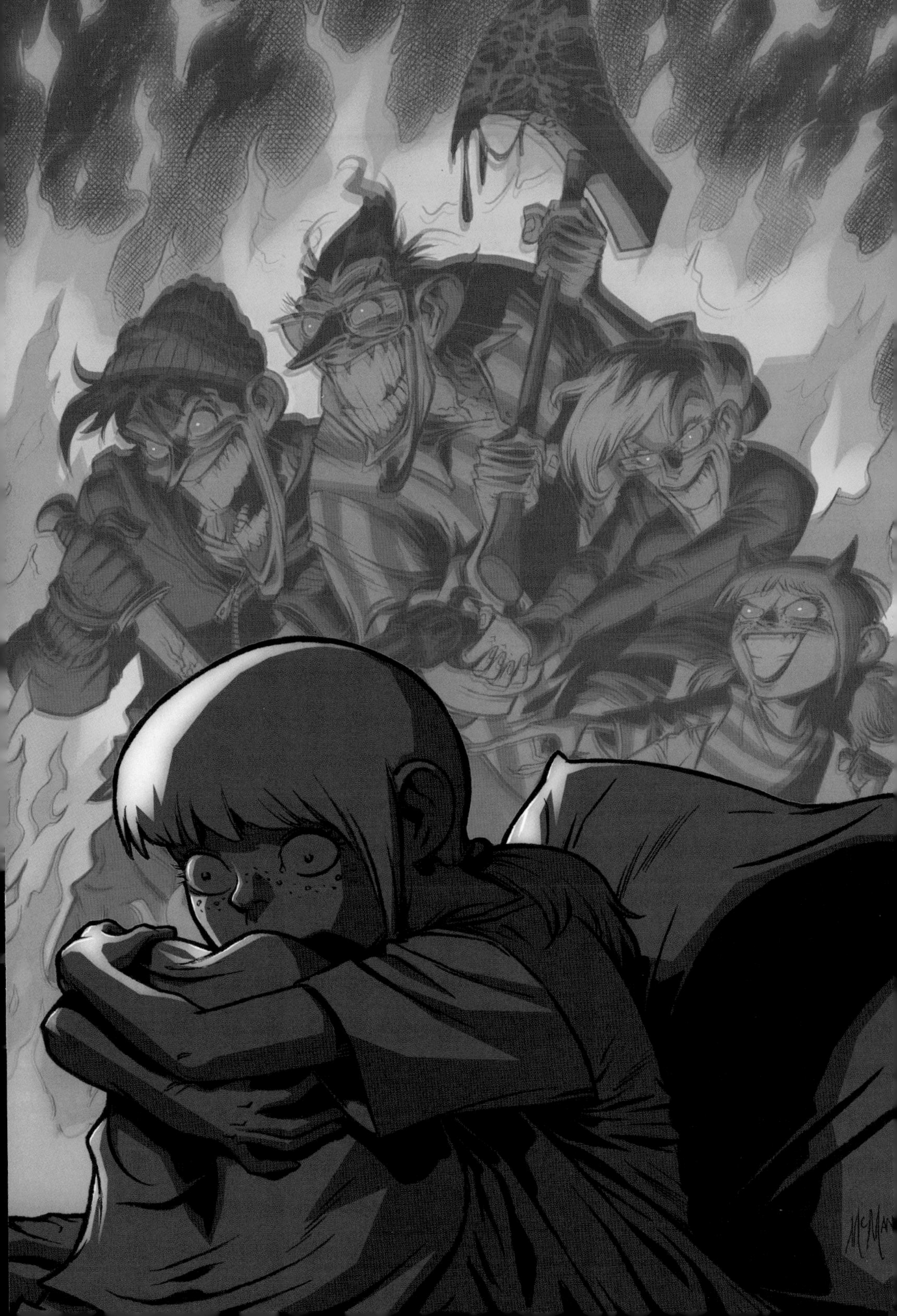

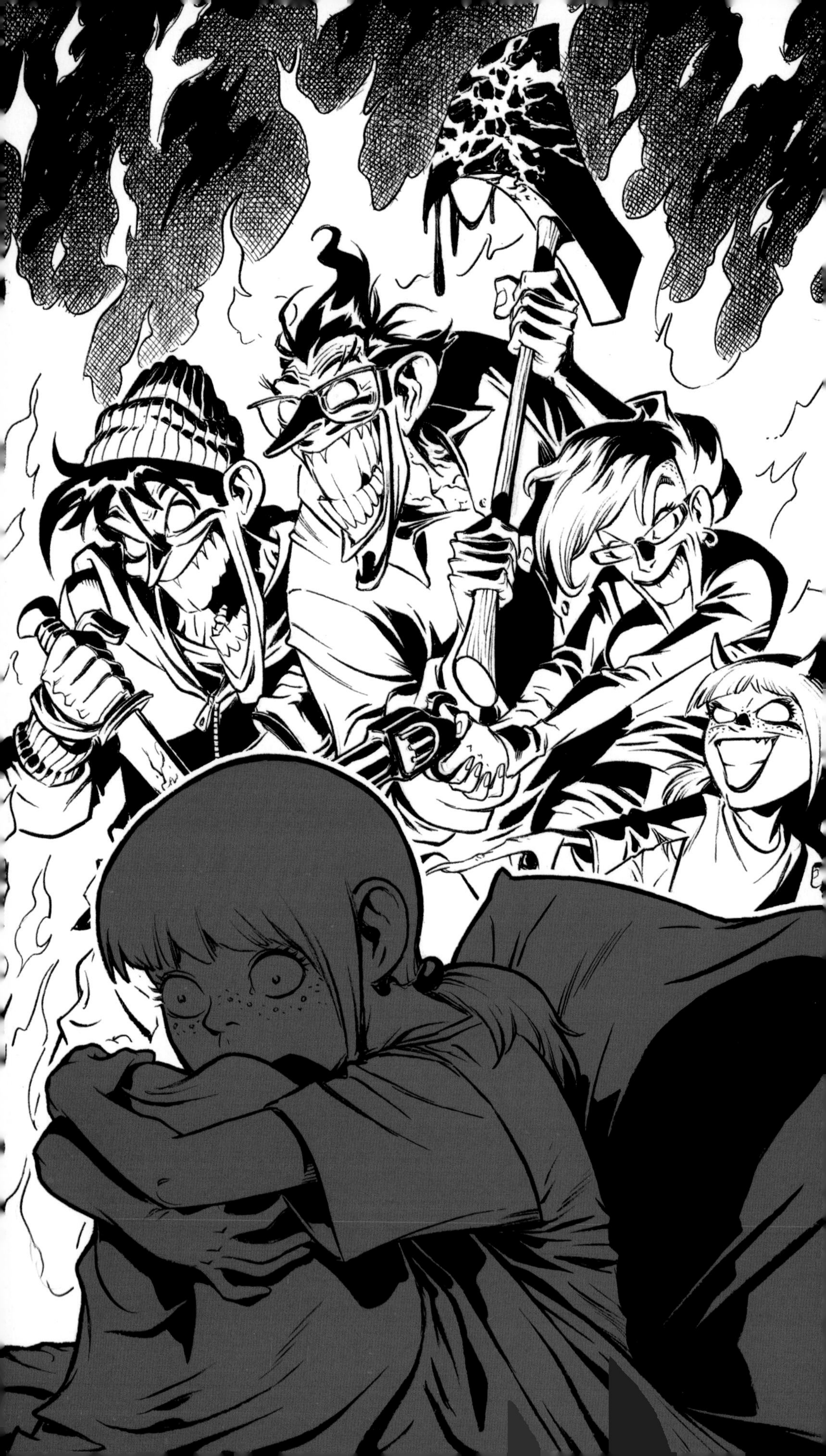

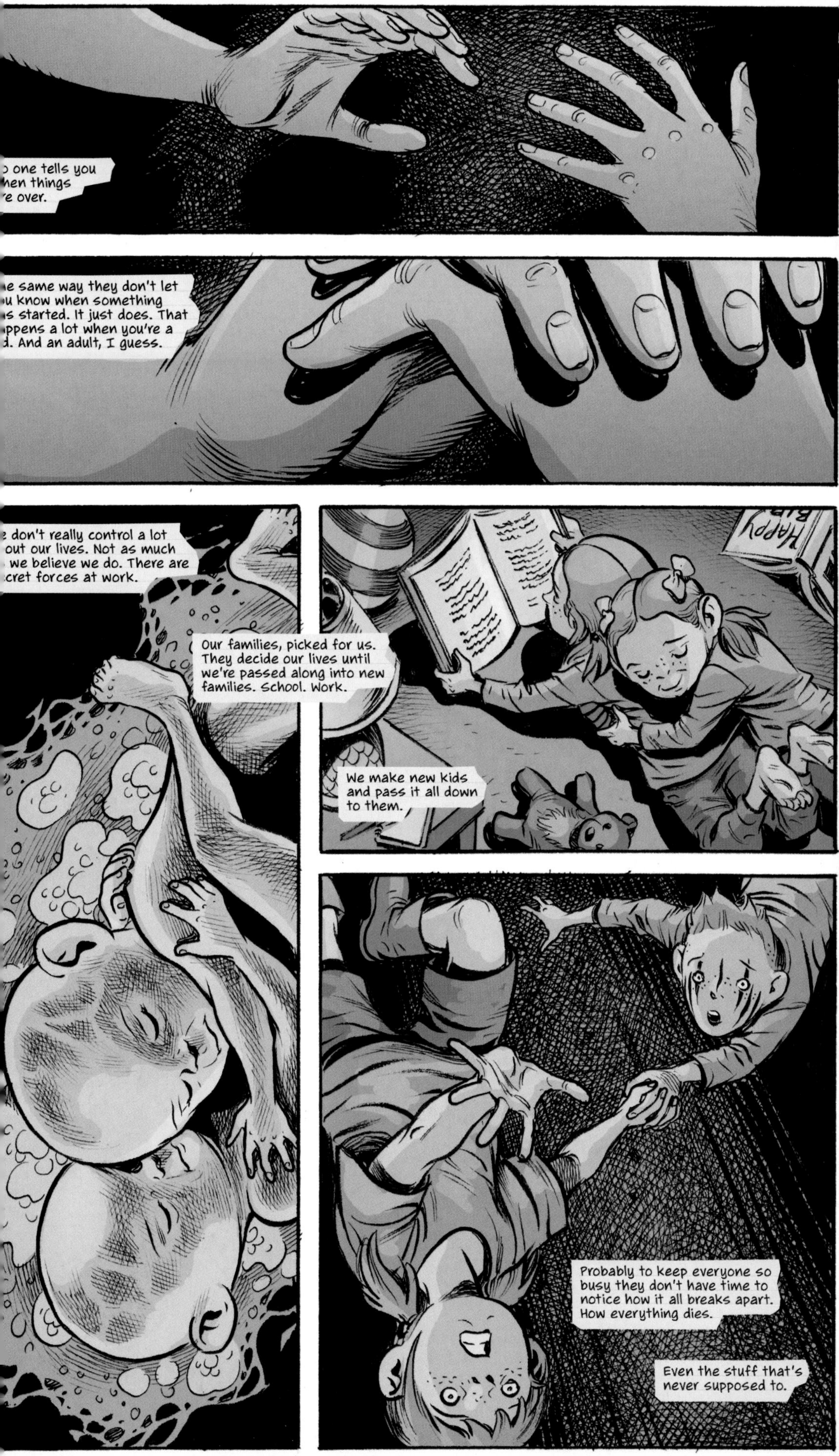

o one tells you
hen things
e over.
e same way they don't let
u know when something
s started. It just does. That
ppens a lot when you're a
d. And an adult, I guess.
e don't really control a lot
out our lives. Not as much
we believe we do. There are
cret forces at work.
Our families, picked for us. They decide our lives until we're passed along into new families. School. Work.
We make new kids and pass it all down to them.
Probably to keep everyone so busy they don't have time to notice how it all breaks apart. How everything dies.
Even the stuff that's never supposed to.

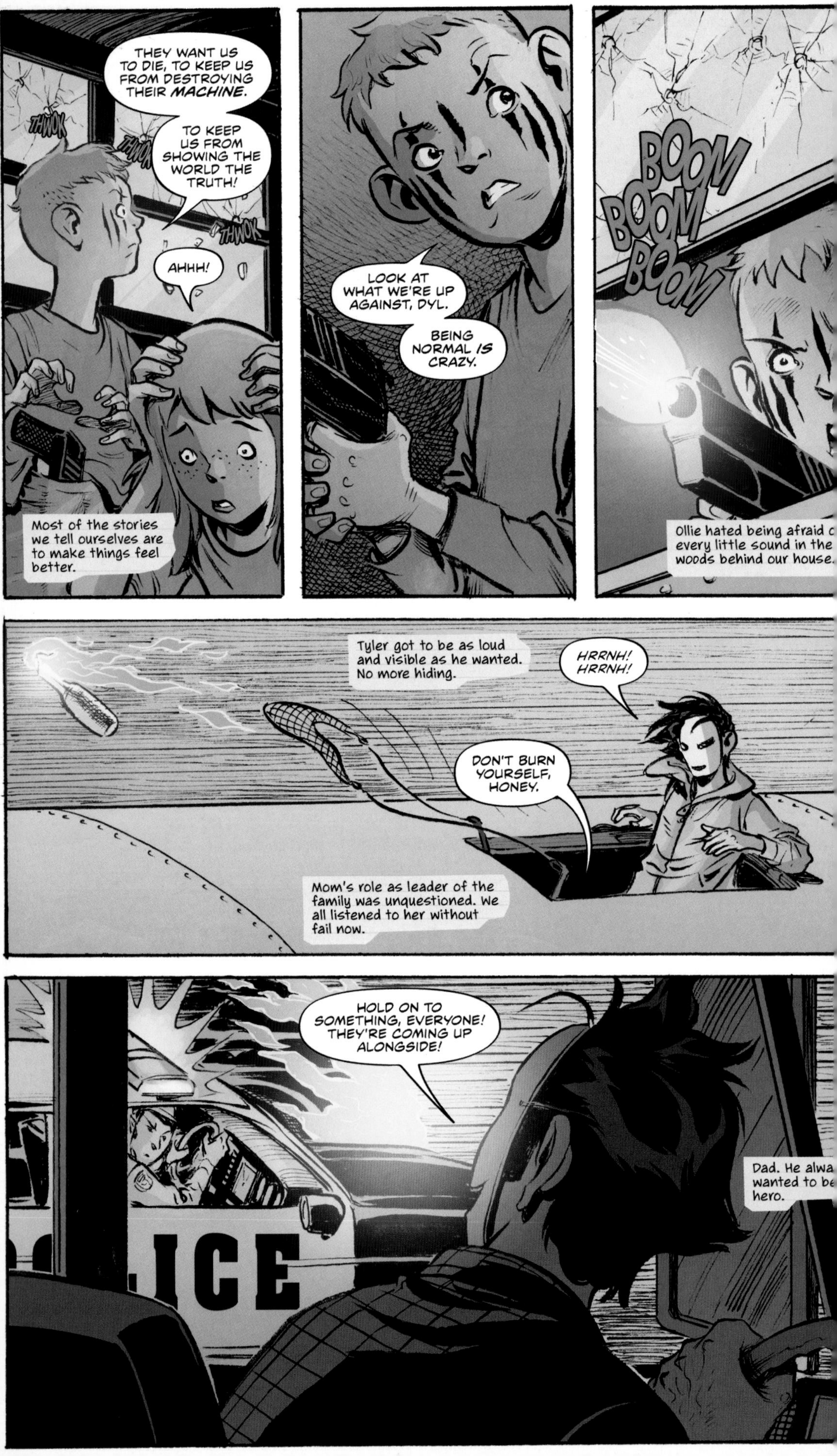

THEY WANT US TO DIE, TO KEEP US FROM DESTROYING THEIR *MACHINE*.
TO KEEP US FROM SHOWING THE WORLD THE TRUTH!
THWOK
THWOK
THWOK
AHHH!
Most of the stories we tell ourselves are to make things feel better.
LOOK AT WHAT WE'RE UP AGAINST, DYL.
BEING NORMAL *IS* CRAZY.
BOOM
BOOM
BOOM
Ollie hated being afraid o
every little sound in the
woods behind our house.
Tyler got to be as loud and visible as he wanted. No more hiding.
HRRNH! HRRNH!
DON'T BURN YOURSELF, HONEY.
Mom's role as leader of the family was unquestioned. We all listened to her without fail now.
HOLD ON TO SOMETHING, EVERYONE! THEY'RE COMING UP ALONGSIDE!
Dad. He alwa
wanted to be
hero.

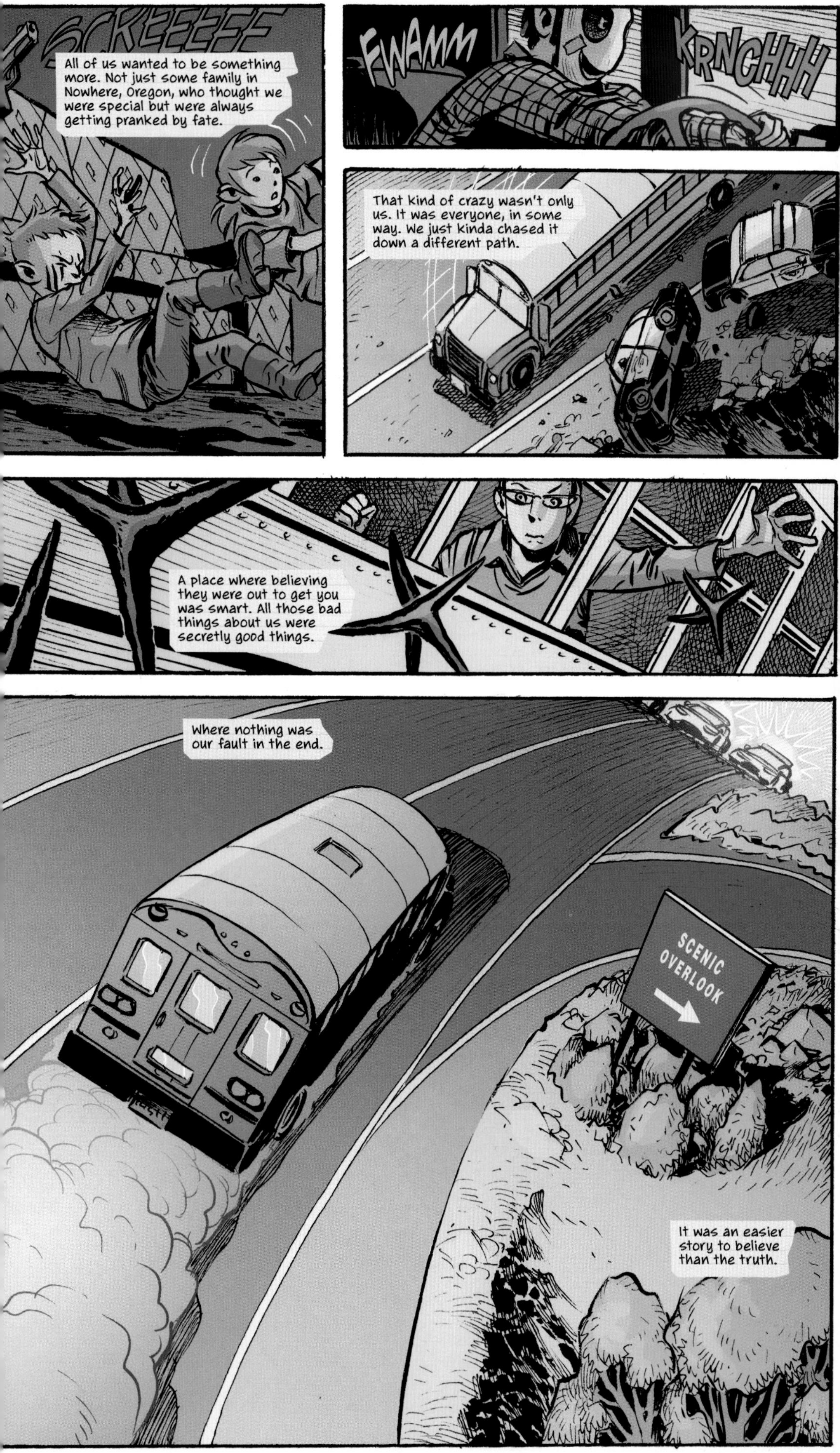
SCREEEEEE
All of us wanted to be something more. Not just some family in Nowhere, Oregon, who thought we were special but were always getting pranked by fate.
FWAMM
KRNCHHH
That kind of crazy wasn't only us. It was everyone, in some way. We just kinda chased it down a different path.
A place where believing they were out to get you was smart. All those bad things about us were secretly good things.
Where nothing was our fault in the end.
SCENIC OVERLOOK
It was an easier story to believe than the truth.

HOUSE AMOK

PART FIVE: WE DISSOLVE

CHRISTOPHER SEBELA
writer

SHAWN McMANUS
artist & cover A

GABRIEL RODRIGUEZ
cover B

TAMRA BONVILLAIN
cover B colorist

Neil Uyetake
letterer

Lee Loughridge
colorist

Megan Brown
assistant editor

Shelly Bond
editor

HOUSE AMOK is created by Sebela & McManus

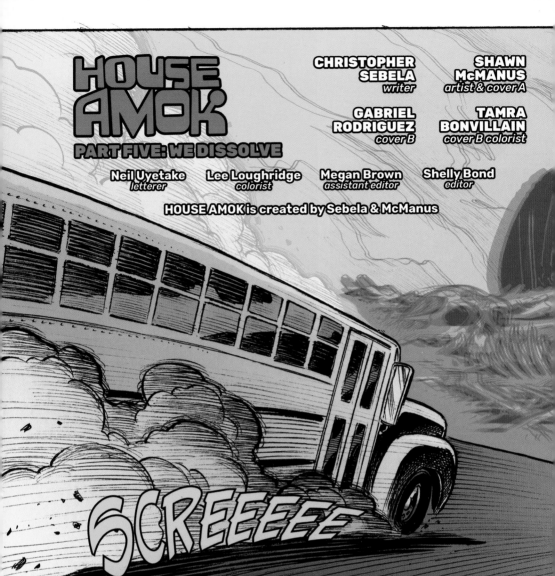

SCREEEEE

OH GOD.

I WANT TO WAKE UP.

BANG BANG
BANG BANG

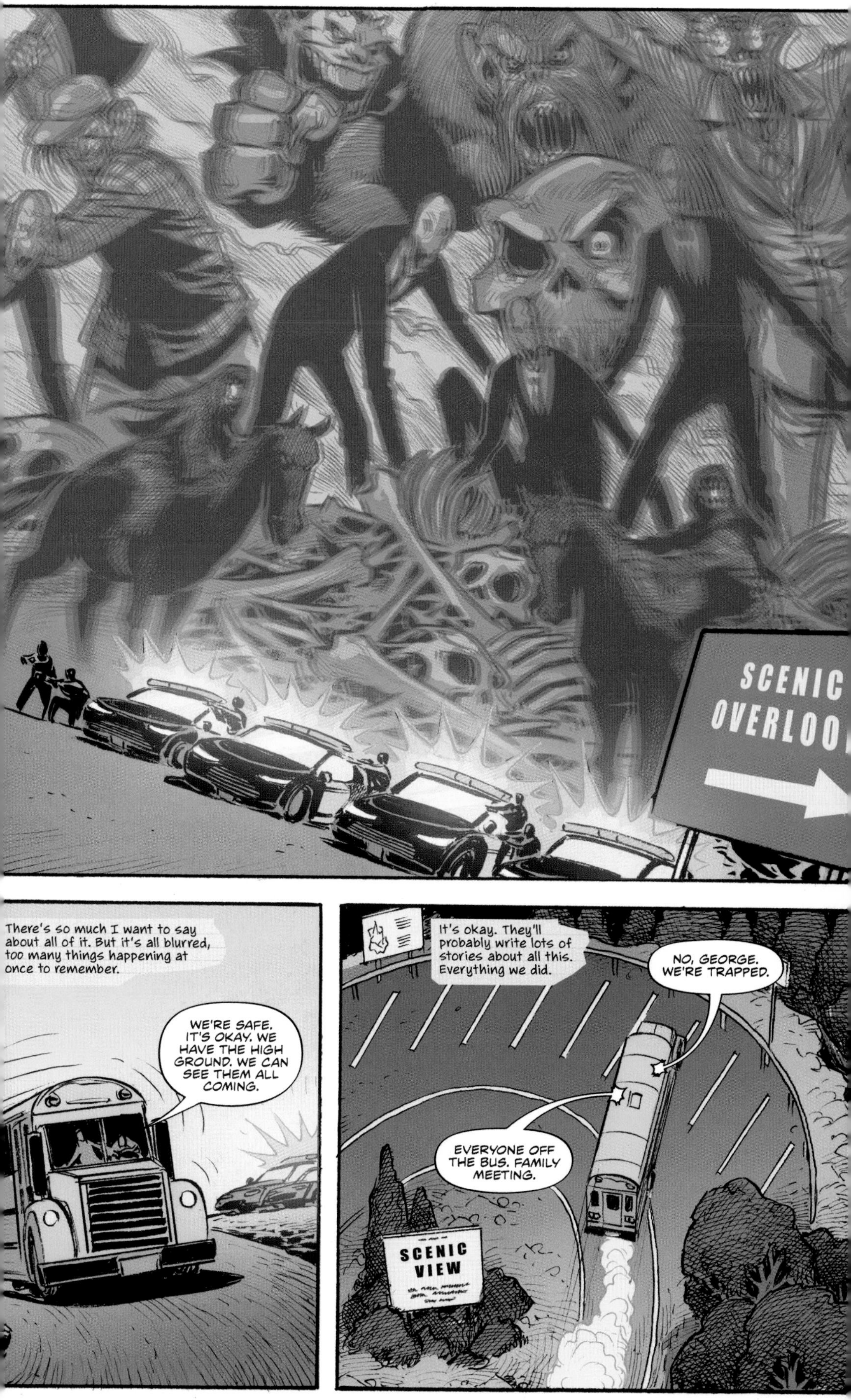
SCENIC
OVERLOO
There's so much I want to say about all of it. But it's all blurred, too many things happening at once to remember.
WE'RE SAFE. IT'S OKAY. WE HAVE THE HIGH GROUND. WE CAN SEE THEM ALL COMING.
It's okay. They'll probably write lots of stories about all this. Everything we did.
NO, GEORGE. WE'RE TRAPPED.
EVERYONE OFF THE BUS. FAMILY MEETING.
SCENIC
VIEW

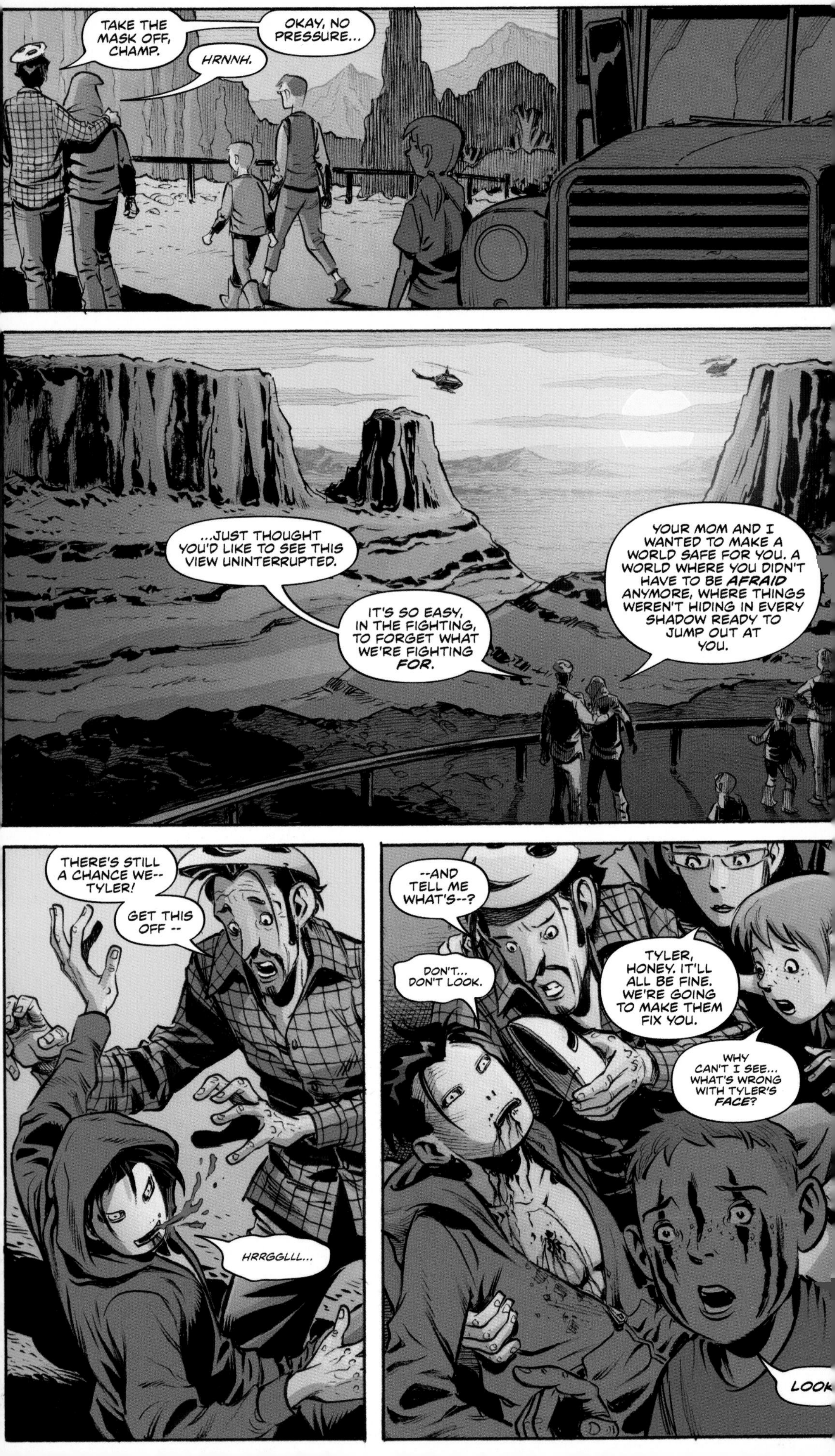
TAKE THE MASK OFF, CHAMP.
OKAY, NO PRESSURE...
HRNNH.
...JUST THOUGHT YOU'D LIKE TO SEE THIS VIEW UNINTERRUPTED.
IT'S SO EASY, IN THE FIGHTING, TO FORGET WHAT WE'RE FIGHTING FOR.
YOUR MOM AND I WANTED TO MAKE A WORLD SAFE FOR YOU. A WORLD WHERE YOU DIDN'T HAVE TO BE AFRAID ANYMORE, WHERE THINGS WEREN'T HIDING IN EVERY SHADOW READY TO JUMP OUT AT YOU.
THERE'S STILL A CHANCE WE-- TYLER!
GET THIS OFF --
HRRGGLLL...
--AND TELL ME WHAT'S--?
DON'T... DON'T LOOK.
TYLER, HONEY. IT'LL ALL BE FINE. WE'RE GOING TO MAKE THEM FIX YOU.
WHY CAN'T I SEE... WHAT'S WRONG WITH TYLER'S FACE?
LOOK

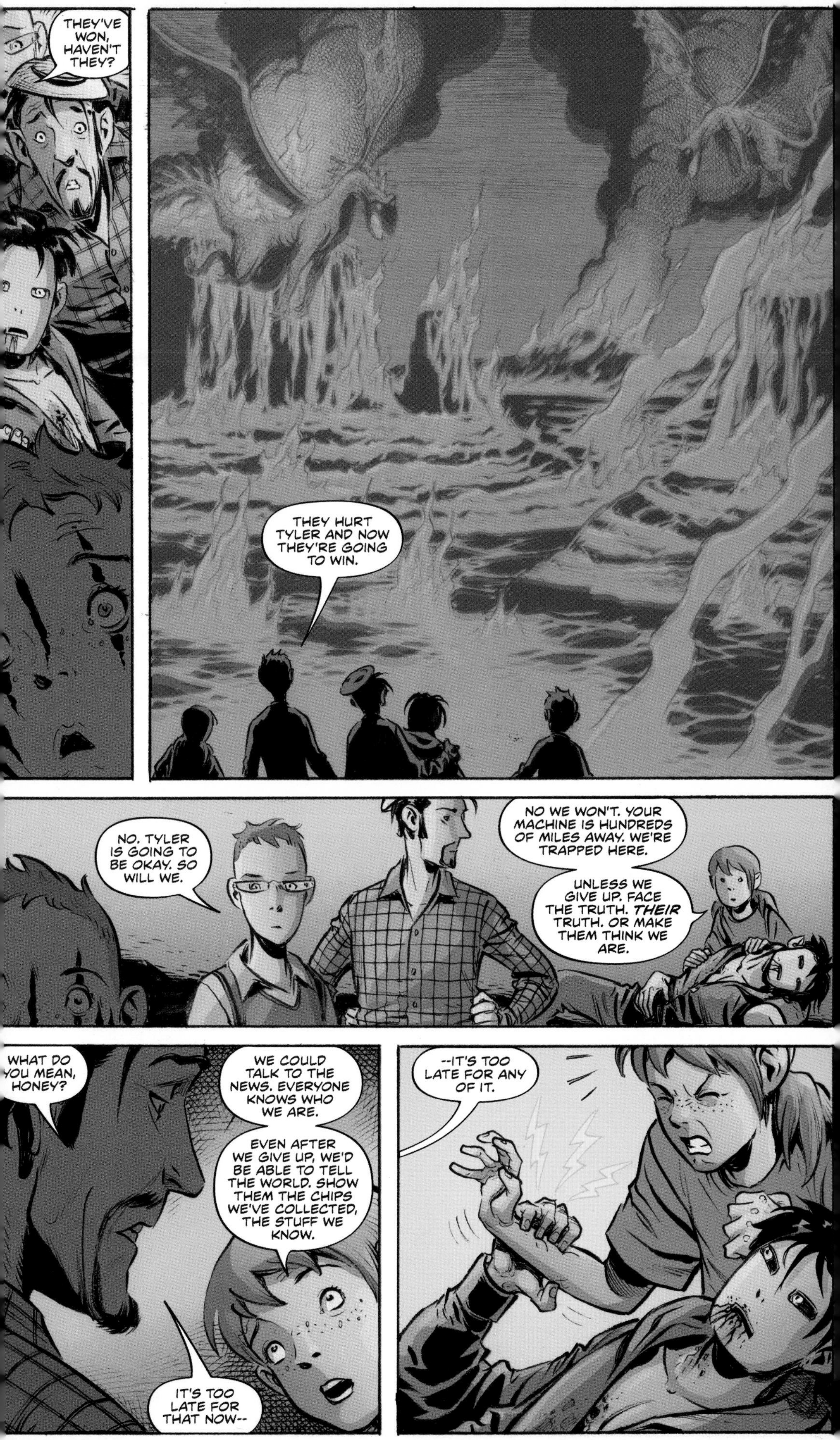
THEY'VE WON, HAVEN'T THEY?
THEY HURT TYLER AND NOW THEY'RE GOING TO WIN.
NO. TYLER IS GOING TO BE OKAY. SO WILL WE.
NO WE WON'T. YOUR MACHINE IS HUNDREDS OF MILES AWAY. WE'RE TRAPPED HERE.
UNLESS WE GIVE UP. FACE THE TRUTH. *THEIR* TRUTH. OR MAKE THEM THINK WE ARE.
WHAT DO YOU MEAN, HONEY?
WE COULD TALK TO THE NEWS. EVERYONE KNOWS WHO WE ARE.
EVEN AFTER WE GIVE UP, WE'D BE ABLE TO TELL THE WORLD. SHOW THEM THE CHIPS WE'VE COLLECTED, THE STUFF WE KNOW.
IT'S TOO LATE FOR THAT NOW--
--IT'S TOO LATE FOR ANY OF IT.

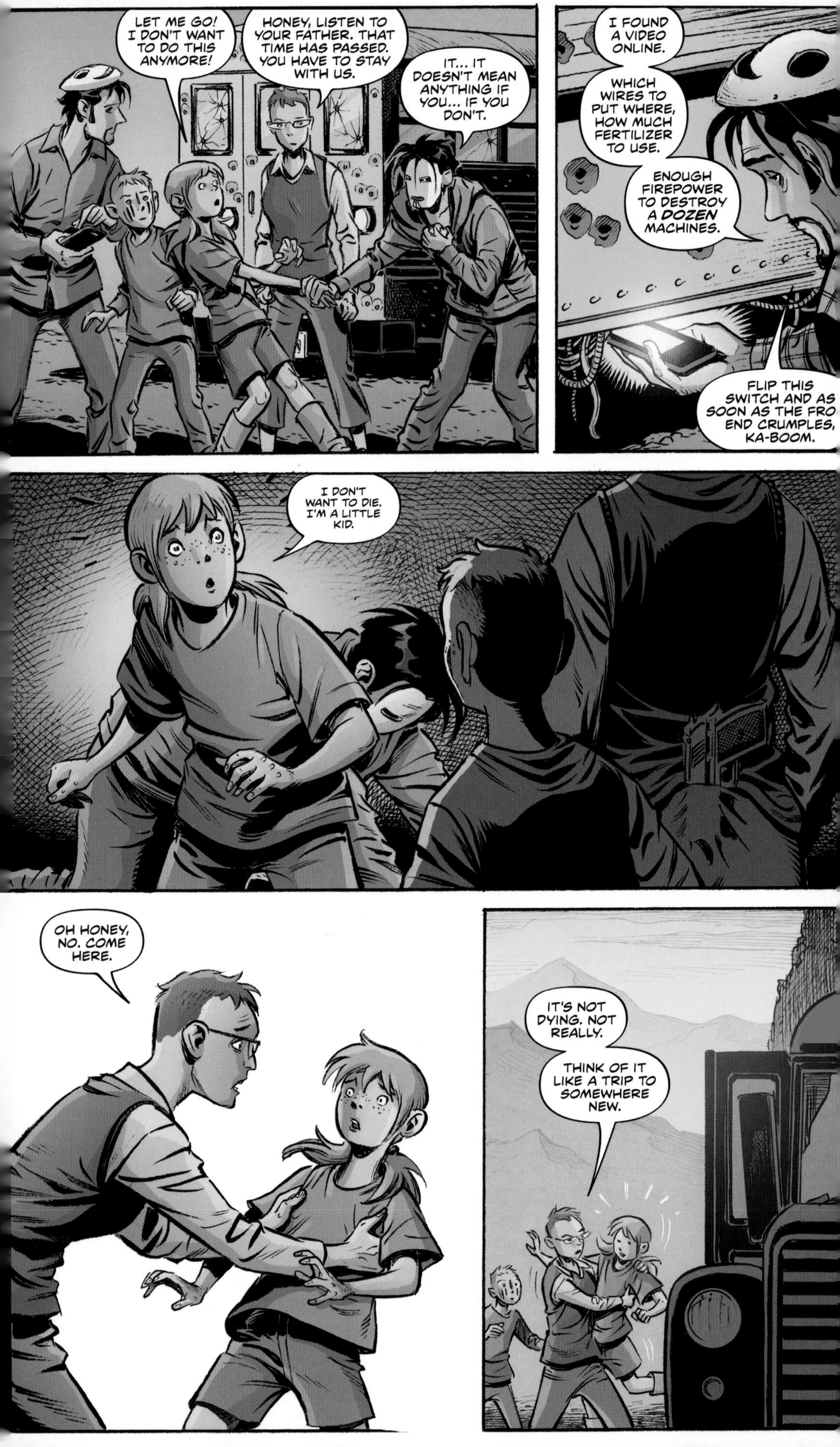
LET ME GO! I DON'T WANT TO DO THIS ANYMORE!
HONEY, LISTEN TO YOUR FATHER. THAT TIME HAS PASSED. YOU HAVE TO STAY WITH US.
IT... IT DOESN'T MEAN ANYTHING IF YOU... IF YOU DON'T.
I FOUND A VIDEO ONLINE.
WHICH WIRES TO PUT WHERE, HOW MUCH FERTILIZER TO USE.
ENOUGH FIREPOWER TO DESTROY A *DOZEN* MACHINES.
FLIP THIS SWITCH AND AS SOON AS THE FRO END CRUMPLES, KA-BOOM.
I DON'T WANT TO DIE. I'M A LITTLE KID.
OH HONEY, NO. COME HERE.
IT'S NOT DYING. NOT REALLY.
THINK OF IT LIKE A TRIP TO SOMEWHERE NEW.

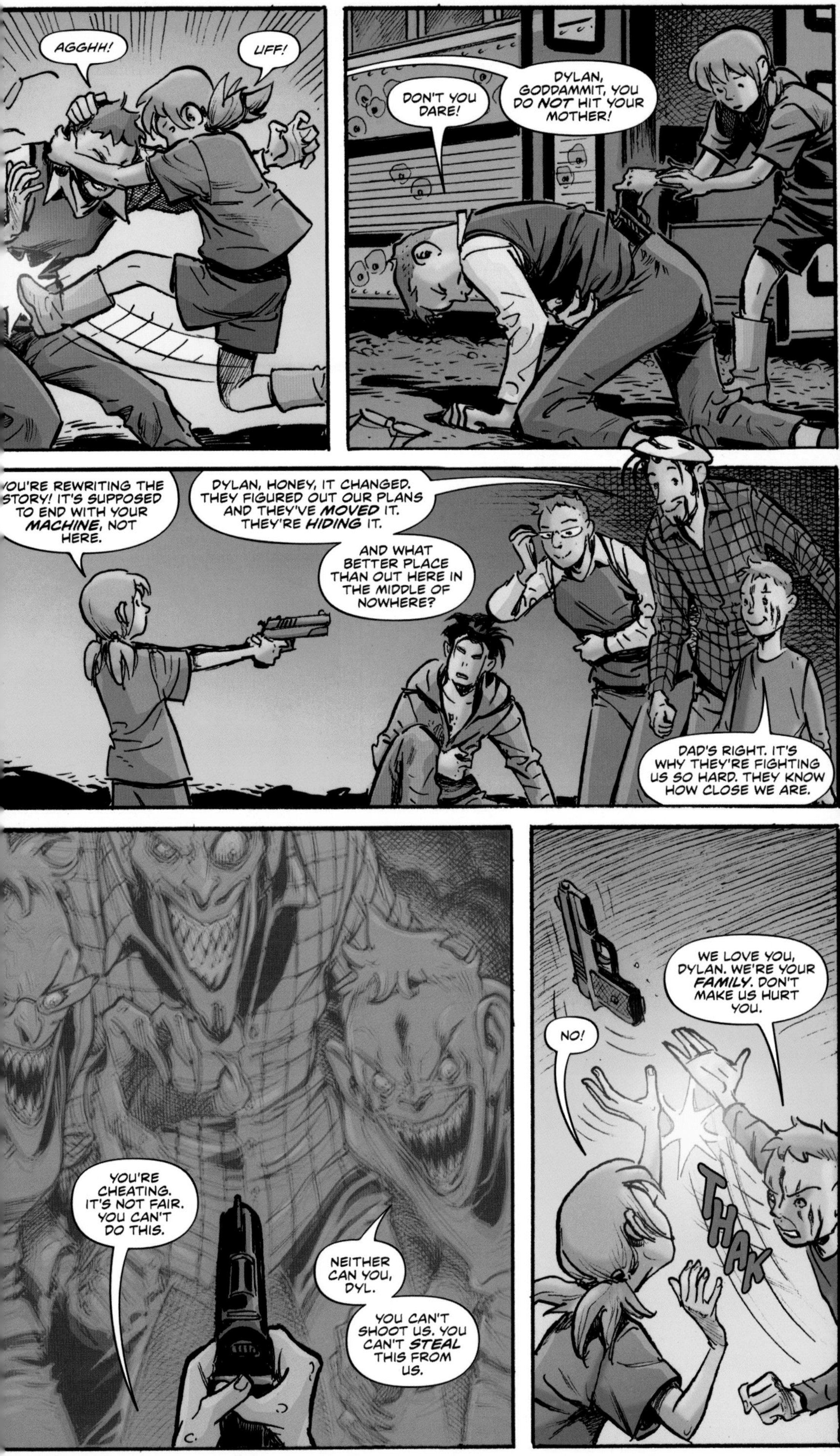
AGGHH!
UFF!
DON'T YOU DARE!
DYLAN, GODDAMMIT, YOU DO NOT HIT YOUR MOTHER!
YOU'RE REWRITING THE STORY! IT'S SUPPOSED TO END WITH YOUR MACHINE, NOT HERE.
DYLAN, HONEY, IT CHANGED. THEY FIGURED OUT OUR PLANS AND THEY'VE MOVED IT. THEY'RE HIDING IT.
AND WHAT BETTER PLACE THAN OUT HERE IN THE MIDDLE OF NOWHERE?
DAD'S RIGHT. IT'S WHY THEY'RE FIGHTING US SO HARD. THEY KNOW HOW CLOSE WE ARE.
YOU'RE CHEATING. IT'S NOT FAIR. YOU CAN'T DO THIS.
NEITHER CAN YOU, DYL.
YOU CAN'T SHOOT US. YOU CAN'T STEAL THIS FROM US.
WE LOVE YOU, DYLAN. WE'RE YOUR FAMILY. DON'T MAKE US HURT YOU.
NO!
THAK

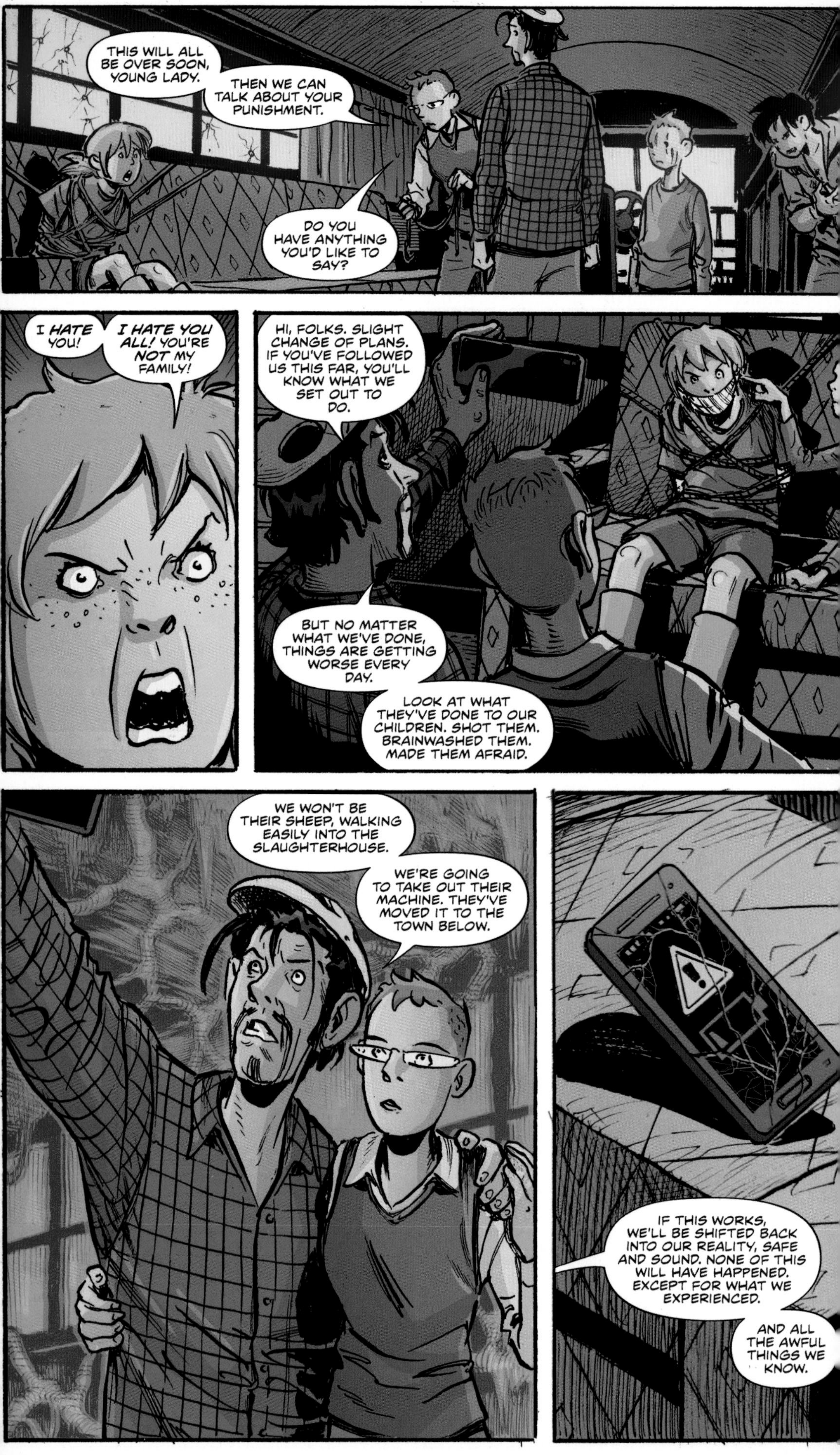
THIS WILL ALL BE OVER SOON, YOUNG LADY.
THEN WE CAN TALK ABOUT YOUR PUNISHMENT.
DO YOU HAVE ANYTHING YOU'D LIKE TO SAY?
I *HATE* YOU!
I HATE YOU ALL! YOU'RE *NOT* MY FAMILY!
HI, FOLKS. SLIGHT CHANGE OF PLANS. IF YOU'VE FOLLOWED US THIS FAR, YOU'LL KNOW WHAT WE SET OUT TO DO.
BUT NO MATTER WHAT WE'VE DONE, THINGS ARE GETTING WORSE EVERY DAY.
LOOK AT WHAT THEY'VE DONE TO OUR CHILDREN. SHOT THEM. BRAINWASHED THEM. MADE THEM AFRAID.
WE WON'T BE THEIR SHEEP, WALKING EASILY INTO THE SLAUGHTERHOUSE.
WE'RE GOING TO TAKE OUT THEIR MACHINE. THEY'VE MOVED IT TO THE TOWN BELOW.
IF THIS WORKS, WE'LL BE SHIFTED BACK INTO OUR REALITY, SAFE AND SOUND. NONE OF THIS WILL HAVE HAPPENED. EXCEPT FOR WHAT WE EXPERIENCED.
AND ALL THE AWFUL THINGS WE KNOW.

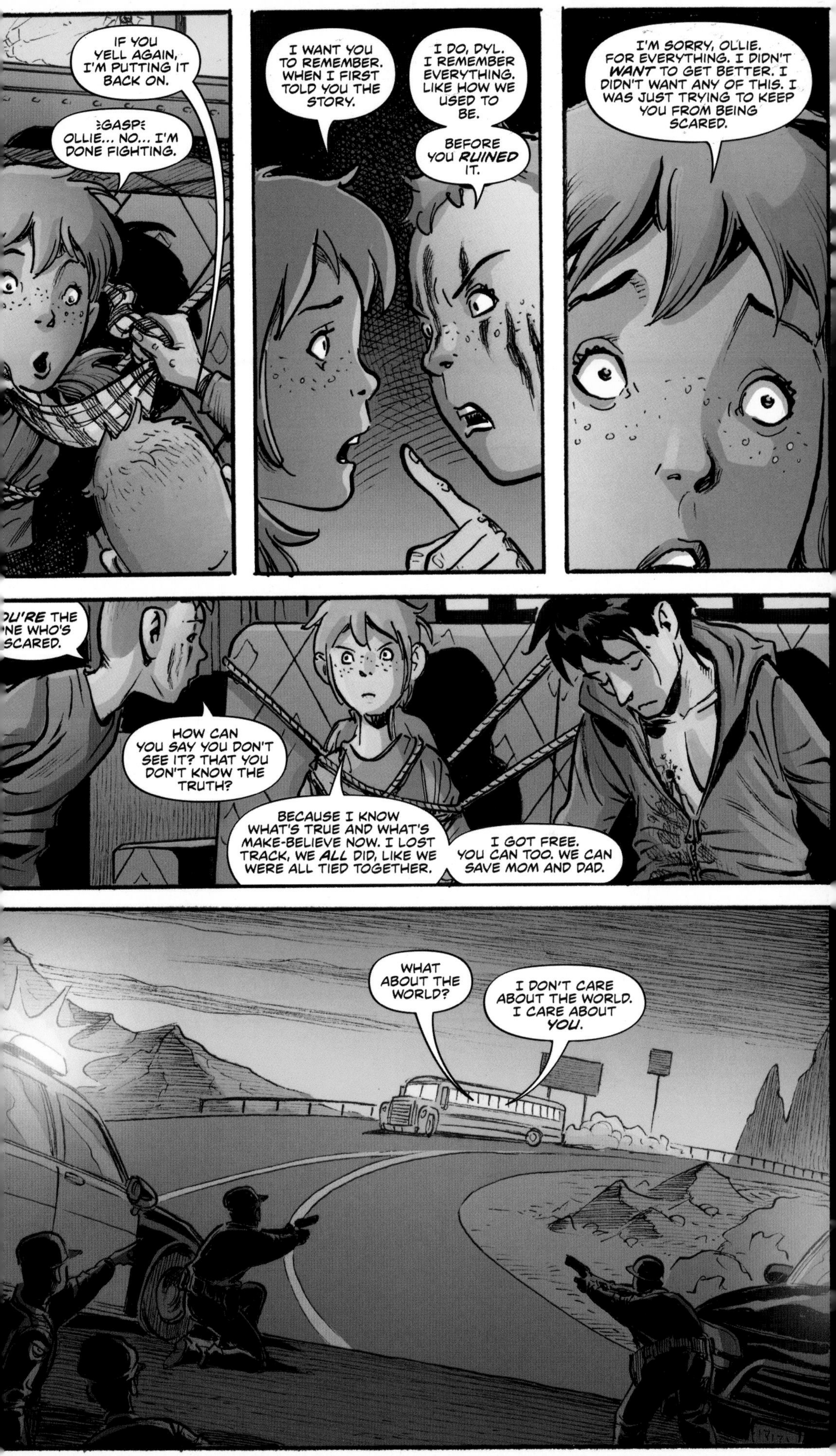
IF YOU YELL AGAIN, I'M PUTTING IT BACK ON.
ƎGASPƎ OLLIE... NO... I'M DONE FIGHTING.
I WANT YOU TO REMEMBER. WHEN I FIRST TOLD YOU THE STORY.
I DO, DYL. I REMEMBER EVERYTHING. LIKE HOW WE USED TO BE.
BEFORE YOU RUINED IT.
I'M SORRY, OLLIE. FOR EVERYTHING. I DIDN'T WANT TO GET BETTER. I DIDN'T WANT ANY OF THIS. I WAS JUST TRYING TO KEEP YOU FROM BEING SCARED.
OU'RE THE NE WHO'S SCARED.
HOW CAN YOU SAY YOU DON'T SEE IT? THAT YOU DON'T KNOW THE TRUTH?
BECAUSE I KNOW WHAT'S TRUE AND WHAT'S MAKE-BELIEVE NOW. I LOST TRACK, WE ALL DID, LIKE WE WERE ALL TIED TOGETHER.
I GOT FREE. YOU CAN TOO. WE CAN SAVE MOM AND DAD.
WHAT ABOUT THE WORLD?
I DON'T CARE ABOUT THE WORLD. I CARE ABOUT YOU.

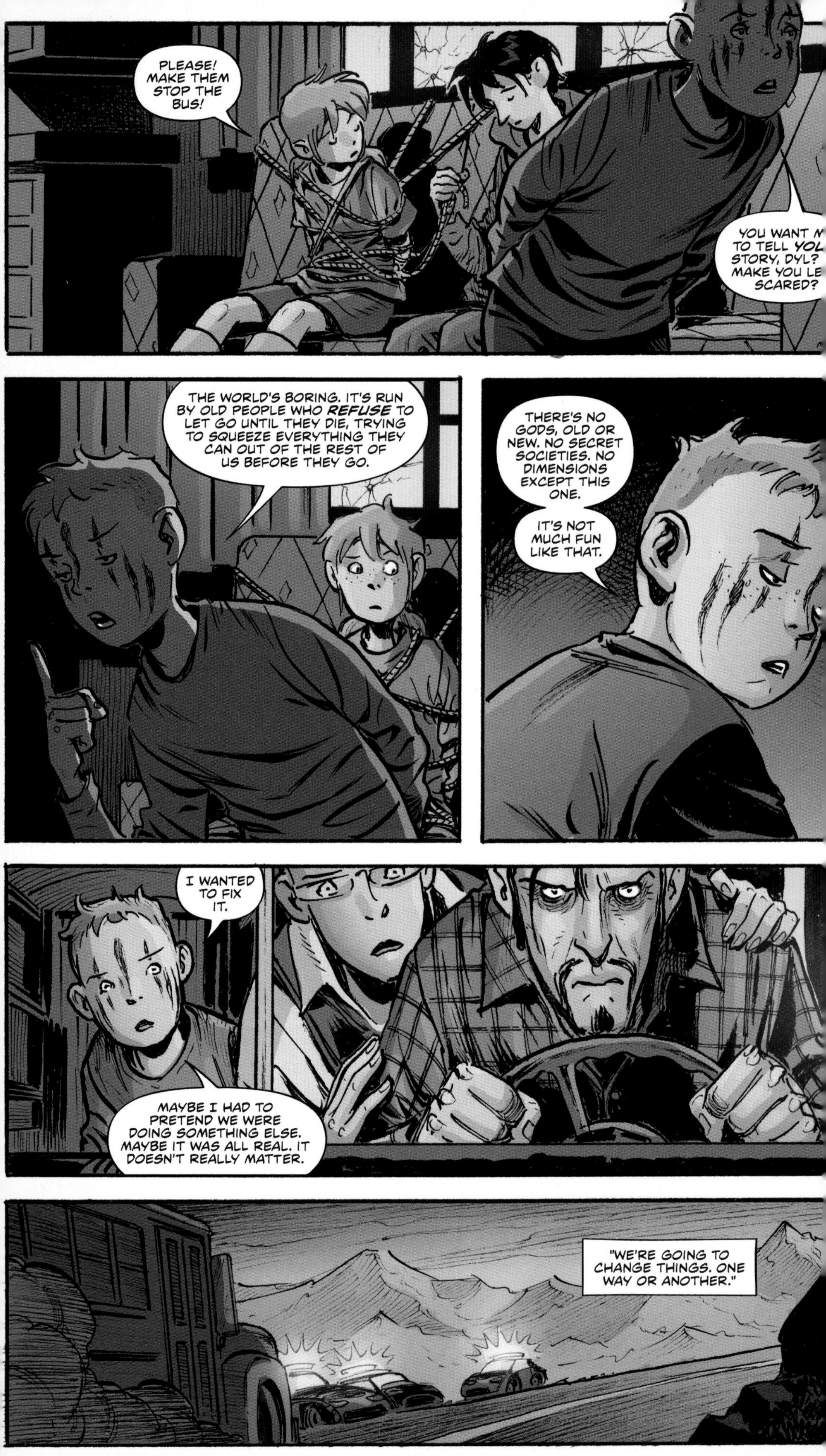
PLEASE! MAKE THEM STOP THE BUS!
YOU WANT M TO TELL YOL STORY, DYL? MAKE YOU LE SCARED?
THE WORLD'S BORING. IT'S RUN BY OLD PEOPLE WHO *REFUSE* TO LET GO UNTIL THEY DIE, TRYING TO SQUEEZE EVERYTHING THEY CAN OUT OF THE REST OF US BEFORE THEY GO.
THERE'S NO GODS, OLD OR NEW. NO SECRET SOCIETIES. NO DIMENSIONS EXCEPT THIS ONE.
IT'S NOT MUCH FUN LIKE THAT.
I WANTED TO FIX IT.
MAYBE I HAD TO PRETEND WE WERE DOING SOMETHING ELSE. MAYBE IT WAS ALL REAL. IT DOESN'T REALLY MATTER.
"WE'RE GOING TO CHANGE THINGS. ONE WAY OR ANOTHER."

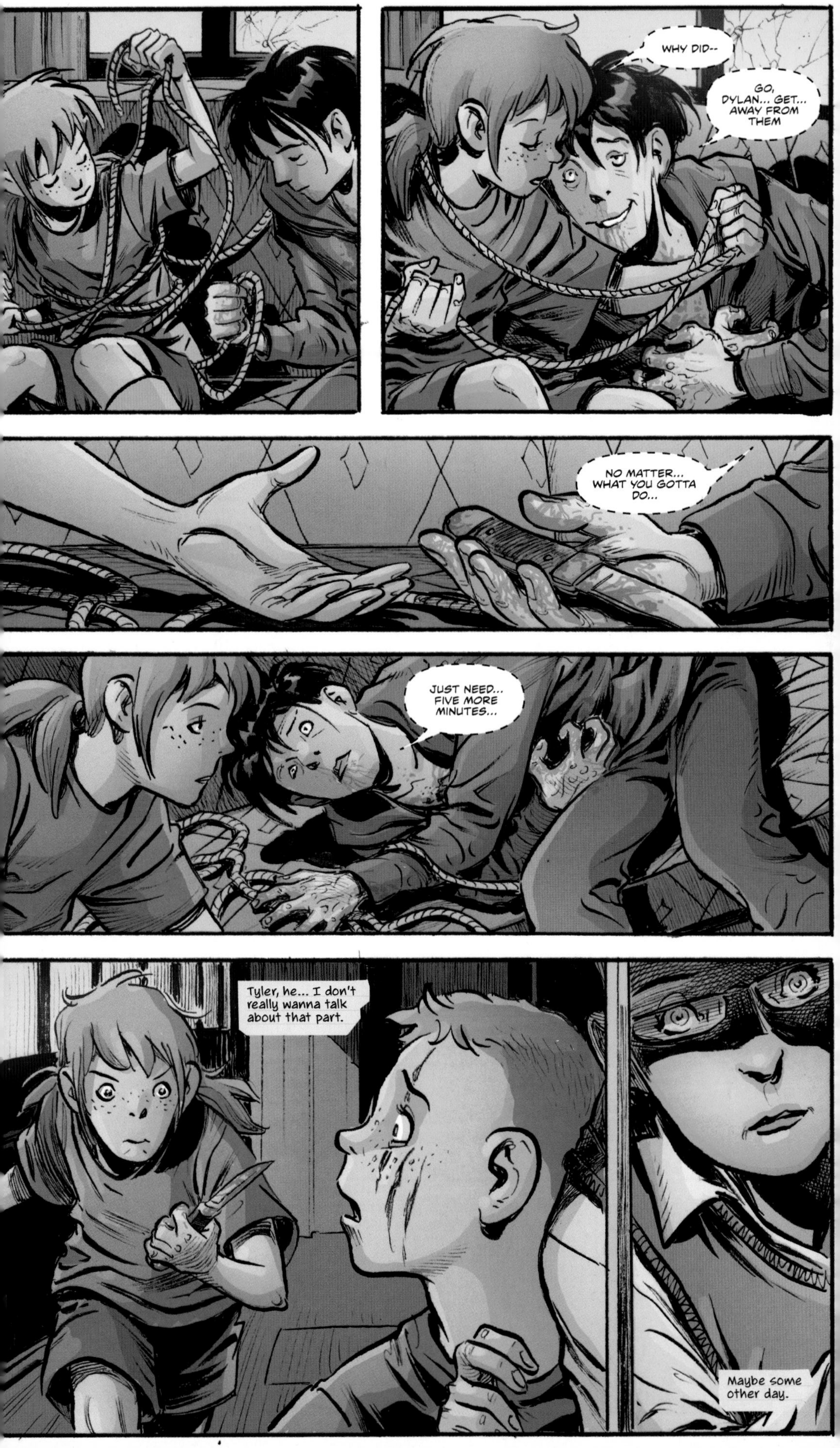
WHY DID--
GO, DYLAN... GET... AWAY FROM THEM
NO MATTER... WHAT YOU GOTTA DO...
JUST NEED... FIVE MORE MINUTES...
Tyler, he... I don't really wanna talk about that part.
Maybe some other day.

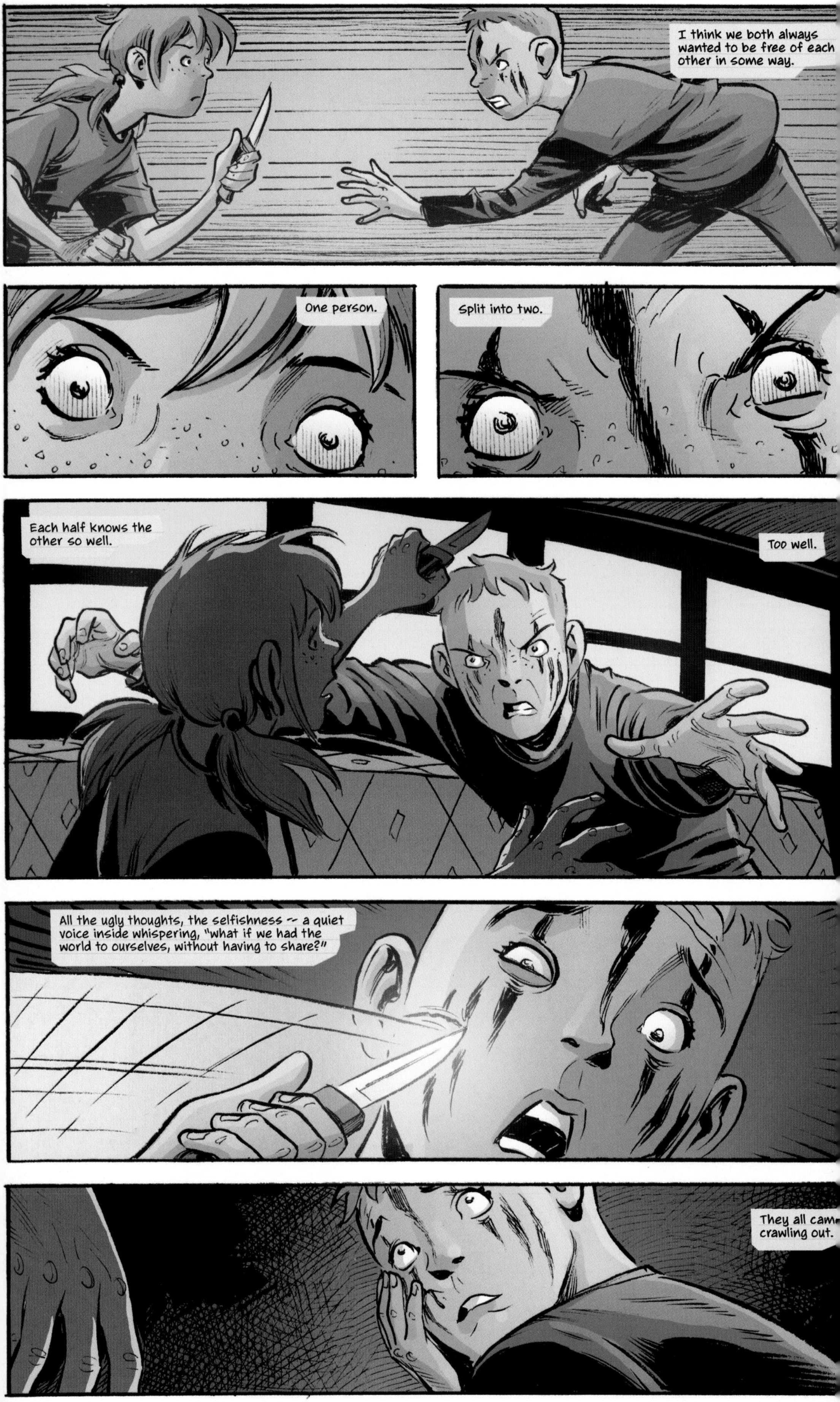

I think we both always wanted to be free of each other in some way.
One person.
Split into two.
Each half knows the other so well.
Too well.
All the ugly thoughts, the selfishness -- a quiet voice inside whispering, "what if we had the world to ourselves, without having to share?"
They all cam
crawling out.

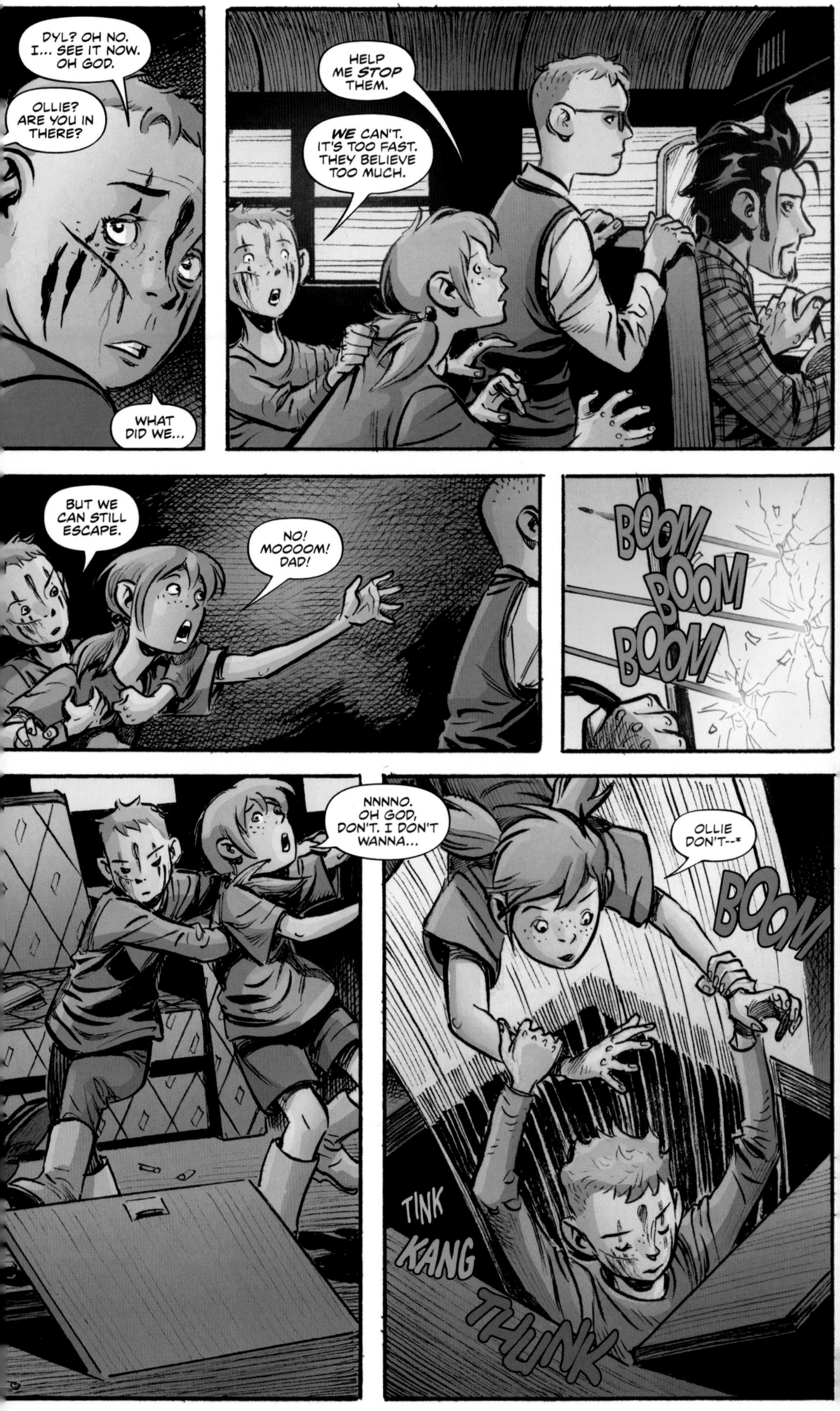
DYL? OH NO. I... SEE IT NOW. OH GOD.
OLLIE? ARE YOU IN THERE?
WHAT DID WE...
HELP ME STOP THEM.
WE CAN'T. IT'S TOO FAST. THEY BELIEVE TOO MUCH.
BUT WE CAN STILL ESCAPE.
NO! MOOOOM! DAD!
BOOM
BOOM
BOOM
NNNNO. OH GOD, DON'T. I DON'T WANNA...
OLLIE DON'T--*
BOOM
TINK
KANG
THUNK

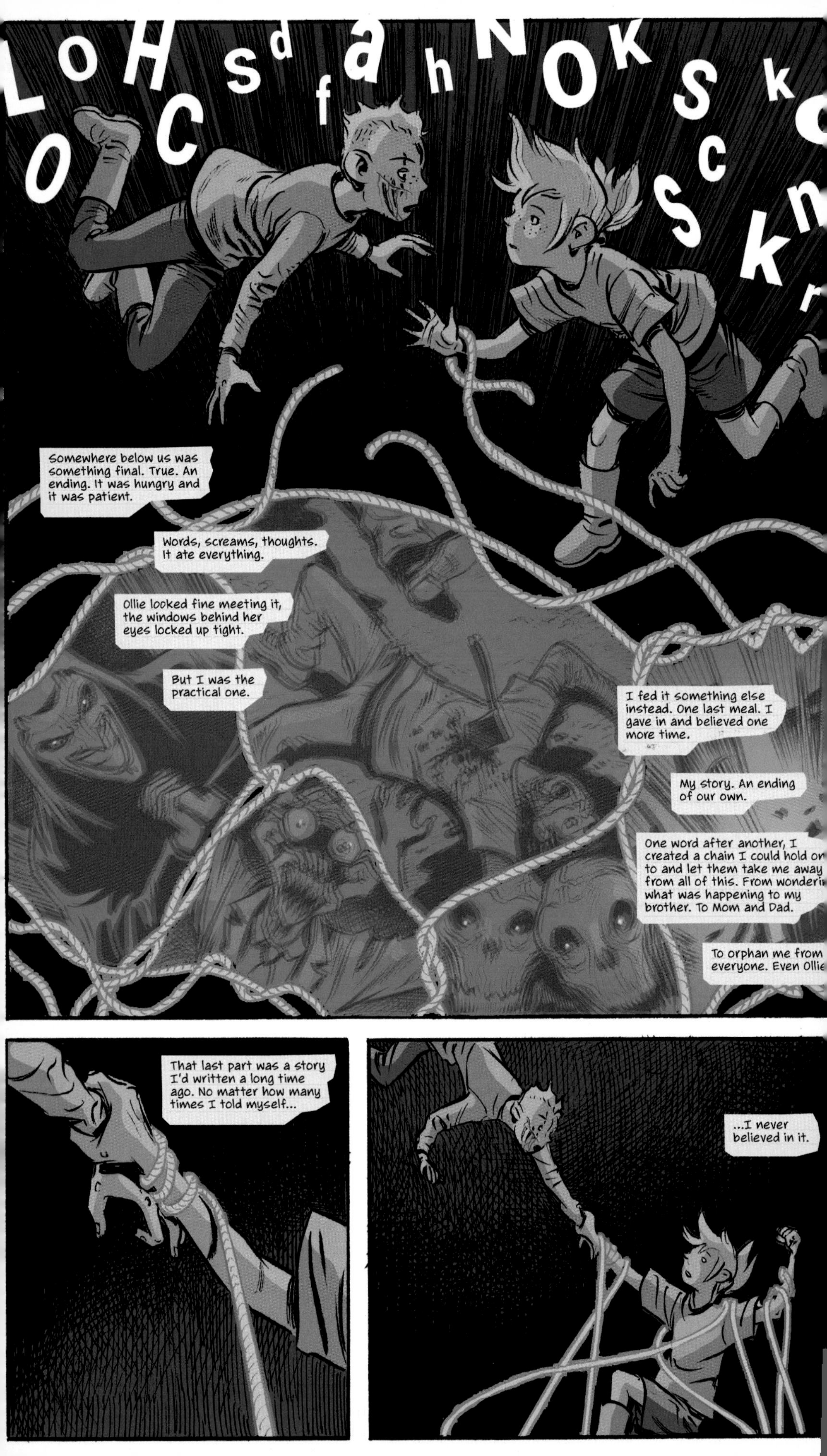
Somewhere below us was something final. True. An ending. It was hungry and it was patient.
Words, screams, thoughts. It ate everything.
Ollie looked fine meeting it, the windows behind her eyes locked up tight.
But I was the practical one.
I fed it something else instead. One last meal. I gave in and believed one more time.
My story. An ending of our own.
One word after another, I created a chain I could hold on to and let them take me away from all of this. From wonderi what was happening to my brother. To Mom and Dad.
To orphan me from everyone. Even Ollie
That last part was a story I'd written a long time ago. No matter how many times I told myself...
...I never believed in it.

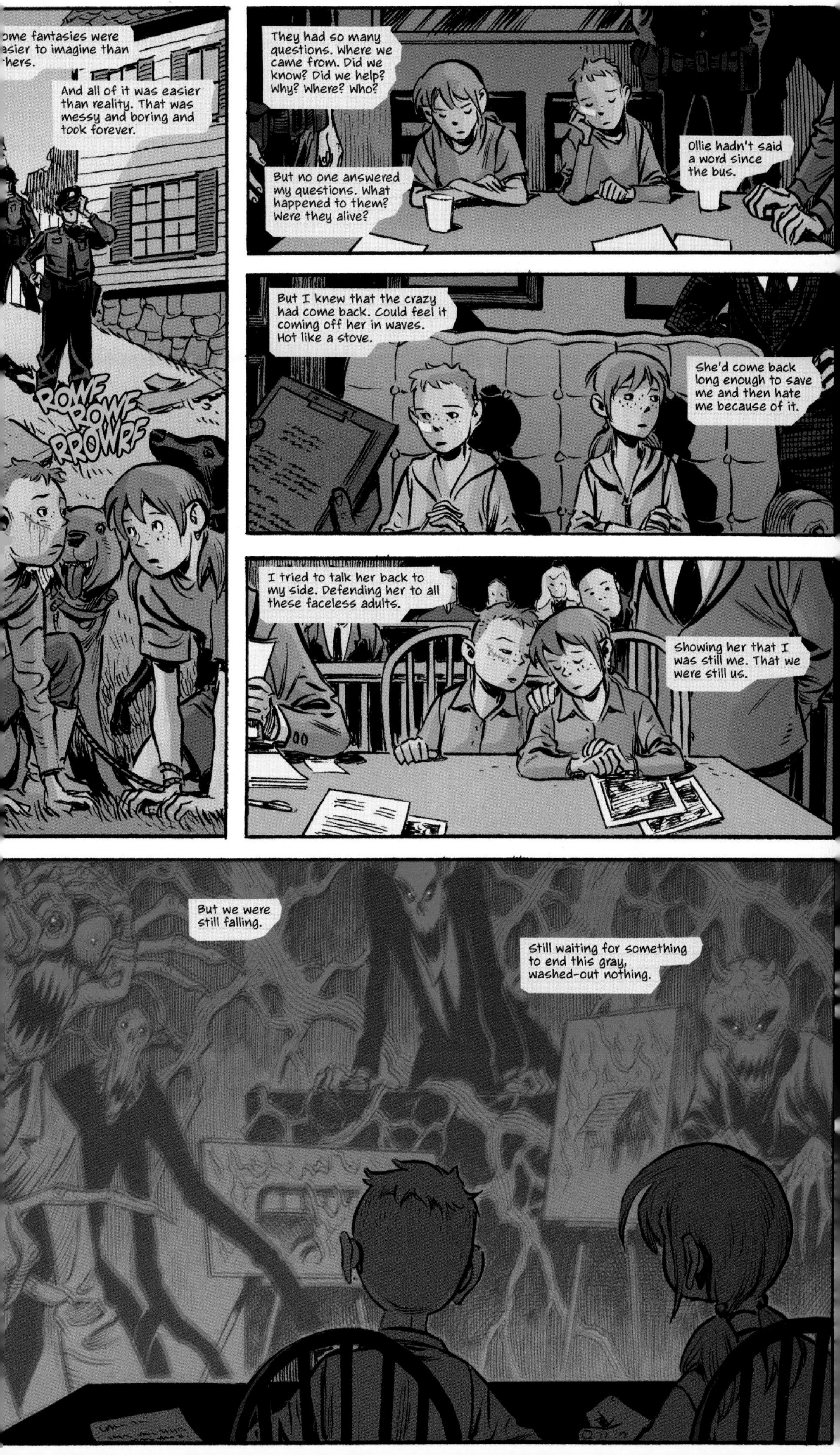
ome fantasies were asier to imagine than hers.
And all of it was easier than reality. That was messy and boring and took forever.
ROWF ROWF RROWRF
They had so many questions. Where we came from. Did we know? Did we help? Why? Where? Who?
But no one answered my questions. What happened to them? Were they alive?
Ollie hadn't said a word since the bus.
But I knew that the crazy had come back. Could feel it coming off her in waves. Hot like a stove.
She'd come back long enough to save me and then hate me because of it.
I tried to talk her back to my side. Defending her to all these faceless adults.
Showing her that I was still me. That we were still us.
But we were still falling.
Still waiting for something to end this gray, washed-out nothing.

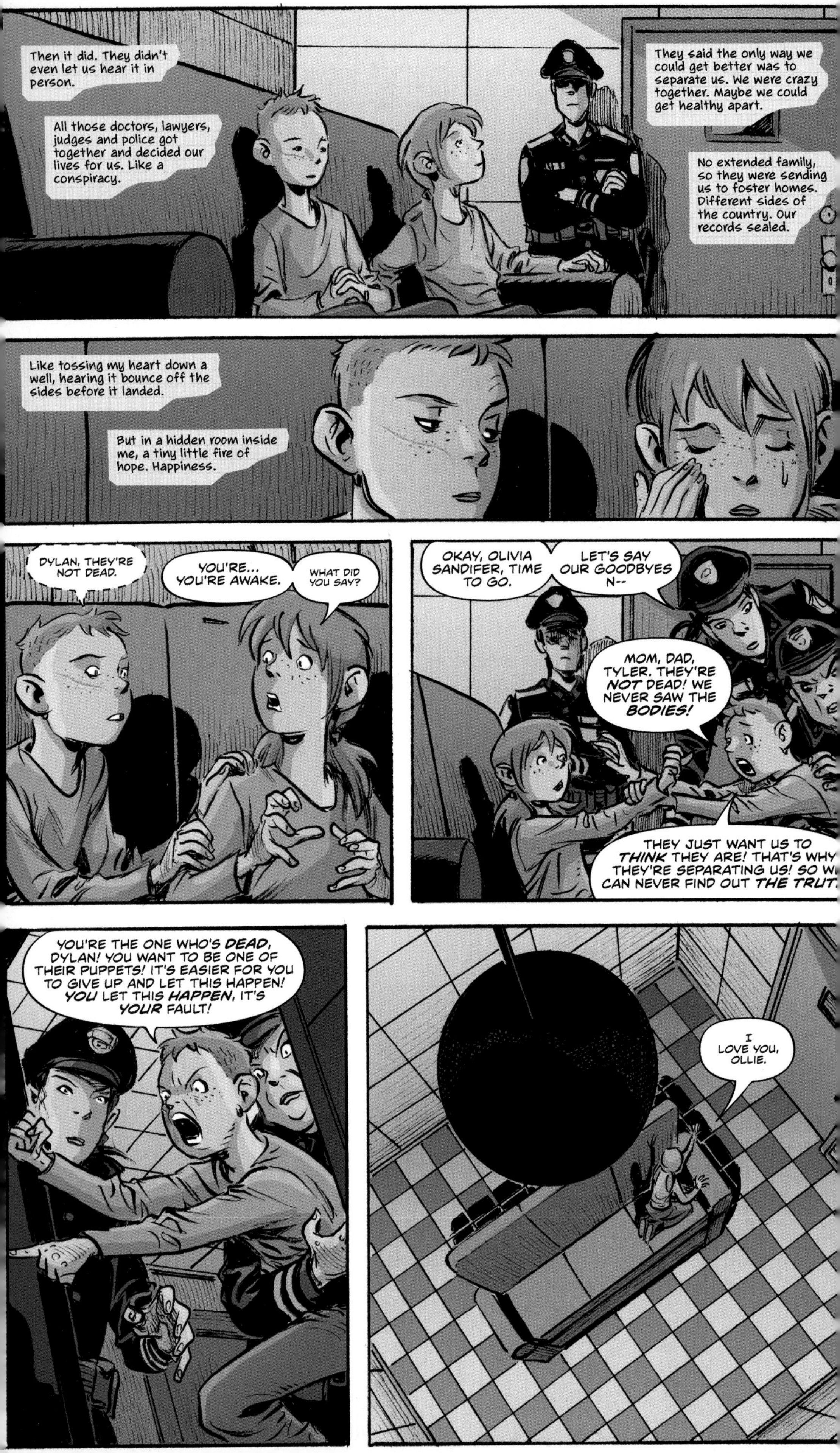
Then it did. They didn't even let us hear it in person.
All those doctors, lawyers, judges and police got together and decided our lives for us. Like a conspiracy.
They said the only way we could get better was to separate us. We were crazy together. Maybe we could get healthy apart.
No extended family, so they were sending us to foster homes. Different sides of the country. Our records sealed.
Like tossing my heart down a well, hearing it bounce off the sides before it landed.
But in a hidden room inside me, a tiny little fire of hope. Happiness.
DYLAN, THEY'RE NOT DEAD.
YOU'RE... YOU'RE AWAKE.
WHAT DID YOU SAY?
OKAY, OLIVIA SANDIFER, TIME TO GO.
LET'S SAY OUR GOODBYES N--
MOM, DAD, TYLER. THEY'RE NOT DEAD! WE NEVER SAW THE BODIES!
THEY JUST WANT US TO THINK THEY ARE! THAT'S WHY THEY'RE SEPARATING US! SO W
CAN NEVER FIND OUT THE TRUT
YOU'RE THE ONE WHO'S DEAD, DYLAN! YOU WANT TO BE ONE OF THEIR PUPPETS! IT'S EASIER FOR YOU TO GIVE UP AND LET THIS HAPPEN! YOU LET THIS HAPPEN, IT'S YOUR FAULT!
I LOVE YOU, OLLIE.

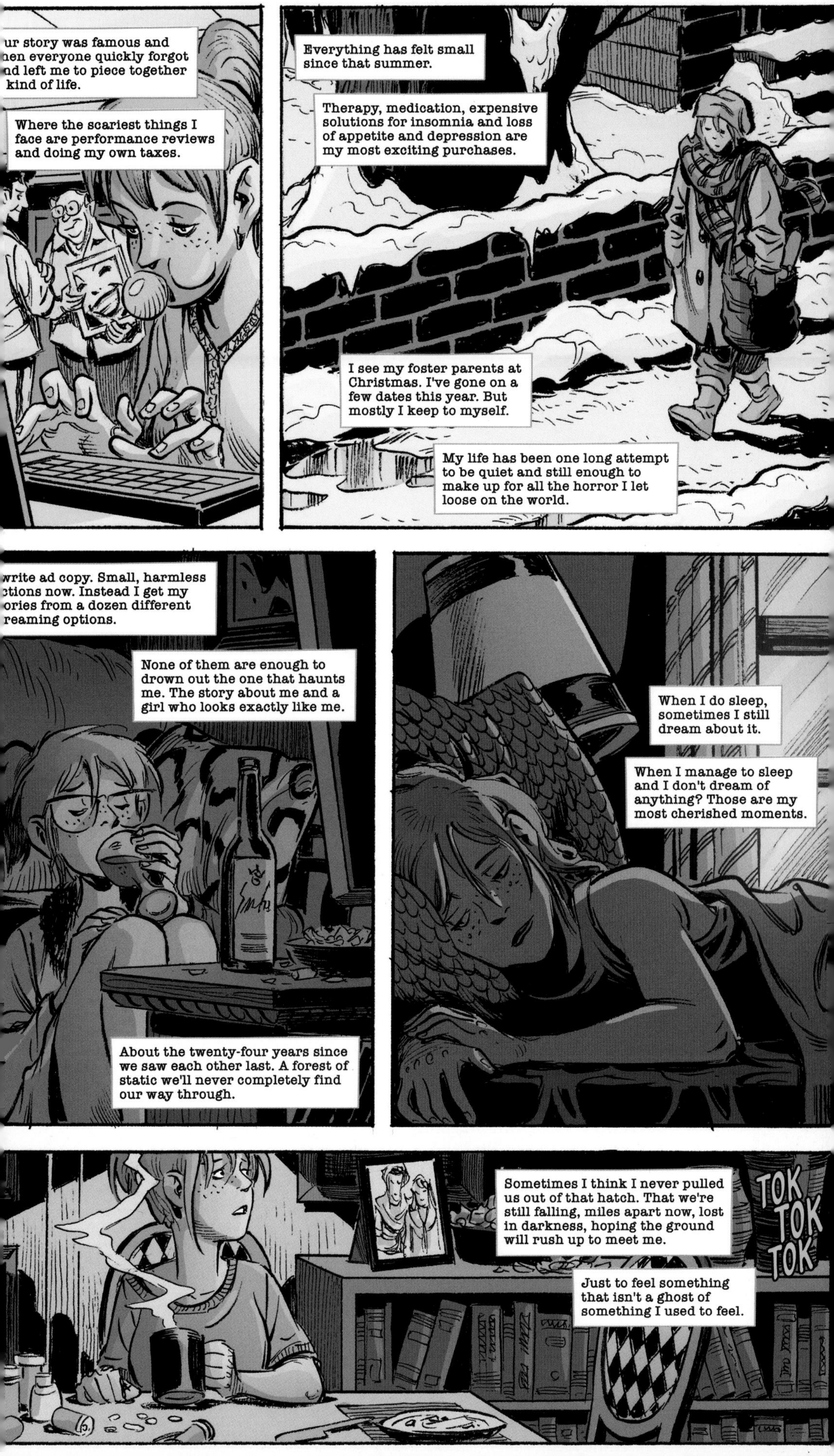
ur story was famous and
nen everyone quickly forgot
nd left me to piece together
kind of life.
Where the scariest things I face are performance reviews and doing my own taxes.
Everything has felt small since that summer.
Therapy, medication, expensive solutions for insomnia and loss of appetite and depression are my most exciting purchases.
I see my foster parents at Christmas. I've gone on a few dates this year. But mostly I keep to myself.
My life has been one long attempt to be quiet and still enough to make up for all the horror I let loose on the world.
write ad copy. Small, harmless
ctions now. Instead I get my
ories from a dozen different
reaming options.
None of them are enough to drown out the one that haunts me. The story about me and a girl who looks exactly like me.
About the twenty-four years since we saw each other last. A forest of static we'll never completely find our way through.
When I do sleep, sometimes I still dream about it.
When I manage to sleep and I don't dream of anything? Those are my most cherished moments.
Sometimes I think I never pulled us out of that hatch. That we're still falling, miles apart now, lost in darkness, hoping the ground will rush up to meet me.
Just to feel something that isn't a ghost of something I used to feel.
TOK TOK TOK

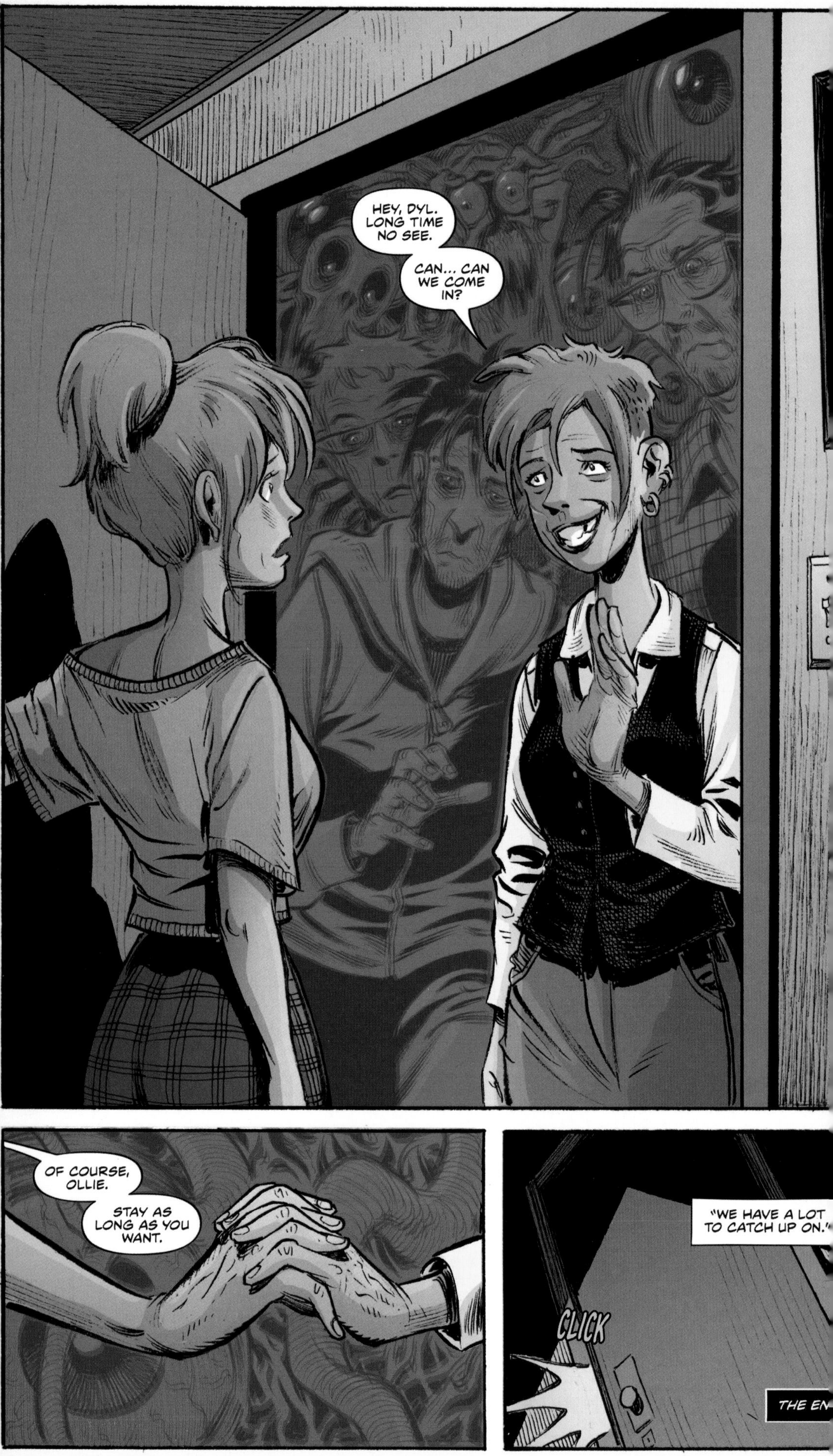
HEY, DYL. LONG TIME NO SEE.
CAN... CAN WE COME IN?
OF COURSE, OLLIE.
STAY AS LONG AS YOU WANT.
CLICK
"WE HAVE A LOT TO CATCH UP ON."
THE EN

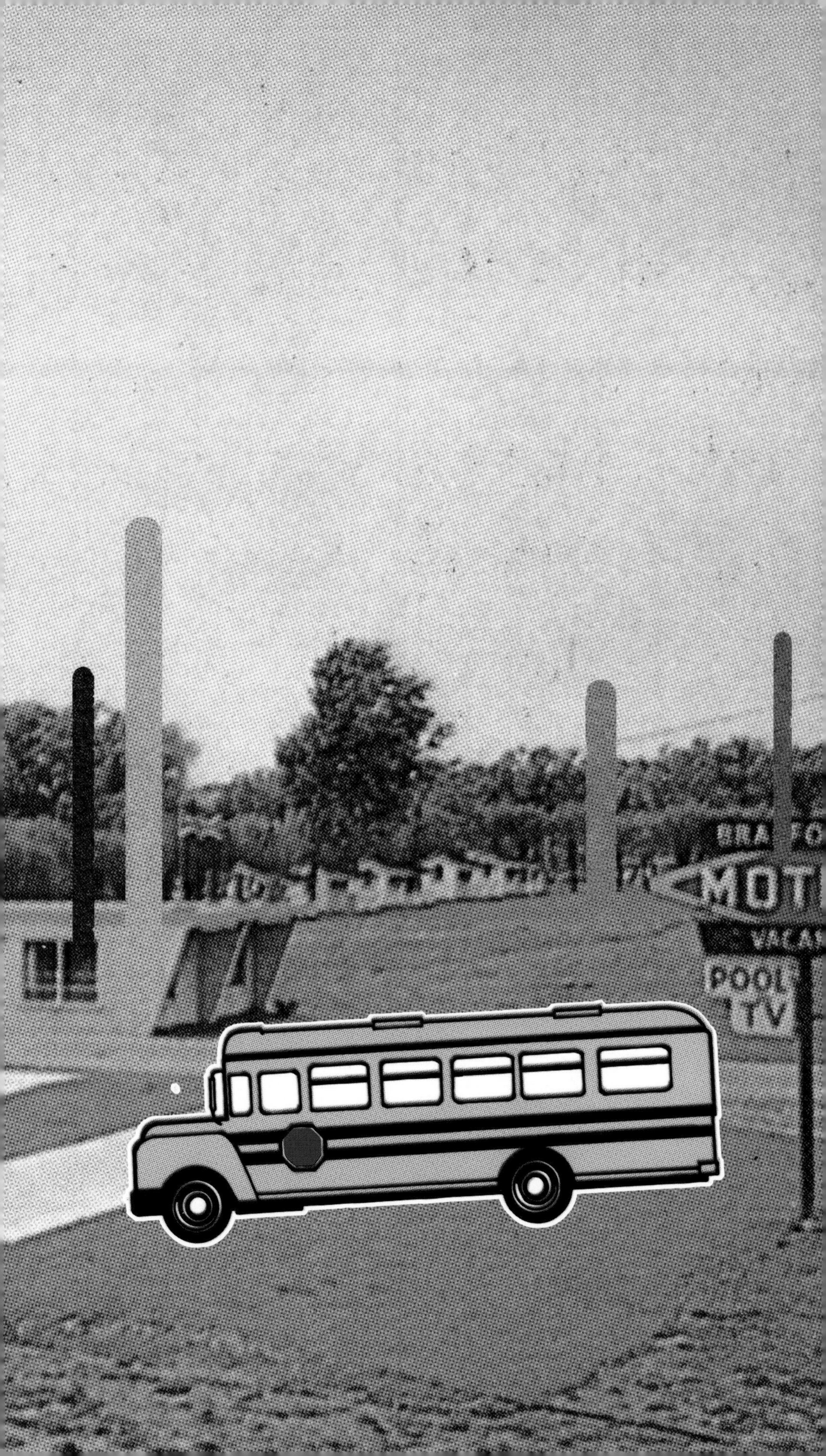
MOT
POOL
TV

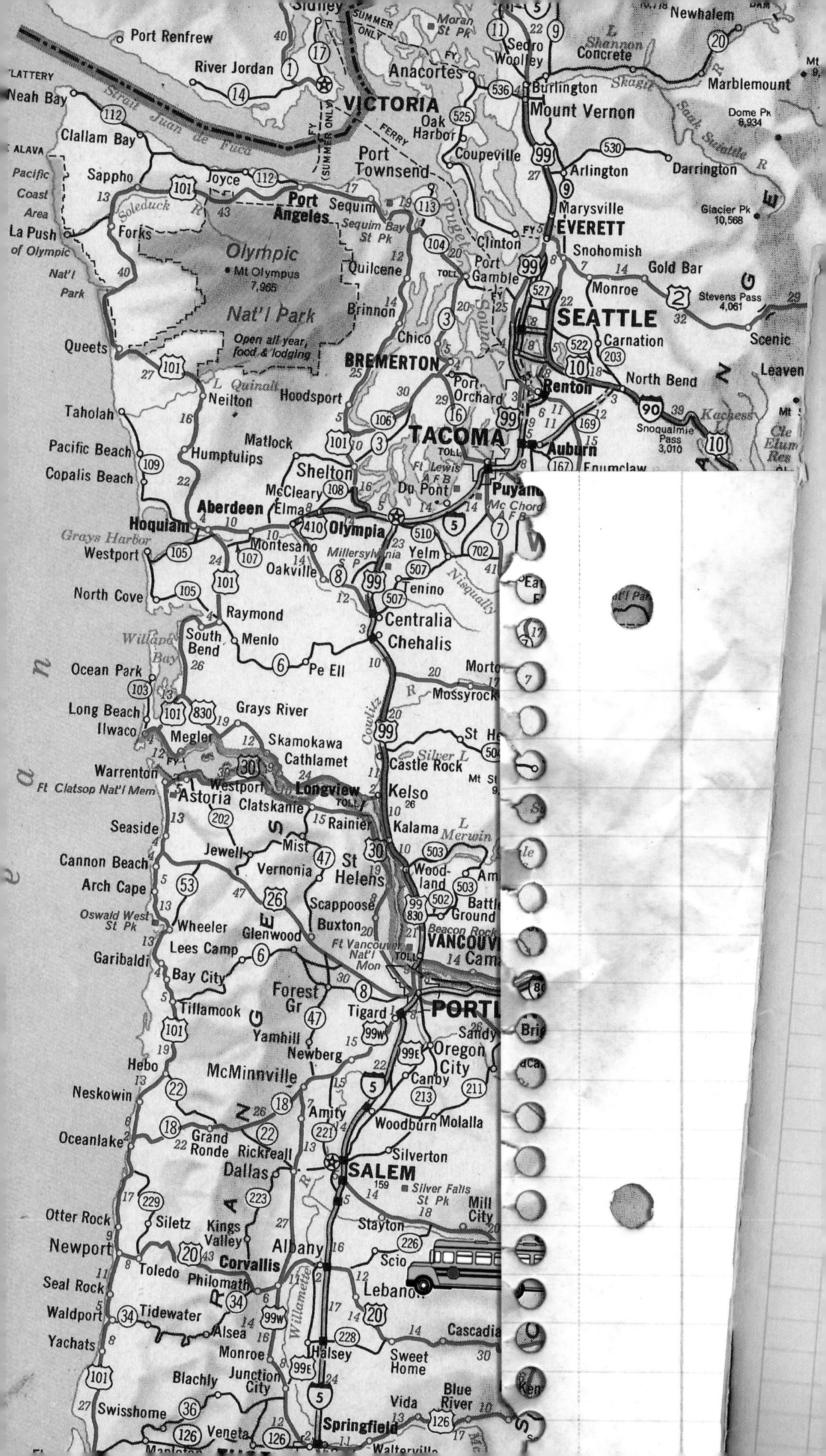

Port Renfrew • River Jordan ① ④⓪ 17

SUMMER ONLY
Moran St Pk
Newhalem
⑤ ⑪ ⑨ Sedro Woolley Concrete ⑳ DAM
Anacortes 536 Burlington Marblemount Mt 9,
LATTERY Neah Bay ⑭ Skagit Dome Pk 8,934
112 VICTORIA Oak Harbor 525 Mount Vernon Saaih Swiatlie R
Clallam Bay Coupeville 99 Arlington Darrington
Pacific Sappho 101 Joyce 112 Port Townsend 27 9 Marysville Glacier Pk 10,568
Coast 13 Soleduck R 43 Port Sequim 19 113 9 EVERETT
Area Angeles Sequim Bay St Pk Clinton Snohomish Gold Bar G
La Push Forks 104 Port 99 7 ⑭ Monroe ② Stevens Pass 4,061 29
of Olympic Olympic Mt Olympus 7,965 Quilcene 20 Gamble 527 Stevens Pass 32 Scenic
Nat'l Park 40 Brinnon 12 TOLL 3 SEATTLE N Leaven
Queets 101 Nat'l Park 3 Chico 522 203 Carnation
27 Open all year, food & lodging BREMERTON Port 4 99 8 522 North Bend
Taholah L Quinault 25 Orchard 8 10 18 Snoqualmie Pass 3,010 Kachess
Neilton Hoodsport 30 99 Renton 11 90 39
Pacific Beach 109 Matlock 101 106 16 TACOMA 99 169 Auburn 167 Enumclaw Cle Elum Res
Copalis Beach 22 Humptulips 3 Ft Lewis AFB Du Pont Puyallup Mc Chord F B 10
Hoquiam Aberdeen McCleary Elma 410 Olympia 510 5 7
Grays Harbor 4 10 108 16 14 702 41
Westport 105 107 Montesano Millersylvania Yelm 507
North Cove 105 24 Oakville 8 99 507 Tenino Nisqually
Raymond Centralia
Ocean Park 103 13 South Bend Menlo 6 Pe Ell 10 Chehalis 20 Morton
Long Beach 101 830 19 Grays River Mossyrock
Ilwaco 12 Megler 12 99 St H 50
Warrenton FY 30 Skamokawa Cathlamet Castle Rock Mt St 9
Ft Clatsop Nat'l Mem Westport 24 Longview Silver L
Astoria Clatskanie TOLL Kelso 26
Seaside 202 13 15 Rainier Kalama Merwin L
Cannon Beach Jewell Mist 47 30 503
Arch Cape 53 Vernonia St Helens 19 Woodland Am 503
Oswald West St Pk 47 26 Scappoose 99 502 Battle
Wheeler Glenwood Buxton 830 Ground
Garibaldi Lees Camp 6 Ft Vancouver Nat'l Mon VANCOUVER Cama
Bay City 30 8 14
Tillamook 101 Forest Gr PORTL
101 47 Tigard Sandy
Yamhill Newberg 15 99W Bri
McMinnville 22 99E Oregon City aCa
18 Canby 211
Neskowin 13 26 Amity 5 213 Molalla
Oceanlake 18 Grand Ronde 22 221 Woodburn
22 Rickreall 13 Silverton
Dallas SALEM Silver Falls St Pk
17 229 Siletz Kings Valley 27 159 Mill City
Otter Rock Stayton 18
Newport 20 43 Corvallis Albany 226 20
Seal Rock Toledo Philomath Scio
Waldport 34 Tidewater 34 Lebanon 12
Yachats Alsea 99W 14 20 Cascadia
101 Monroe 228 14 Sweet Home 30
Blachly Junction City 99E Blue River
Swisshome 36 Veneta 5 Vida
126 126 Springfield Walterville

Tonasket
Sherman Pass 5,575
Evans
Tiger
Nordman
Bonners Ferry 1,773
Naples
Republic
Kettle Falls
Colville
Winthrop
Riverside
Omak
Callspell Pk 6,837
Priest L
Colburn
Rice
Coulee Dam
Addy
Cusick
Sandpoint
Kootenai
Hope
Okanogan
Inchelium
Gifford
Nat l Rec Area
Chewelah
Franklin D Roosevelt L
Nespelem
Columbia R
Newport
Priest River
Clark
Pend Oreille L
Brewster
Keller
Loon Lake
Pateros
Coulee Dam
Hunters
Springdale
Bridgeport
CHIEF JOSEPH DAM
GRAND COULEE DAM
FREE FY
Ford
Deer Park
Spirit Lake
Athol
Miles
Pend Oreille R
Sanpoil
Okanogan
Rathdrum

THIS HANDY CHART TO RECORD YOUR TRIP EXPENSES

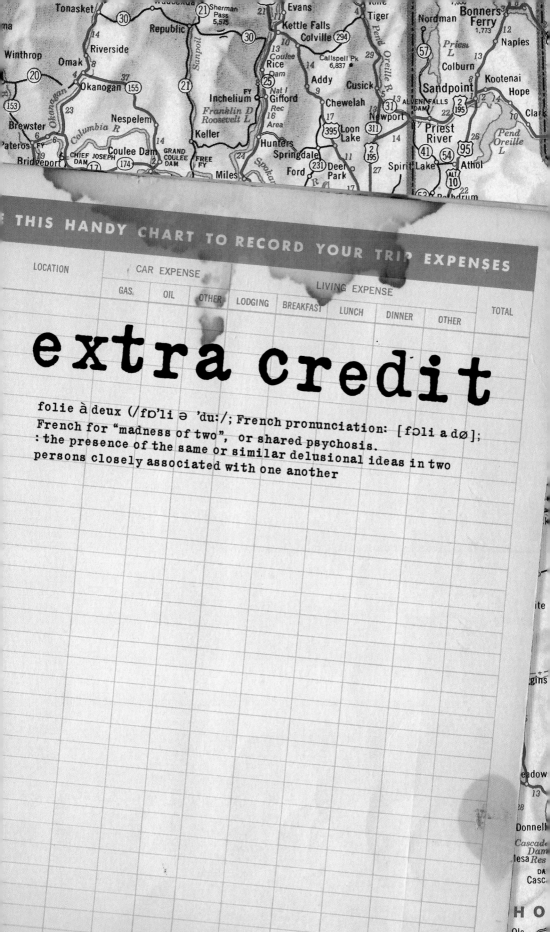

LOCATION	CAR EXPENSE			LIVING EXPENSE						TOTAL
	GAS	OIL	OTHER	LODGING	BREAKFAST	LUNCH	DINNER	OTHER		

extra credit

folie à deux (/fɒ'li ə 'du:/; French pronunciation: [fɔli a dø];
French for "madness of two", or shared psychosis.
: the presence of the same or similar delusional ideas in two persons closely associated with one another

HOUSE AMOK #1 variant cover by Tony Sandoval

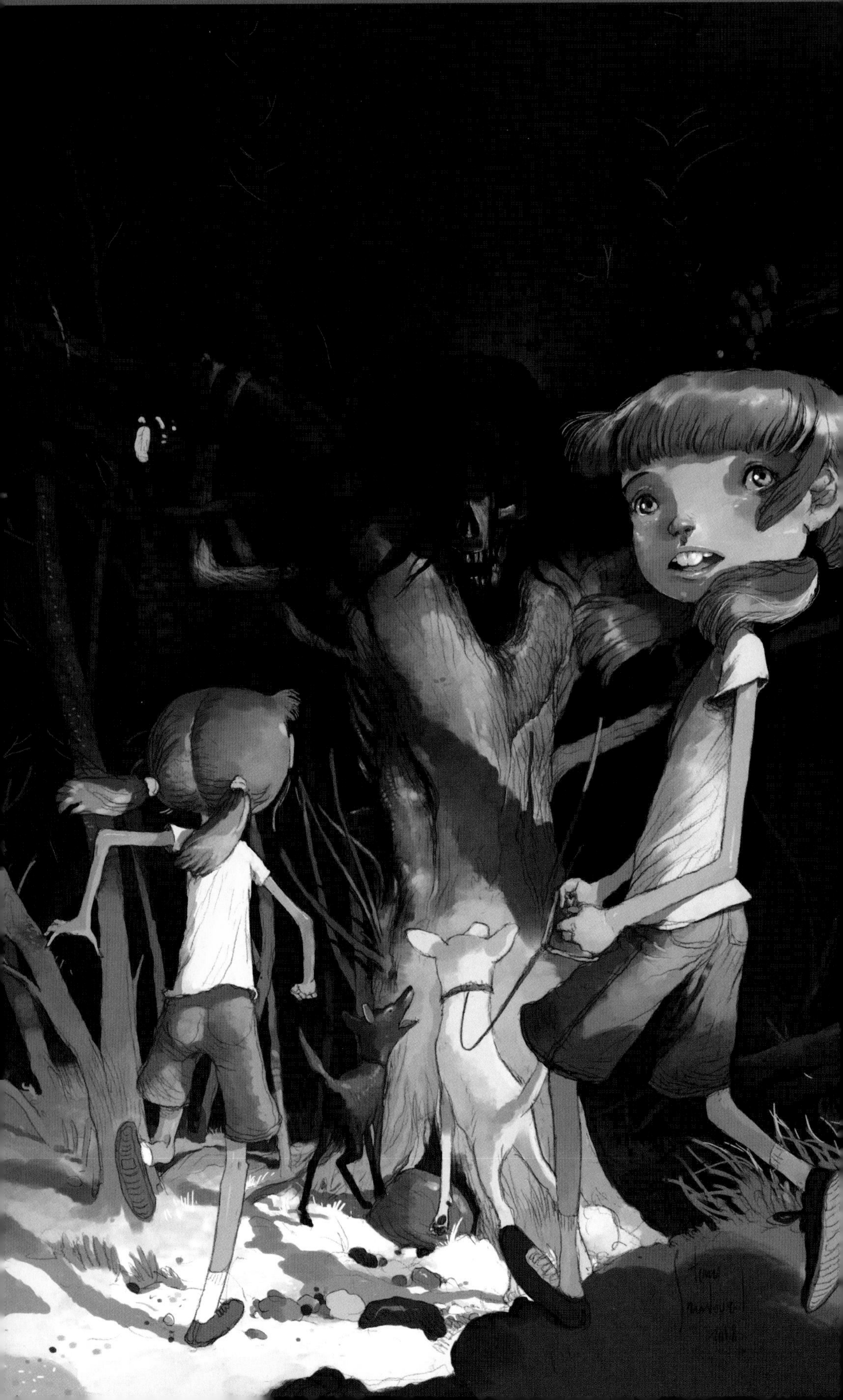

HOUSE AMOK #2 variant cover by Caitlin Yarsky

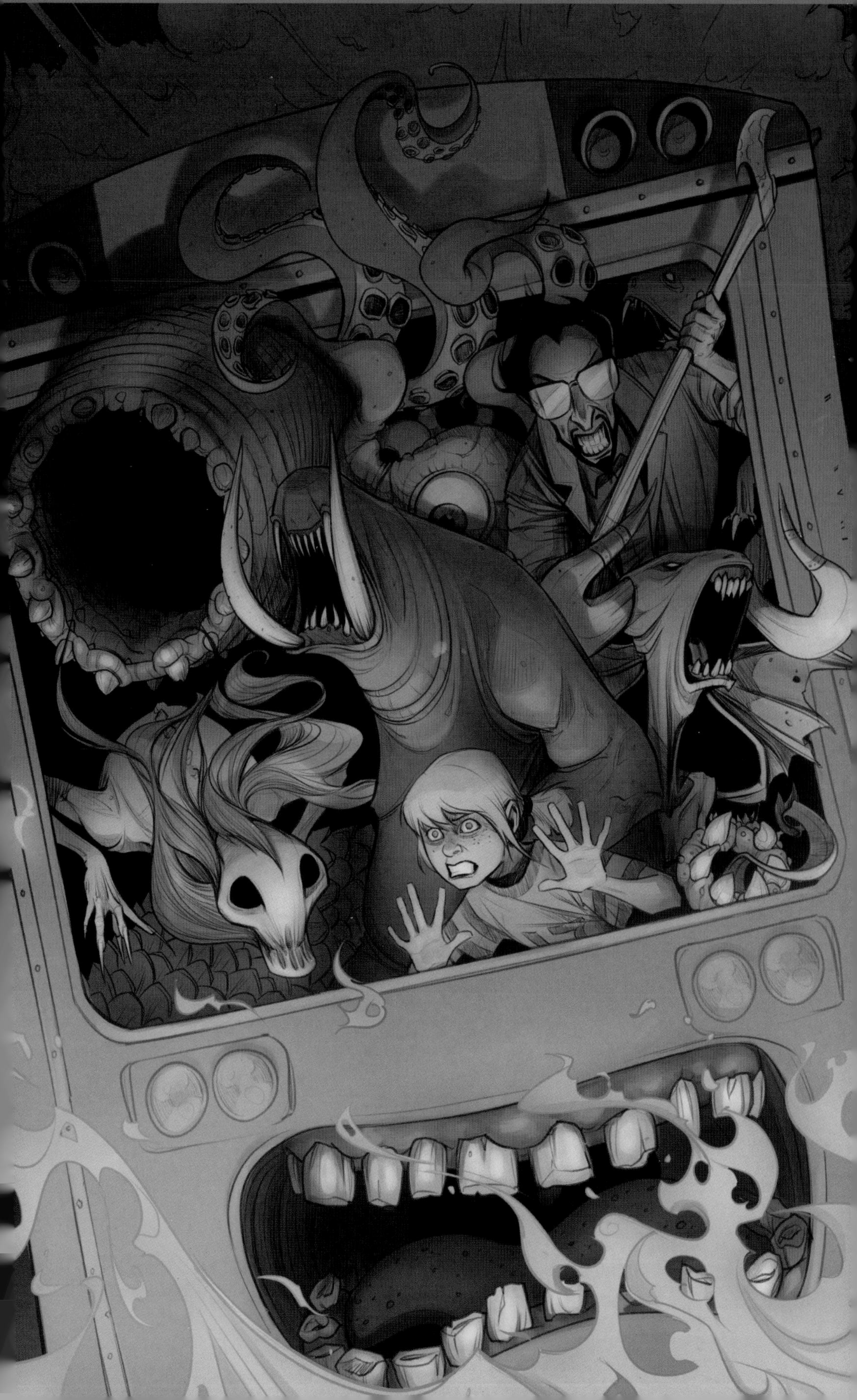

HOUSE AMOK #3 variant cover by Jonathan Edwards

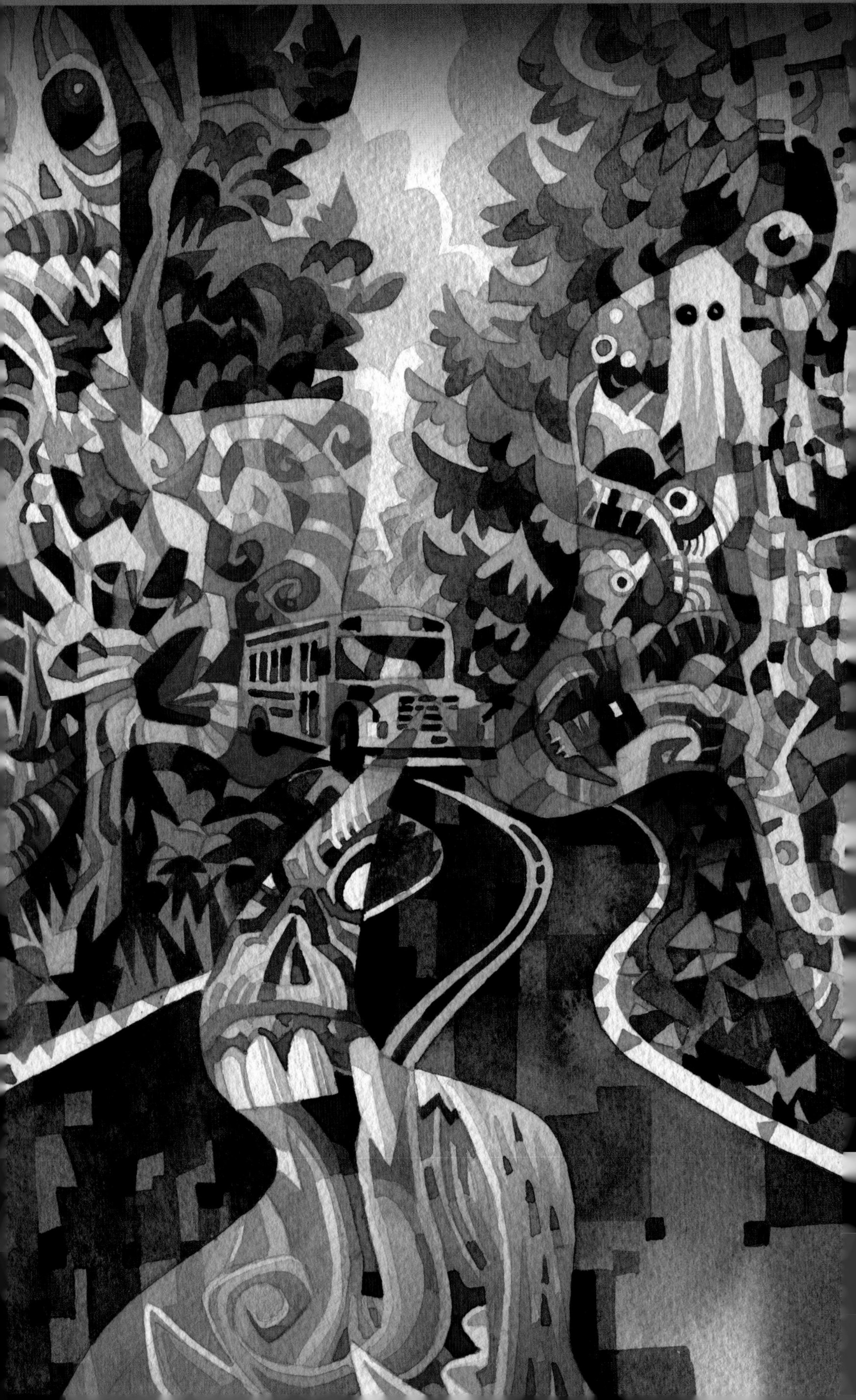

HOUSE AMOK #4 variant cover by Dilraj Mann

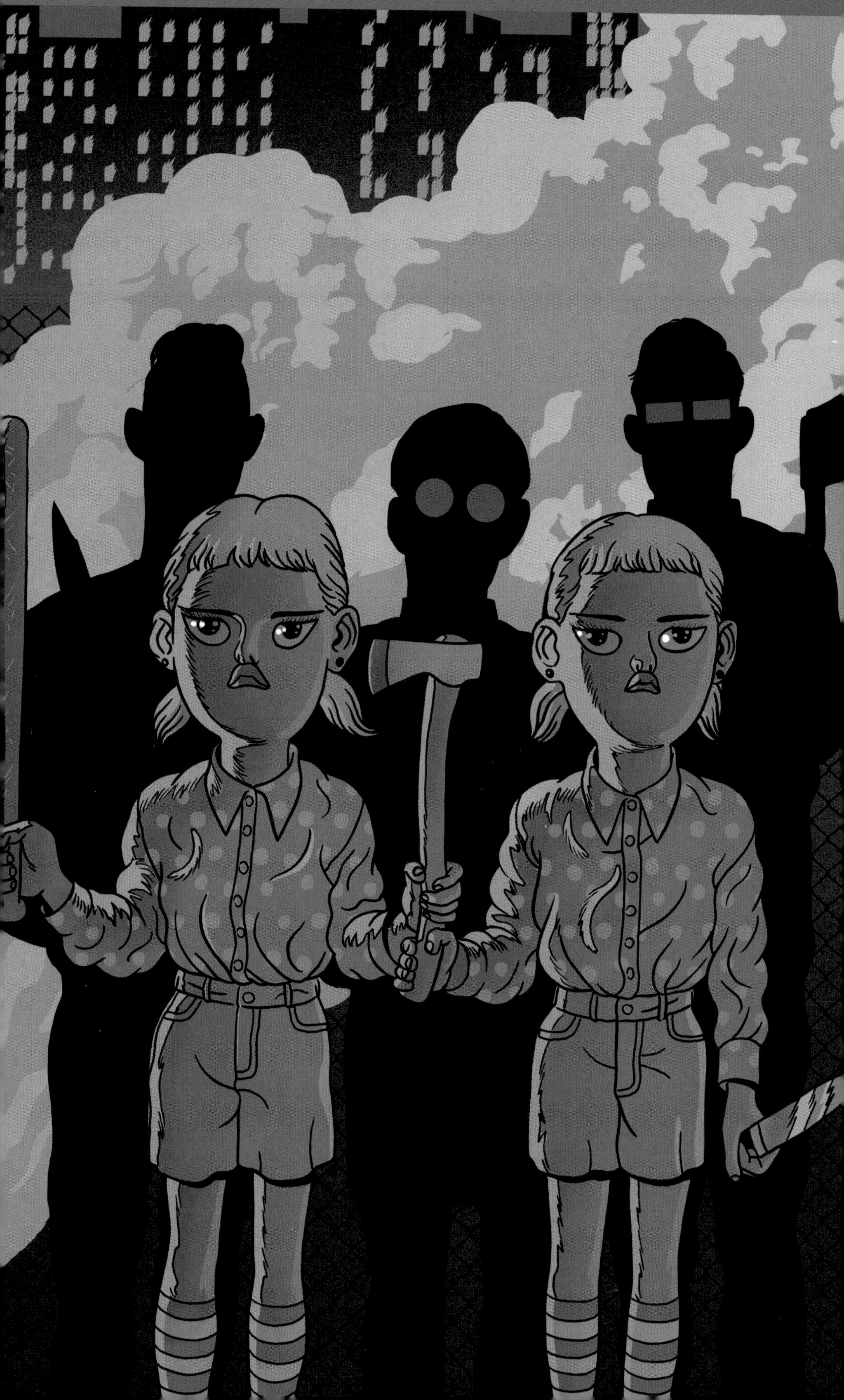

HOUSE AMOK #5 variant cover
by Gabriel Rodriguez and Tamra Bonvillain

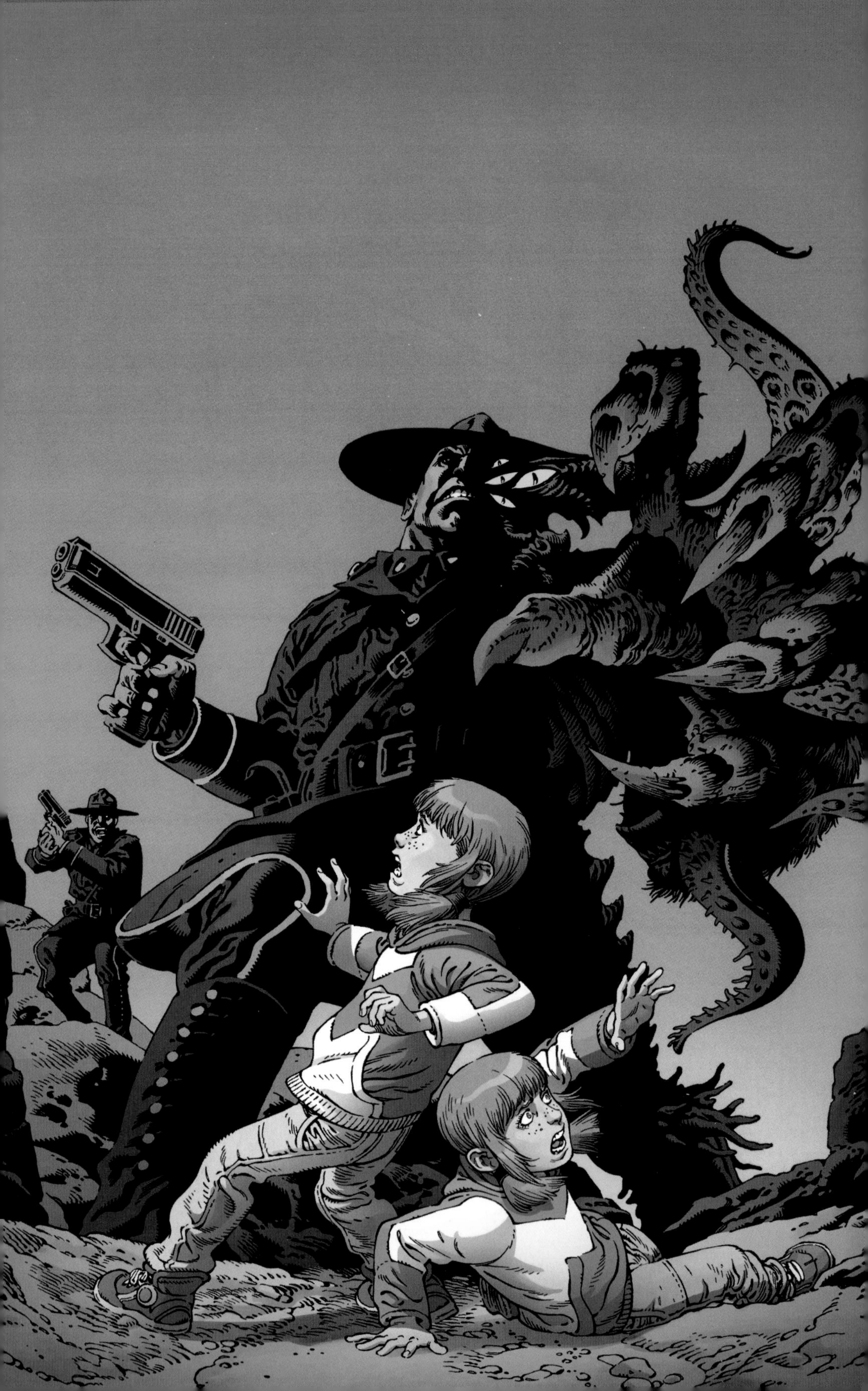

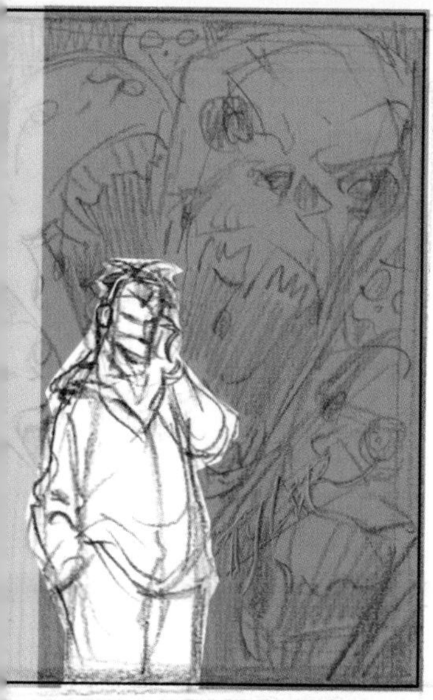

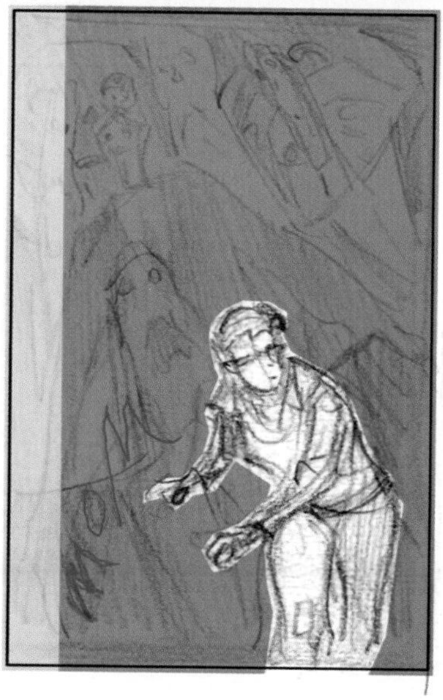

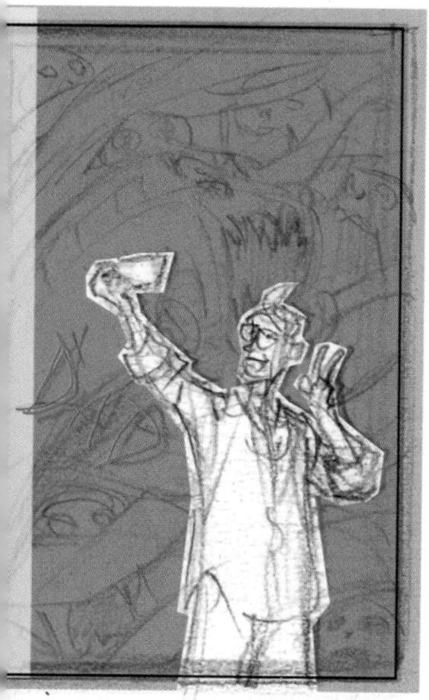

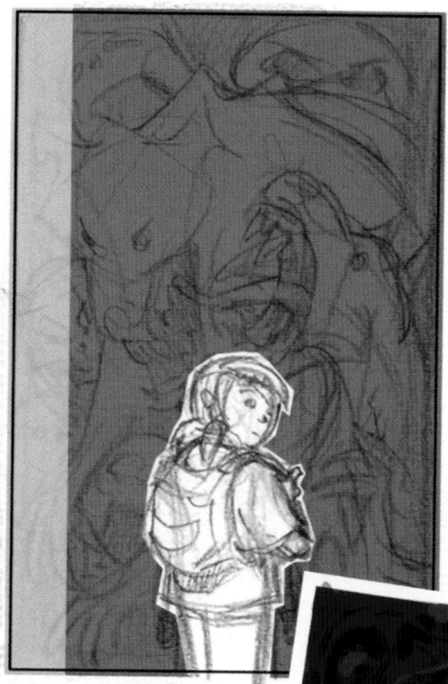

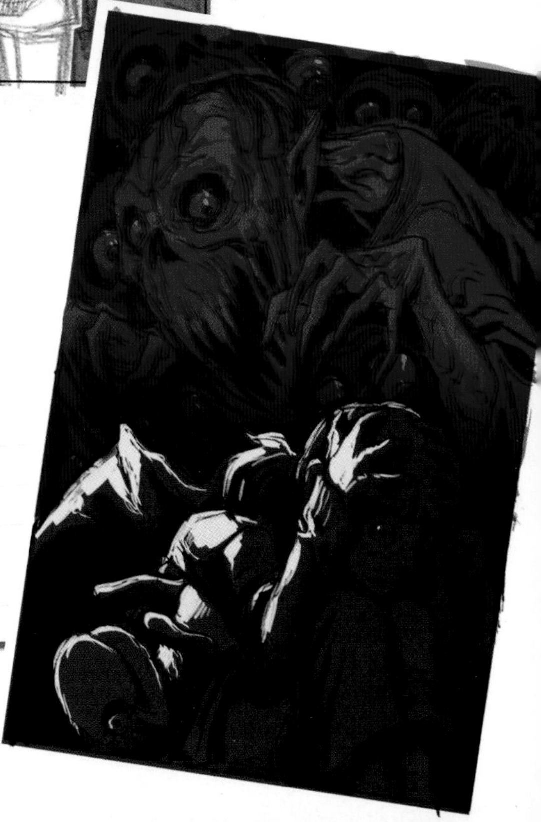

Early cover roughs by
Shawn McManus

From the original HOUSE AMOK series proposal by Christopher Sebela:

"The Sandifers were a calm, centered family of five until they began to be persecuted by Reality Adjusters, agents in charge of changing small pieces of reality, like going back and changing it so that the "Berenstein" everyone remembers is now spelled "Berenstain", destroying all traces of a Sinbad film called "Shazam"-- tiny tweaks that butterfly-effect into huge changes that sweep the world in the direction the cabal wants it to go."

"Ollie and Dylan are 10-year-old fraternal twin sisters who have similar haircuts and dress somewhat alike, a family within a family sharing a secret bond and language none of the others understand."

"Tyler is 16, starting to get anxious and wanting to roam at a time when his family has been thrown closer together than ever, moving out to the middle of nowhere and turning him into a prisoner right as his life was getting started."

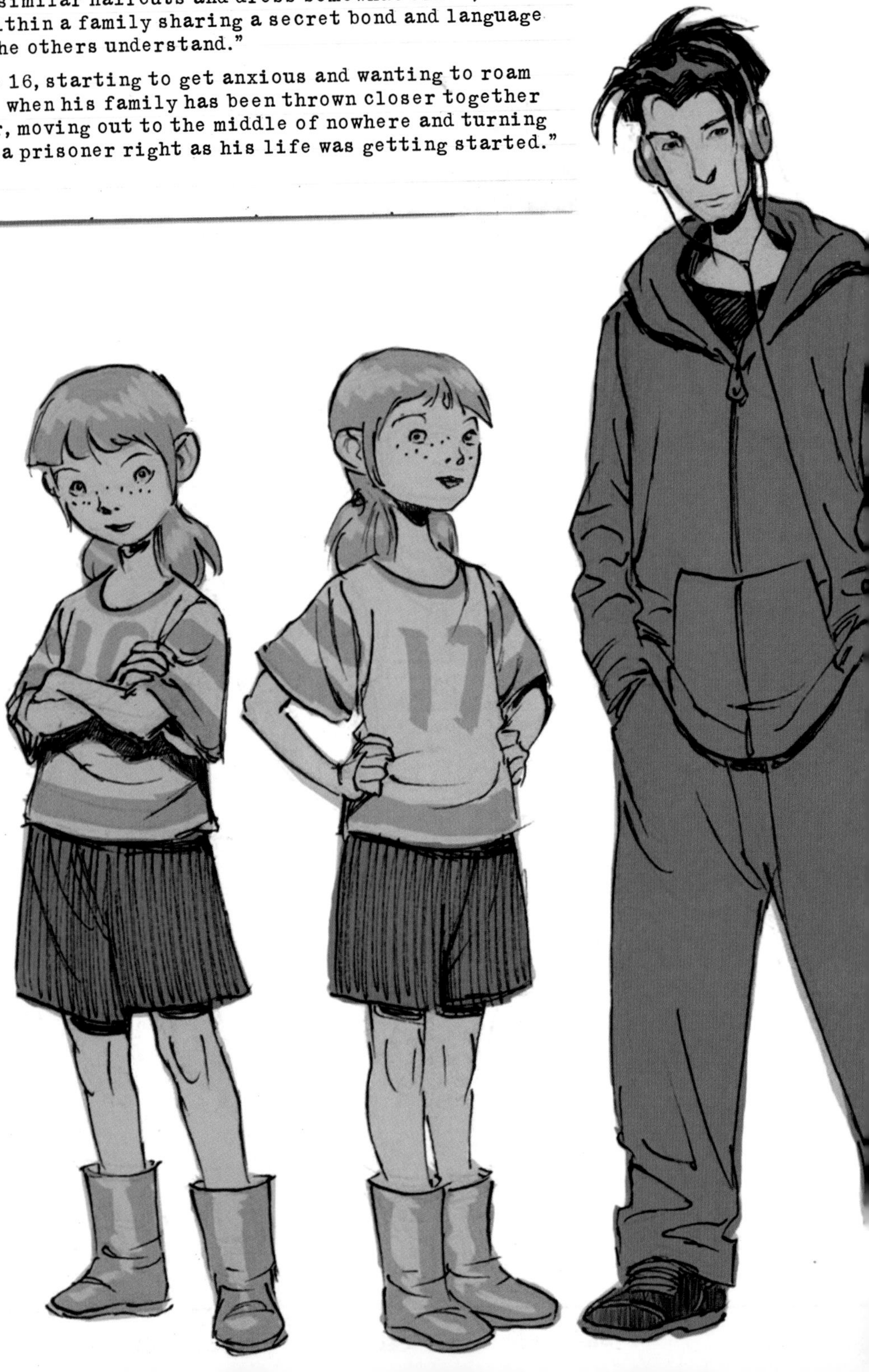

“George is the dad, a blogger who has made the Sandifers mildly Internet famous as he documents his life home-schooling the twins, retrofitting an old school bus as a home for a family of five, mining his family for content to keep comments and revenues coming.”

“Karen is the mother and breadwinner, an accountant who handles the books for every small business, farm, and landowner in the Oregon Valley; a woman who brooks no judgment in doing what’s right for her family.”

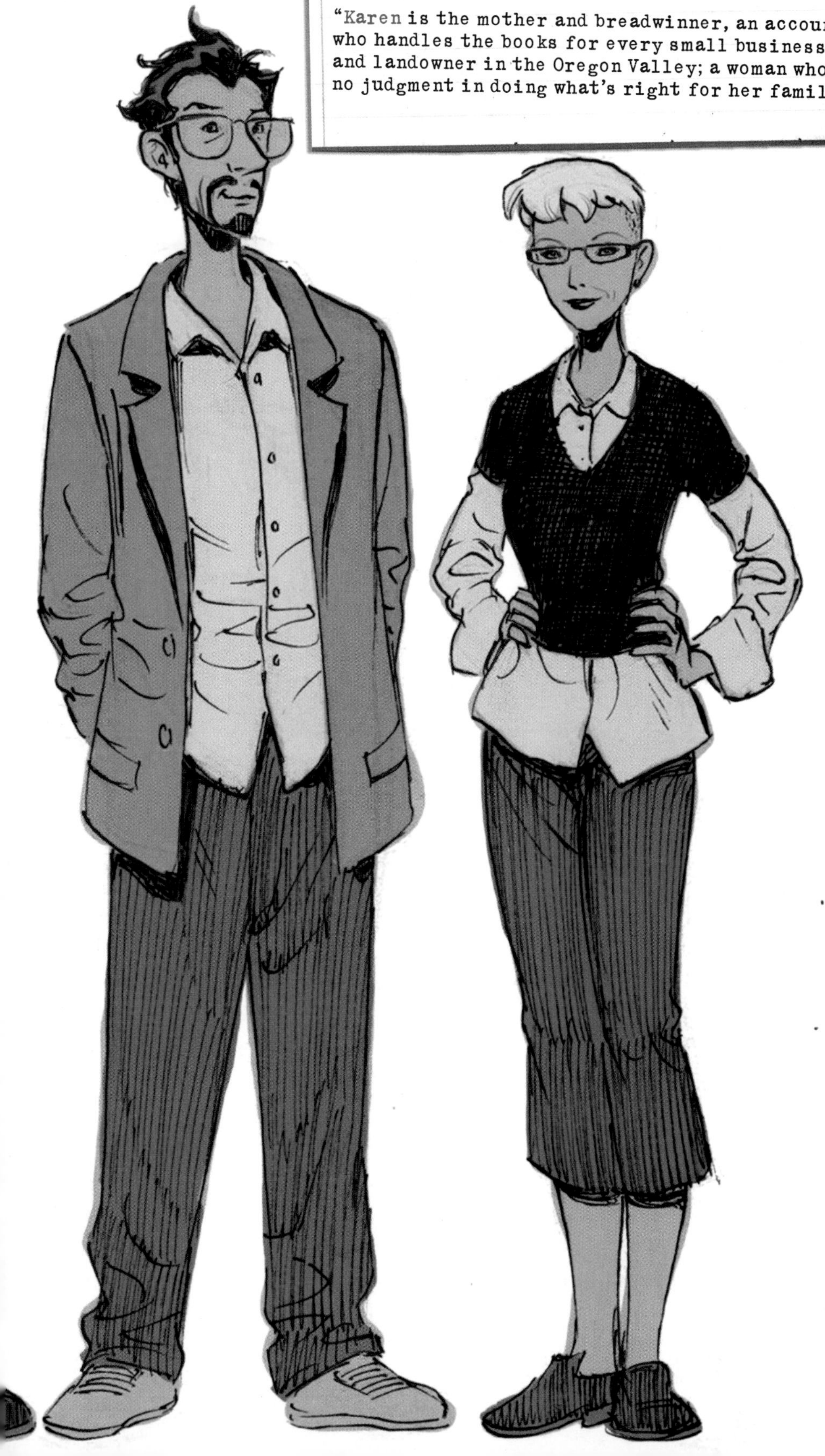

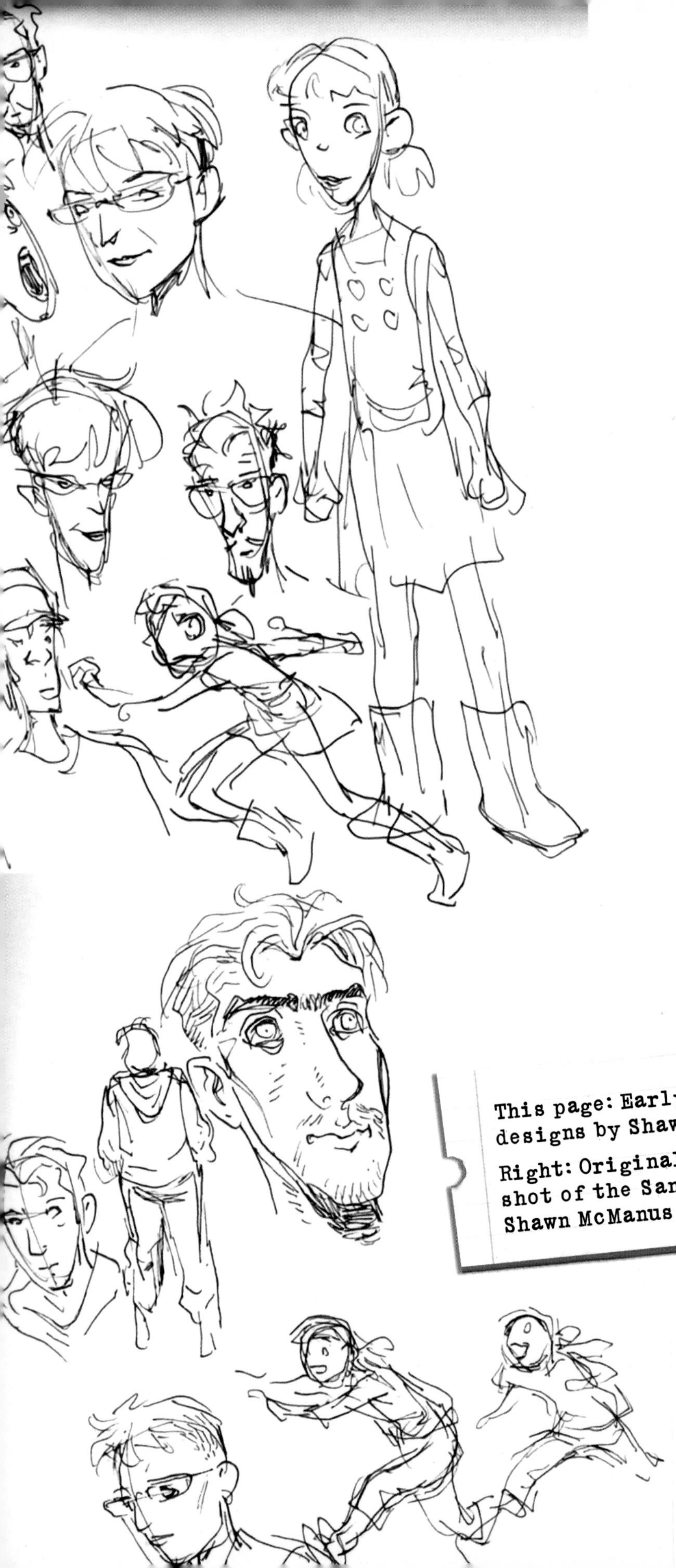

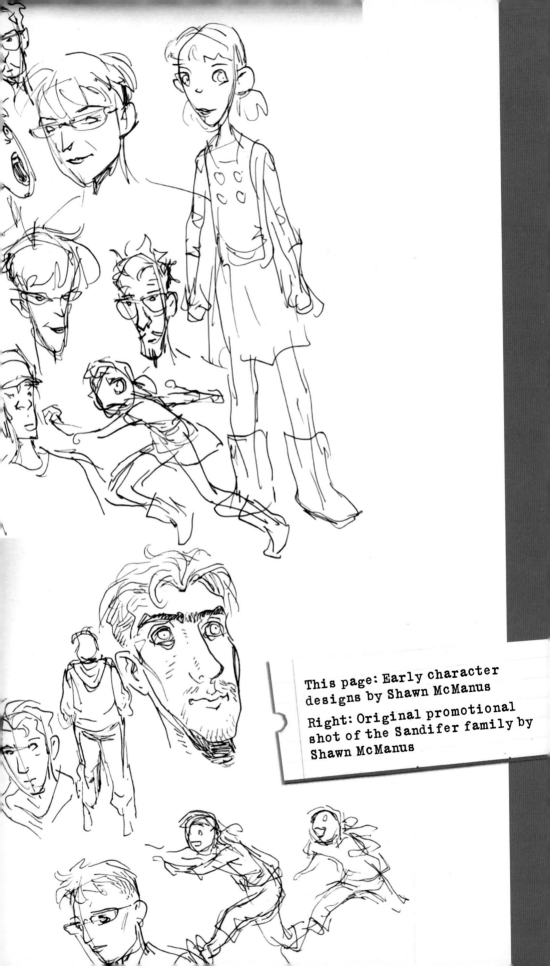

This page: Early character designs by Shawn McManus

Right: Original promotional shot of the Sandifer family by Shawn McManus

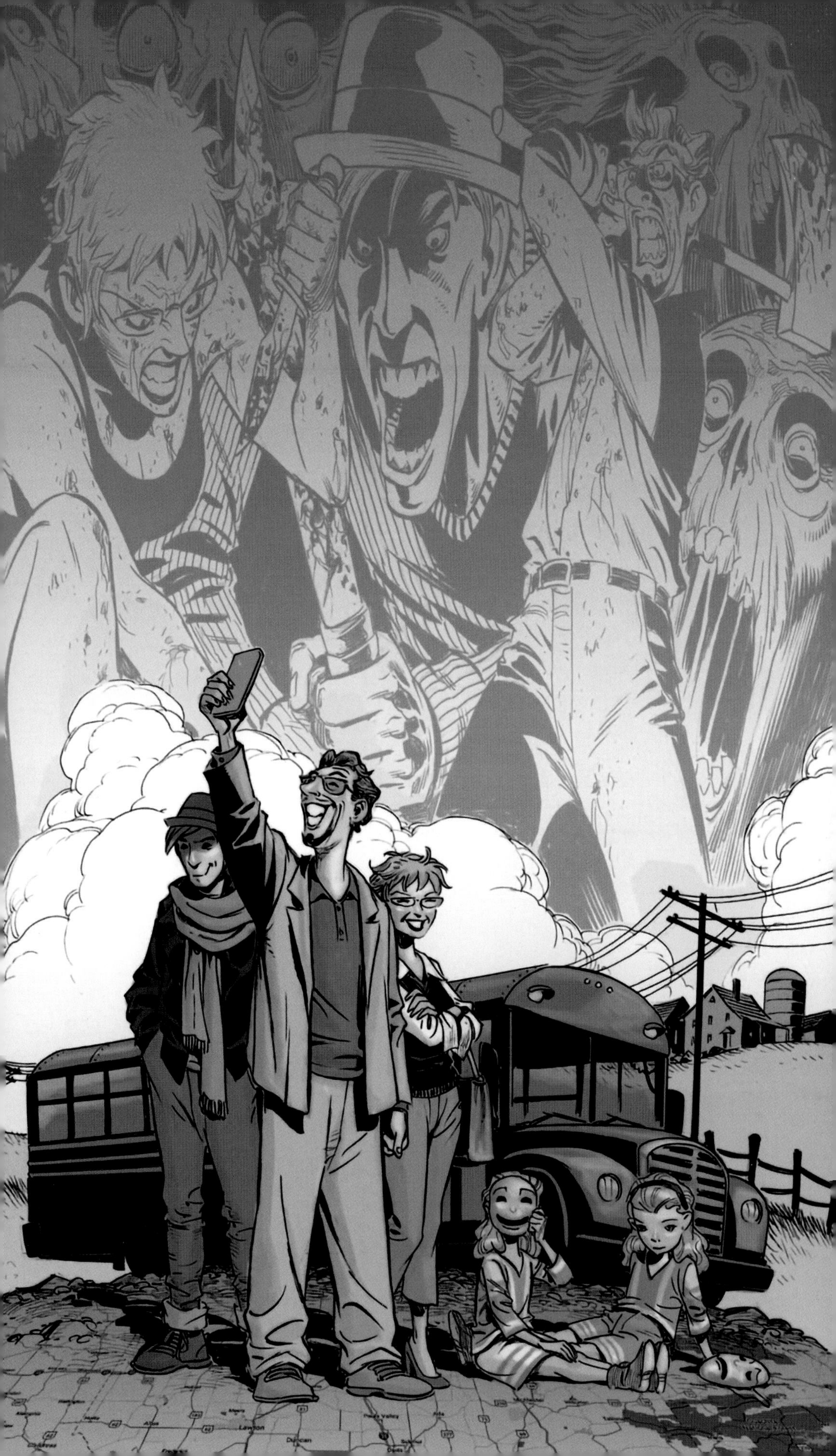

TOUR GUIDES

CHRISTOPHER SEBELA

is a two-time Eisner-nominated writer, designer and publisher living in Portland, Oregon. He's the co-creator of *Crowded*, *Shanghai Red*, *High Crimes*, *Heartthrob*, *We(l)come Back*, *Dead Letters*, *Short Order Crooks* and *The Death Defying*. He also writes things in other people's sandboxes sometimes. He is catnip for weirdos, father to a blockheaded dog named Zola, consumer of toxic amounts of coffee, and a fan of horror movies since he was a little kid.

SHAWN McMANUS

is an American artist who has worked extensiv over three decades, notably for DC's origin Vertigo imprint on *The Sandman* and *Fables* seri When he's not watching episodes of *Curb Y Enthusiasm* or *Baskets* or admiring the magic Frank Godwin's line work, he can be found chain to his drawing board trying to meet a deadline.

LEE LOUGHRIDGE

is the colorist on HOUSE AMOK, EUTHANAUTS and KID LOBOTOMY.

ADITYA BIDIKAR

is BLACK CROWN's esteemed house letterer and the recipient of Broken Frontier's 2017 & 2018 Best Letterer Award. He designed the fonts and lettered the first two issues of HOUSE AMOK. Based in India, Adi also letters *Motor Crush* and *Grafity's Wall*. @adityab adityab.net.

NEIL UYETAKE

is the letterer of HOUSE AM issues 3, 4 and 5.

MEGAN BROWN

is an Assistant Editor and BLACK CROWN's San Diego connection. When she's not racking up a tab at the Black Crown Pub, you can find her at one of the coffee shops around town, perfecting the art of being a struggling writer.
@megan_mb

CHASE MAROTZ

is the Associate Editor of BLACK CROWN.
A self-proclaimed "Johnny-on-the-spot," he provides much-needed eyes, ears, hands and feet between the Los Angeles-based BCHQ and the IDW mothership in San Diego.
@thrillothechase

SHELLY BOND

is the editor and curator BLACK CROWN. Driven to e + curate comic books, cr deadlines and innovate for o a quarter-century, Bond li in Los Angeles with husba Philip, son Spencer, five guit a drum kit and one thousand pens.
@sxbond @blackcrownhq

TALOGUE

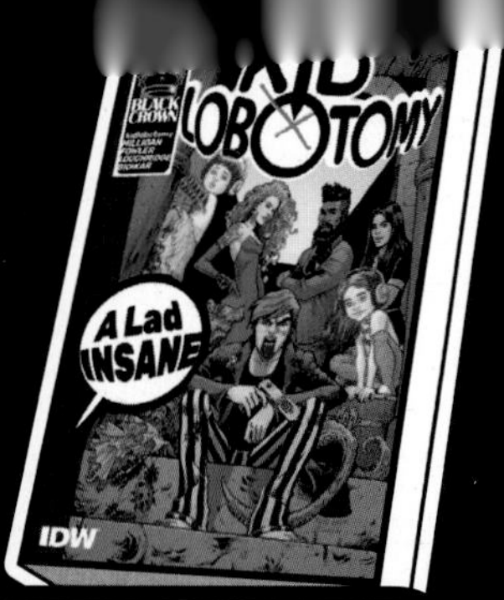
KID LOBOTOMY
A Lad INSANE
IDW

KID LOBOTOMY
Almost Rockstar. Awkward Hotelier. Definitive Madman.
by Peter Milligan + Tess Fowler

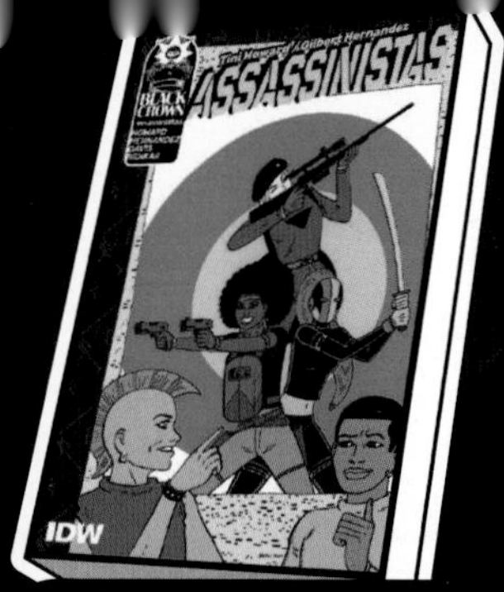
Tini Howard / Gilbert Hernandez
ASSASSINISTAS
IDW

ASSASSINISTAS
Modern Family. Retro Sass. Highly Trained to Kick Your Ass.
by Tini Howard + Gilbert Hernandez

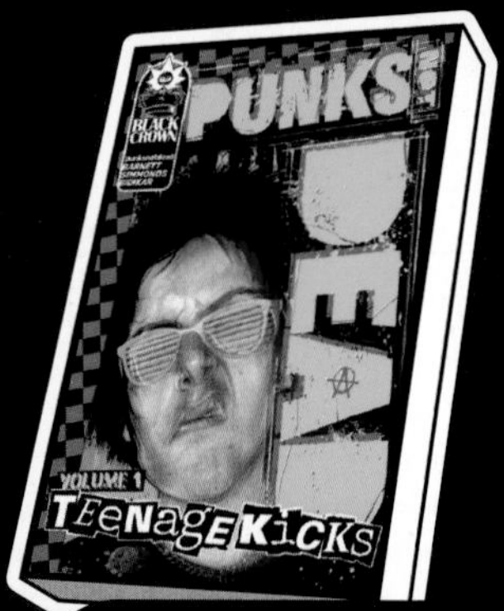
PUNKS NOT DEAD
VOLUME 1
TEENAGE KICKS

PUNKS NOT DEAD
The Ghost. The Geek. The Geriatric Mod Superspy. Everything & the Bollocks
by David Barnett + Martin Simmonds

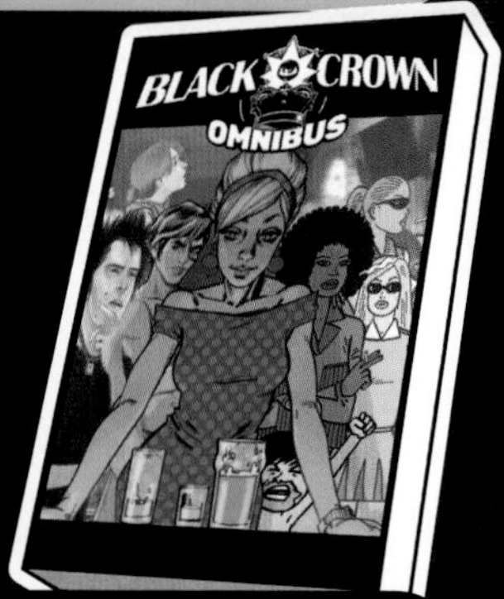
BLACK CROWN
OMNIBUS

BLACK CROWN OMNIBUS
The Compendium of Comics, Culture & Cool featuring Tales from the BC Pub.
by Rob Davis, CUD + others

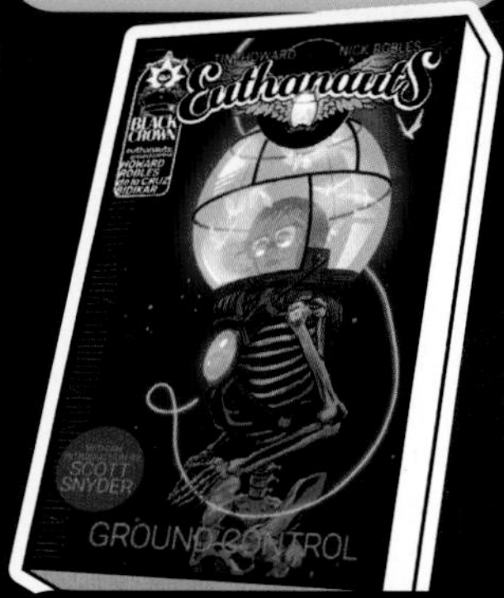
Euthanauts
SCOTT SNYDER
GROUND CONTROL

EUTHANAUTS
Tethers to the Great Beyond. Psychonautic Mindspaces.
by Tini Howard + Nick Robles

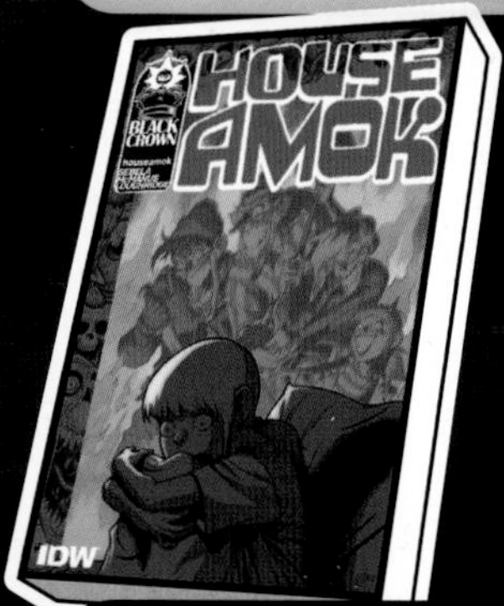
HOUSE AMOK
IDW

HOUSE AMOK
Conspiracy theories come to life. Shared Family Madness & Murder.
by Christopher Sebela + Shawn McManus

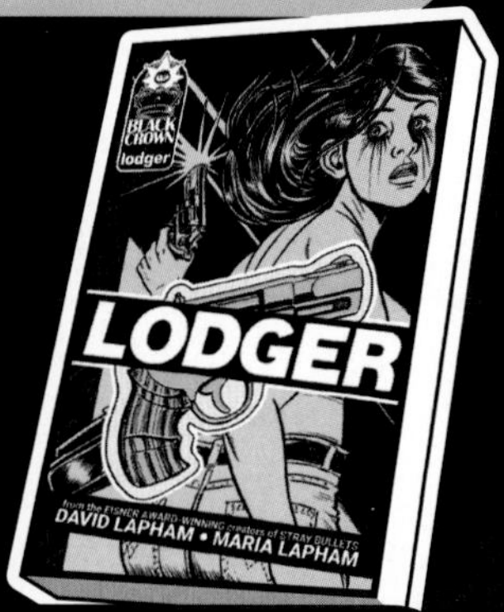
LODGER
DAVID LAPHAM • MARIA LAPHAM

LODGER
A serial killer hides in plain sight as a travel blogger in a game of cat & mouse.
By The Laphams of Stray Bullets

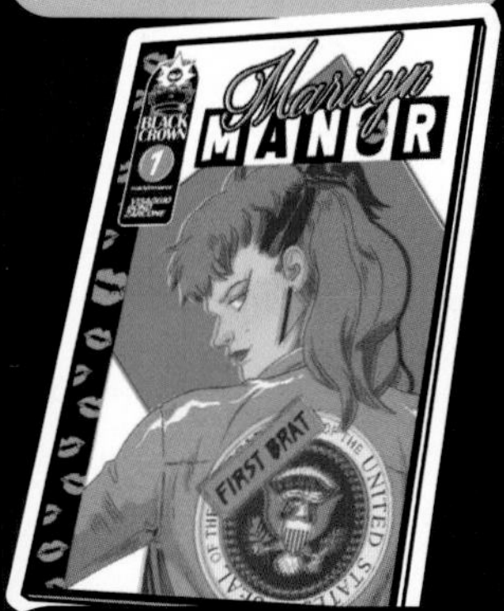
Marilyn MANOR
FIRST BRAT

MARILYN MANOR
It's 1981 and the President's daughter throws a rager in the White House!
by Mags Visaggio + Marley Zarcone

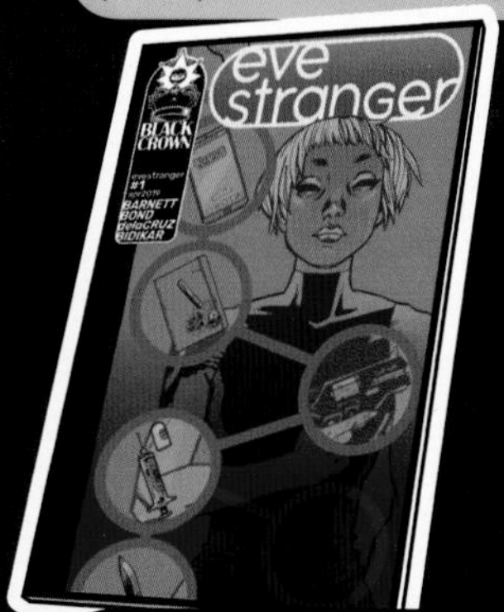
eve stranger

EVE STRANGER
High-Octane Thrills! Weird Science! Doomed Romance!
by David Barnett + Philip Bond

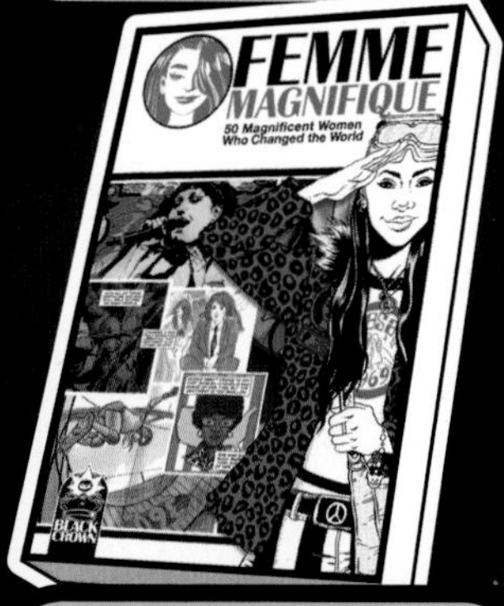
FEMME MAGNIFIQUE
50 Magnificent Women Who Changed the World

FEMME MAGNIFIQUE
A salute to personal icons who shatter ceilings in pop, politics, art & science.
by 100+ A-list writers & artists

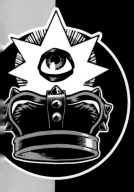

blackcrown.pub
@blackcrownhq

#therulingclass

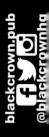

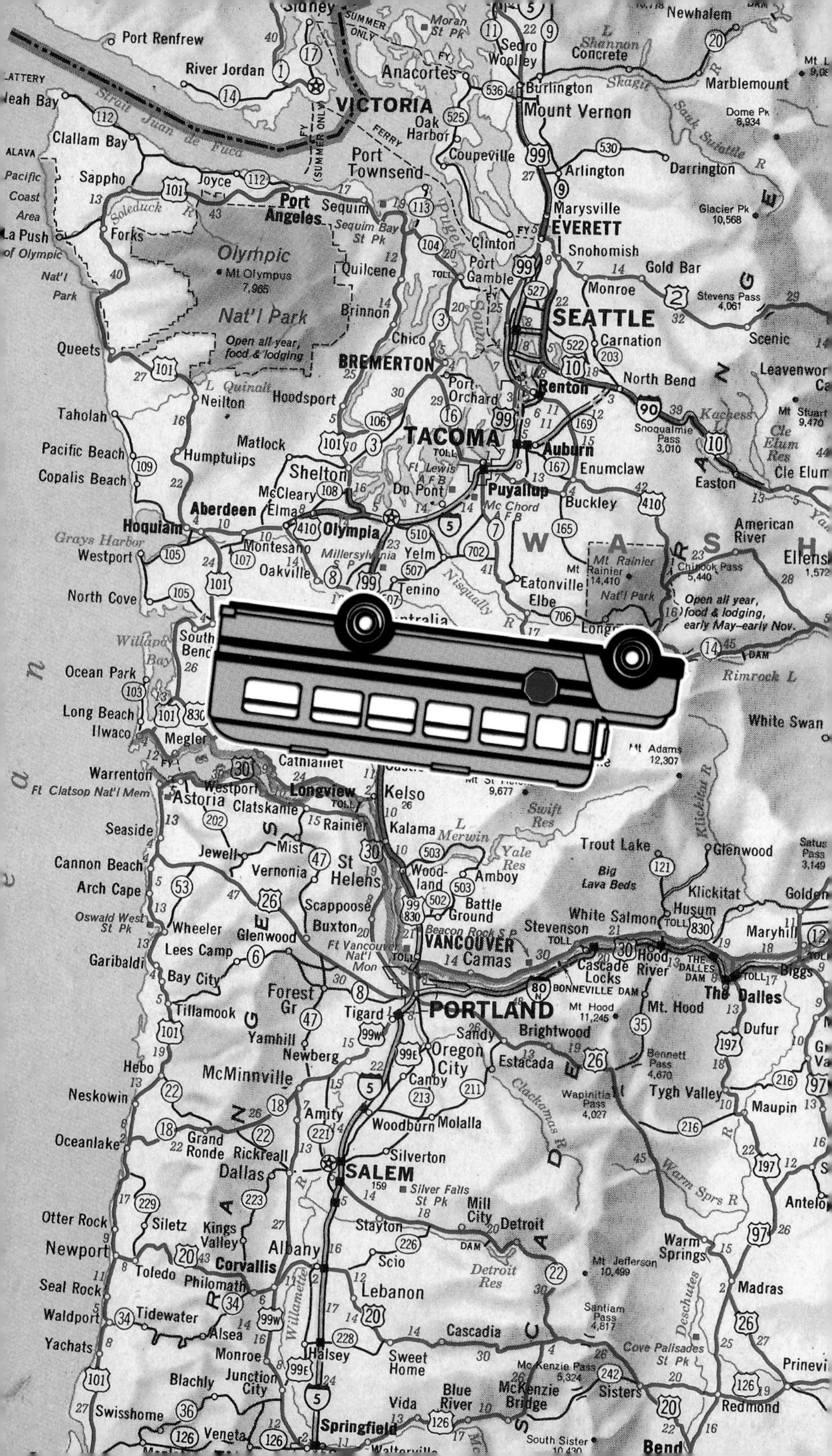

Newhalem
Port Renfrew
River Jordan
Sidney
SUMMER ONLY
Moran St Pk
Sedro Woolley
Shannon
Concrete
Anacortes
Burlington
Skagit
Marblemount
VICTORIA
Oak Harbor
Mount Vernon
Dome Pk 8,934
Neah Bay
Strait of Juan de Fuca
FERRY
(SUMMER ONLY)
Clallam Bay
Coupeville
Port Townsend
Arlington
Darrington
Sauk
Suiattle R
Pacific Coast Area
Sappho
Joyce
Port Angeles
Sequim
Marysville
EVERETT
Glacier Pk 10,568
La Push
Soleduck R
Forks
Sequim Bay St Pk
Puget
Clinton
Snohomish
Olympic
Mt Olympus 7,965
Quilcene
Port Gamble
Gold Bar
of Olympic Nat'l Park
Nat'l Park
Monroe
Stevens Pass 4,061
Brinnon
Sound
SEATTLE
Carnation
Queets
Open all year, food & lodging
Chico
Scenic
BREMERTON
Leavenworth
L Quinault
Neilton
Hoodsport
Port Orchard
Renton
North Bend
Taholah
Snoqualmie Pass 3,010
Kachess
Mt Stuart 9,470
Cle Elum Res
TACOMA
Matlock
Auburn
Pacific Beach
Humptulips
Ft Lewis A F B
Enumclaw
Cle Elum
Copalis Beach
Shelton
McCleary
Du Pont
Puyallup
Easton
Aberdeen
Elma
Mc Chord A F B
Buckley
Hoquiam
Olympia
American River
Grays Harbor
Montesano
Millersylvania S P
Yelm
W A S H
Westport
Mt Rainier 14,410
Mt Rainier Nat'l Park
Chinook Pass 5,440
Oakville
Tenino
Nisqually
Eatonville
North Cove
Elbe
Open all year, food & lodging early May–early Nov.
Willapa Bay
South Bend
DAM
Rimrock L
Ocean Park
Long Beach
White Swan
Ilwaco
Megler
Mt Adams 12,307
Cathlamet
Warrenton
Ft Clatsop Nat'l Mem
Westport
Longview
Kelso
Mt St Helens 9,677
Astoria
Clatskanie
Swift Res
Seaside
Rainier
Kalama
L Merwin
Trout Lake
Glenwood
Satus Pass 3,149
Jewell
Mist
Yale Res
Cannon Beach
Vernonia
St Helens
Wood-land
Amboy
Big Lava Beds
Arch Cape
Klickitat
Goldendale
Oswald West St Pk
Scappoose
Battle Ground
Husum
White Salmon
Wheeler
Buxton
Beacon Rock S P
Stevenson
Maryhill
Glenwood
VANCOUVER
Ft Vancouver Nat'l Mon
Lees Camp
Camas
Cascade Locks
Hood River
Garibaldi
THE DALLES DAM
Biggs
Bay City
Forest Gr
BONNEVILLE DAM
The Dalles
Tillamook
PORTLAND
Mt Hood 11,245
Mt. Hood
Tigard
Sandy
Brightwood
Dufur
Yamhill
Newberg
Oregon City
Estacada
Bennett Pass 4,670
Hebo
McMinnville
Canby
Tygh Valley
Neskowin
Clackamas R
Wapinitia Pass 4,027
Maupin
Amity
Woodburn
Molalla
Oceanlake
Grand Ronde
Rickreall
Silverton
Dallas
SALEM
Warm Sprs R
Silver Falls St Pk
Antelope
Otter Rock
Siletz
Kings Valley
Stayton
Mill City
Detroit
Warm Springs
Newport
Albany
Scio
DAM
Toledo
Corvallis
Detroit Res
Mt Jefferson 10,499
Seal Rock
Philomath
Lebanon
Madras
Waldport
Tidewater
Alsea
Willamette
Santiam Pass 4,817
Deschutes
Yachats
Cascadia
Cove Palisades St Pk
Monroe
Halsey
Sweet Home
Mc Kenzie Pass 5,324
Prineville
Blachly
Junction City
Blue River
McKenzie Bridge
Sisters
Vida
Redmond
Swisshome
Springfield
Veneta
South Sister 10,430
Walterville
Bend